Lecture Notes in Computer Science 2613

Edited by G. Goos, J. Hartmanis, and J. van Leeuwen

T0216045

Springer
Berlin
Heidelberg
New York
Hong Kong
London
Milan
Paris
Tokyo

Fabien A.P. Petitcolas   Hyoung Joong Kim (Eds.)

Digital Watermarking

First International Workshop, IWDW 2002
Seoul, Korea, November 21-22, 2002
Revised Papers

 Springer

Series Editors

Gerhard Goos, Karlsruhe University, Germany
Juris Hartmanis, Cornell University, NY, USA
Jan van Leeuwen, Utrecht University, The Netherlands

Volume Editors

Fabien A.P. Petitcolas
Microsoft Research
7 J. J. Thomson Avenue, Cambridge, CB3 0FB, UK
E-mail: fabienpe@microsoft.com

Hyoung Joong Kim
Kangwon National University
Department of Control and Instrumentation Engineering
Chunchon 200-701, Korea
E-mail: khj@kangwon.ac.kr

Cataloging-in-Publication Data applied for

A catalog record for this book is available from the Library of Congress.

Bibliographic information published by Die Deutsche Bibliothek
Die Deutsche Bibliothek lists this publication in the Deutsche Nationalbibliografie;
detailed bibliographic data is available in the Internet at <http://dnb.ddb.de>.

CR Subject Classification (1998): K.4.1, K.6.5, H.5.1, D.4.6, E.3, E.4, F.2.2, H.3, I.4,
I.7

ISSN 0302-9743
ISBN 3-540-01217-6 Springer-Verlag Berlin Heidelberg New York

This work is subject to copyright. All rights are reserved, whether the whole or part of the material is
concerned, specifically the rights of translation, reprinting, re-use of illustrations, recitation, broadcasting,
reproduction on microfilms or in any other way, and storage in data banks. Duplication of this publication
or parts thereof is permitted only under the provisions of the German Copyright Law of September 9, 1965,
in its current version, and permission for use must always be obtained from Springer-Verlag. Violations are
liable for prosecution under the German Copyright Law.

Springer-Verlag Berlin Heidelberg New York
a member of BertelsmannSpringer Science+Business Media GmbH

http://www.springer.de

© Springer-Verlag Berlin Heidelberg 2003
Printed in Germany

Typesetting: Camera-ready by author, data conversion by PTP-Berlin GmbH
Printed on acid-free paper   SPIN: 10872881   06/3142   5 4 3 2 1 0

Preface

The 1st International Workshop on Digital Watermarking (IWDW), the conference covering all aspects of digital watermarking, was held at the Hotel Riviera situated along the beautiful Han River in Seoul, Korea from November 21 to 22, 2002. These proceedings contain 21 papers that were accepted for presentation at the conference. These papers were selected from 67 submissions including 3 invited papers. They went through a thorough review process by the Program Committee and were selected on the basis of excellence and novelty.

The following is a brief description of the history of this conference and reviewing process: In August 2001 some members of the Special Interest Group on Multimedia Protection (SIGMP) of the Korea Institute of Information Security and Cryptology (KIISC) agreed to create the IWDW. In November 2001 we set up a Program Committee and solicited papers while asking Springer-Verlag to publish the proceedings of the workshop in their Lecture Notes in Computer Science series. In July 2002 we received 64 submissions from 14 countries using Microsoft's conference management site (http://cmt.research.microsoft.com/iwdw2002/). Each submission was assigned a number automatically by the conference management tool and the paper was sent to the Program Committee members for their review. We also encouraged different sets of experts to join for fair reviews. Thanks to the quality and size of the Program Committee, we were able to match manuscripts for almost all submissions according to the interests and expertise of specific committee members. To balance the program, we invited 3 papers.

In September 2002 we selected 21 submissions as regular presentations and 5 papers for a poster session according to the input of the reviewers. Of these 19 regular papers and the 2 invited papers are published here. These 21 papers were revised after the conference for better quality. The invited speakers were Zheng Liu (M.Ken, Japan), Pierre Moulin (University of Illinois, USA), and Matt L. Miller (NEC Research Institute, USA).

We would like to take this opportunity to sincerely thank the Program Committee for their time and for conscientious reviewing. Also, the Organizing Committee Chair, Byeungwoo Jeon at Sungkyunkwan University, and the Secretariat, Judy Kang of Judy & Communications, deserve acknowledgments for their dedicated work on the local arrangements and correspondence with authors and participants. It is also a pleasure to once again thank the KIISC for hosting, and the Secure Digital Content Association (SEDICA) for cohosting and supporting this conference. Special thanks go to the DRM Forum, SDM Forum, and MarkAny for their sponsorship.

We hope that these proceedings will be useful for future research on digital watermarking.

November 2002

Fabien A.P. Petitcolas
Hyoung Joong Kim

Committee Listings

General Chair
Dong-Ho Won (Sungkyunkwan University, Korea)

Advisory Committee
Sang Uk Lee (Seoul National University, Korea)
Chee Deuk Ahn (ETRI, Korea)
Won Geun Oh (ETRI, Korea)
Myung Joon Kim (ETRI, Korea)
Soo Ngee Koh (Nanyang Technological University, Singapore)
Paul Seo (KETI, Korea)

Program Committee Chair
Fabien A.P. Petitcolas (Microsoft Research, UK)

Program Committee Co-chair
Hyoung Joong Kim (Kangwon National University, Korea)

Program Committee
Jean Luc Dugelay (Institut Eurecom, France)
Touradj Ebrahimi (EPFL, Switzerland)
Jin Woo Hong (ETRI, Korea)
Hideki Imai (University of Tokyo, Japan)
Ton Kalker (Philips Research Eindhoven, The Netherlands)
Mohan Kankanhalli (National University of Singapore, Singapore)
Sung Whan Kim (University of Seoul, Korea)
Reginald L. Lagendijk (Technical University of Delft, The Netherlands)
Heung Kyu Lee (KAIST, Korea)
Hong-Yung Mark Liao (Academia Sinica, Taiwan)
Steven Low (Caltech, USA)
Ji-Hwan Park (Pukyong National University, Korea)
Fernando Perez-Gonzalez (University of Vigo, Spain)
Alessandro Piva (Universita di Firenze, Italy)
Ioannis Pitas (University of Thessaloniki, Greece)
Christine I. Podilchuk (Bell Laboratories, USA)
Shan Suthaharan (North Carolina University, USA)
Andrew Tirkel (Monash University, Australia)
Chee Sun Won (Dongguk University, Korea)
Min Wu (University of Maryland, USA)

Organizing Committee Chair
Byeungwoo Jeon (Sungkyunkwan University, Korea)

Table of Contents

Invited Talks

Information–Hiding Games 1
  Pierre Moulin

Informed Embedding for Multi-bit Watermarks 13
  Matt L. Miller, Gwenaël J. Doërr, Ingemar J. Cox

I. Fundamentals I

The Design and Application of DWT-Domain Optimum Decoders 22
  Yongjian Hu, Sam Kwong, Y.K. Chan

Enhanced Watermarking Scheme Based on Removal of Local Means 31
  Hyun Soo Kang, Jin Woo Hong, Kwang Yong Kim

II. New Algorithms

A Multi-user Based Watermarking System with
Two-Security-Level Keys 40
  Feng-Hsing Wang, Lakhmi Jain, Jeng-Shyang Pan

A New Blind Watermarking Technique Based on Independent
Component Analysis 51
  Dan Yu, Farook Sattar

A New Collusion Attack and Its Performance Evaluation 64
  Viktor Wahadaniah, Yong Liang Guan, Hock Chuan Chua

A Multistage VQ Based Watermarking Technique
with Fake Watermarks 81
  Jeng-Shyang Pan, Feng-Hsing Wang, Lakhmi Jain,
  Nikhil Ichalkaranje

III. Fundamentals II

BER Formulation for the Blind Retrieval of MPEG Video Watermark ... 91
  Sugiri Pranata, Yong Liang Guan, Hock Chuan Chua

Optimal Detection of Transform Domain Additive Watermark
by Using Low Density Diversity 105
    Yafei Shao, Guowei Wu, Xinggang Lin

IV. Watermarking Unusual Content

Implications for Image Watermarking of Recent Work in Image
Analysis and Representation 113
    Ana Georgina Flesia, David L. Donoho

On Watermarking Numeric Sets 130
    Radu Sion, Mikhail Atallah, Sunil Prabhakar

Watermarking Techniques for Electronic Circuit Design 147
    Edoardo Charbon, Ilhami Torunoglu

V. Fragile Watermarking

A SVD-Based Fragile Watermarking Scheme for Image
Authentication 170
    Sung-Cheal Byun, Sang-Kwang Lee, Ahmed H. Tewfik,
    Byung-Ha Ahn

A DWT-Based Fragile Watermarking Tolerant of JPEG Compression 179
    Junquan Hu, Jiwu Huang, Daren Huang, Yun Q. Shi

VI. Robust Watermarking

Robust Local Watermarking on Salient Image Areas 189
    Yi Feng, Ebroul Izquierdo

Image Normalization Using Invariant Centroid for RST Invariant
Digital Image Watermarking 202
    Bum-Soo Kim, Jae-Gark Choi, Kil-Houm Park

An Image Watermarking Algorithm Robust to Geometric Distortion 212
    Xiangui Kang, Jiwu Huang, Yun Q. Shi

VII. Adaptive Watermarking

Spatial Frequency Band Division in Human Visual System
Based Watermarking 224
    Yong Ju Jung, Minsoo Hahn, Yong Man Ro

Two-Step Detection Algorithm in a HVS-Based Blind Watermarking
of Still Images 235
    Yong C. Kim, Byeong C. Choi

Content Adaptive Watermark Embedding in the Multiwavelet
Transform Using a Stochastic Image Model. 249
    Ki-Ryong Kwon, Seong-Geun Kwon, Je-Ho Nam, Ahmed H. Tewfik

Author Index 265

Information–Hiding Games*

Pierre Moulin

University of Illinois, Beckman Inst., Coord. Sci. Lab & ECE Dept.
Urbana, IL 61801, USA
moulin@ifp.uiuc.edu

Abstract. This paper reviews recent research on information-theoretic aspects of information hiding. Emphasis is placed on applications requiring high payload (e.g., covert communications). Information hiding may be viewed as a game between two teams (embedder/decoder vs. attacker), and optimal information-embedding and attack strategies may be developed in this context. This paper focuses on several such strategies, including a framework for developing near-optimal codes and universal decoders. The suboptimality of spread-spectrum strategies follows from the analysis. The theory is applied to image watermarking examples.

1 Introduction

Watermarking (WM) and data hiding (DH) are now major research areas in signal, image and video processing. The goal is to conceal information (such as copyright information, annotations, movie subtitles, secret data, etc.) within a host data set. This hidden information should be decodable even if the watermarked data are modified (to some extent) by an adversary (attacker).

Beginning around 1990, a variety of WM and DH algorithms have been proposed in the literature, with mixed success. Many algorithms would be unable to resist even simple attacks, or they would use relatively naive data embedding techniques. In the second part of the 1990's, it was realized that information theory plays a natural role in WM and DH, due to the need to reliably communicate information to a receiver. The theory also guides the development of good DH codes. The main challenge was to formulate a precise mathematical framework taking the following properties into account:

1. The watermarking process should introduce limited distortion in the host signal. Likewise, the attack should introduce limited distortion.
2. While the host signal is known to the information embedder, it may be unknown to the decoder (blind WM/DH). Additional side information (such as a cryptographic key) may be shared by the encoder and decoder.
3. The communication channel is under control of the attacker.

The essential ingredients of the information-theoretic approach are as follows:

---

* Work supported by NSF grants CDA 96-24396, MIP-97-07633 and CCR 00-81268.

F. Petitcolas and H.J. Kim (Eds.): IWDW 2002, LNCS 2613, pp. 1–12, 2003.
© Springer-Verlag Berlin Heidelberg 2003

1. Distortion metrics are used to define a broad class of admissible embedding functions and a class of attack channels.
2. Statistical models for the host data, the message, and the secret key are used to meaningfully define probabilities of error.
3. Reliable communication is sought under any attack channel in the prescribed class [1]. Game theory plays a natural role under this setup: one party (embedder/decoder team) tries to minimize probability of error, and the other party (attacker) tries to maximize it.

There is a cost in defining an overly restricted class of embedding functions, and a danger in defining an overly restricted class of attacks. In the first case, the WM/DH system may have unnecessarily low performance – in particular, we will see why spread-spectrum systems [2] are generally not competitive with quantization-based systems [3]. In the second case, the WM/DH system may have catastrophic performance – for instance because the embedding algorithm was designed to resist white noise attacks, but not geometric attacks.

Application of information theory has revealed the following fundamental concept, which until early 1999 [3,4,5] had been overlooked in the watermarking literature: Even if the host signal S^N is not available at the decoder (*blind watermarking*), the fact that the encoder knows S^N signifies that achievable rates are higher than if S^N was some unknown interference. (Spread-spectrum systems do not exploit that property.) The watermarking problem falls in the category of communication problems where encoder and decoder have access to side information [6, Ch. 14.9] [7,8].

Notation. We use capital letters to denote random variables, small letters to denote their individual values, calligraphic fonts to denote sets, and a superscript N to denote length-N vectors. For instance, $p(x), x \in \mathcal{X}$ denotes the probability mass function (p.m.f.) of a random variable X taking its values in the set $\mathcal{X}$. The notation $Pr[\mathcal{E}]$ denotes the probability of an event $\mathcal{E}$, and the symbol $\mathbb{E}$ denotes mathematical expectation.

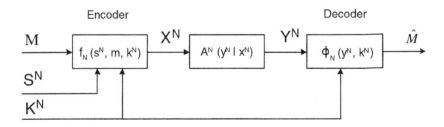

Fig. 1. Formulation of information hiding as a communication problem.

2   Model for Data Hiding

Referring to Fig. 1 [5], assume that a message M is to be embedded in a length-N host-data sequence $S^N = (S_1, \cdots, S_N)$: typically data from an host image, video, or audio signal. Side information $K^N = (K_1, \cdots, K_N)$ (possibly correlated with S^N) is shared by the encoder and decoder. The watermarked data $X^N = (X_1, \cdots, X_N)$ are subject to attacks that attempt to remove any trace of M from the modified data $Y^N = (Y_1, \cdots, Y_N)$. The mapping from X^N to Y^N is generally stochastic and is represented by a p.m.f. $A^N(y^N|x^N)$. The decoder has access to Y^N and K^N and produces an estimate $\hat{M}$ for the message that was originally transmitted. A decoding error occurs if $\hat{M} \neq M$. The variables S_i, K_i, X_i, Y_i take their values in finite sets $\mathcal{S}, \mathcal{K}, \mathcal{X}$ and $\mathcal{Y}$, respectively.

Data Embedding. Consider a bounded distortion function $d_1 : \mathcal{S} \times \mathcal{X} \to \mathbb{R}^+$. The distortion function is extended to a distortion on N-vectors by $d_1^N(s^N, x^N) = \frac{1}{N} \sum_{k=1}^N d_1(s_k, x_k)$. A length-$N$ watermarking code subject to distortion D_1 is defined as a triple $(\mathcal{M}, f_N, \phi_N)$, where:

- $\mathcal{M}$ is the message set of cardinality $|\mathcal{M}|$;
- $f_N : \mathcal{S}^N \times \mathcal{M} \times \mathcal{K}^N \to \mathcal{X}^N$ is the encoder which produces the sequence $x^N = f_N(s^N, m, k^N)$. The mapping f_N is subject to the average distortion constraint

$$\mathbb{E}[d_1^N(S^N, X^N)] \leq D_1; \tag{1}$$

- $\phi_N : \mathcal{Y}^N \times \mathcal{K}^N \to \mathcal{M}$ is the decoder which produces the decoded message $\hat{m} = \phi_N(y^N, k^N)$.

The definition of the distortion constraint (1) involves an averaging with respect to the distribution $p(s^N, k^N)$ and with respect to a uniform distribution on the messages. An alternative is to replace (1) with *almost-sure (a.s.) distortion constraints* [16]:

$$Pr[d_1^N(s^N, X^N) \leq D_1] = 1, \quad \forall s^N \in \mathcal{S}^N. \tag{2}$$

Attacker. Consider a distortion function $d_2 : \mathcal{X} \times \mathcal{Y} \to \mathbb{R}^+$. An *attack channel with memory, subject to distortion D_2*, is defined as a sequence of conditional p.m.f.'s $A^N(y^N|x^N)$ from $\mathcal{X}^N$ to $\mathcal{Y}^N$, such that

$$\mathbb{E}[d_2^N(X^N, Y^N)] \leq D_2. \tag{3}$$

In addition to distortion constraints, other restrictions may be imposed on the attack channels. For instance, for analysis purposes, the attack channel may be constrained to be memoryless, or blockwise memoryless. Denote by $\mathcal{A}^N$ the class of attack channels considered. Two alternatives to the average distortion constraint (3) are a.s. constraints:

$$Pr[d_2^N(x^N, Y^N) \leq D_2] = 1, \quad \forall x^N \in \mathcal{X}^N, \tag{4}$$

and an average distortion constraint with respect to the host data:

$$\mathbb{E}[d_2^N(S^N, Y^N)] \leq D_2. \tag{5}$$

(The attacker is assumed to know f_N and all probability distributions.)

Decoder. If the decoder knows the attack channel A^N, it can implement the Maximum a Posteriori (MAP) decoding rule, which minimizes the probability of error:

$$\hat{m} = \underset{m \in \mathcal{M}}{\operatorname{argmax}} \, p(m|y^N, k^N). \tag{6}$$

If the decoder does not know A^N, one needs a *universal decoder* for the class $\mathcal{A}^N$ [1], with guaranteed performance level for all $A^N \in \mathcal{A}^N$, see Sec. 3. Heuristic decoding rules (such as the correlation rules and normalized correlation rules that are often used in the watermarking literature) might result in low rates of reliable transmission against an astute attacker.

3   Data-Hiding Capacity

The rate of the DH code $(\mathcal{M}, f_N, \phi_N)$ is $R = \frac{1}{N} \log |\mathcal{M}|$, and the average probability of error is

$$P_{e,N} = \frac{1}{|\mathcal{M}|} \sum_{m \in \mathcal{M}} Pr[\phi_N(Y^N, K^N) \neq m \mid M = m]. \tag{7}$$

A rate R is said to be achievable for distortion D_1 and for a class of attack channels $\mathcal{A}^N, N \geq 1$, if there is a sequence of codes subject to distortion D_1, with rate R, such that $P_{e,N} \to 0$ as $N \to \infty$, for any sequence of attacks in $\mathcal{A}^N$. The *data-hiding capacity* $C(D_1, \{\mathcal{A}^N\})$ is then defined as the supremum of all achievable rates for distortion D_1 and attacks in the class $\{\mathcal{A}^N\}$.

3.1   Main Result

Consider the average distortion constraints (1) and (3), and assume the host signal and the attack channel are memoryless. The data-capacity defined above turns out to be the solution of a certain mutual-information game and is given in the theorem below. Let $U \in \mathcal{U}$ be an auxiliary random variable such that $(U, S) \to X \to Y$ forms a Markov chain. Let $\mathcal{Q}(D_1)$ be the set of *covert channels* Q that satisfy the constraint

$$\sum_{x,s,k,u} d_1(s,x)Q(x,u|s,k)p(s,k) \leq D_1, \tag{8}$$

$\mathcal{A}(D_2)$ be the set of attack channels A that satisfy the constraint

$$\sum_{s,x,k,y} d_2(x,y)A(y|x)p(x|s,k)p(s,k) \leq D_2, \tag{9}$$

and $\mathcal{A}$ be an arbitrary subset of $\mathcal{A}(D_2)$.

Theorem 1. *[5] Assume the attacker knows the encoding function f_N and the decoder knows f_N and the attack channel A. A rate R is achievable for distortion D_1 and attacks in the class $\mathcal{A}$ if and only if $R < C$, where C is given by*

$$C = \max_{Q(x,u|s,k) \in \mathcal{Q}(D_1)} \min_{A(y|x) \in \mathcal{A}} J(Q, A) \qquad (10)$$

where $|\mathcal{U}| \leq |\mathcal{X}||\Omega| + 2$, Ω is the support set of $p(s, k)$, and

$$J(Q, A) = I(U; Y|K) - I(U; S|K) \qquad (11)$$

where $I(X; Y|Z) \stackrel{\triangle}{=} \sum_{x,y,z} p(x, y, z) \log \frac{p(x,y|z)}{p(x|z)p(y|z)}$ denotes conditional mutual information [6].

Gel'fand–Pinsker. The capacity result (10) is closely related to a key result by Gel'fand and Pinsker [7] in 1980. They derived the capacity of a memoryless channel whose state is known to the encoder but not to the decoder. The encoder may exploit the state information using a binning technique, as discussed below. The role of the channel state is analogous to the role of the host signal in blind DH. Key differences with the Gel'fand–Pinsker problem include the existence of distortion constraints, the availability of K^N at both the encoder and decoder, and the fact that the attack channel is unknown to the encoder – whence the minimization over A in (10).

Binning Schemes. In principle, the capacity bound can be approached using a *random binning* coding technique [6,7], which exemplifies the role of the covert channel Q, see Fig. 2. A size-$2^{N(I(U;Y,K)-\epsilon)}$ codebook $\mathcal{C}$ is constructed for the variable U^N by randomly sampling the optimal distribution $p(u^N)$, and partitioning the samples into $|\mathcal{M}|$ equal-size subsets (lists). The actual embedding of a message $m \in \mathcal{M}$ proceeds as follows: first identify an element $u^N(m)$ from the list of elements indexed by m in the codebook $\mathcal{C}$, in such a way that $u^N(m)$ is statistically typical with the current (s^N, k^N), then generate watermarked data x^N according to the p.m.f. $p(x^N|u^N(m), s^N, k^N)$. The decoder finds $\hat{u}^N$ that is statistically typical with (y^N, k^N), and obtains $\hat{m}$ as the index of the list to which $\hat{u}^N$ belongs. However, memory and computational requirements grow exponentially with block length N, and so such approaches are known to be infeasible in practice. Developing structured binning schemes that approach the capacity bound is a active research area [3,9,10,11,12], see Sec. 4.

Recent Extensions. Recently, Somekh-Baruch and Merhav [13] have shown that the capacity formula (10) holds under milder assumptions on the attacks and decoder. They assume the a.s. distortion constraints (2) and (4). The decoder does not know the attack channel A^N, which is any channel that satisfies (4) (A^N has arbitrary memory). Capacity can again be achieved using a random binning scheme similar to the one described above, and a particular universal decoder based on the method of types [1,6], i.e., based on the empirical first-order statistics of the pairs (u^N, y^N), for all $u^N \in \mathcal{C}$.

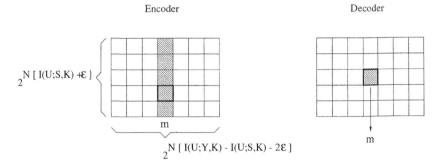

Fig. 2. Random binning technique.

3.2 Gaussian Channels

Theorem 1 can be generalized to the case of infinite alphabets $\mathcal{S}, \mathcal{X}, \mathcal{Y}, \mathcal{U}, \mathcal{K}$. The case of Gaussian S and squared–error distortion measure is of considerable practical and theoretical interest, as it becomes possible to explicitly compute the distributions that achieve capacity and to obtain insightful results. We refer to this case as the Gaussian channel. Let $\mathcal{S} = \mathcal{X} = \mathcal{Y}$ be the set $\mathbb{R}$ of real numbers, and $d_1(x, y) = d_2(x, y) = d(x, y) = (x - y)^2$. Also let $S \sim \mathcal{N}(0, \sigma^2)$, meaning that S follows a Gaussian distribution with mean 0 and variance σ^2.

A remarkable result is that *the data-hiding capacity is the same for both blind and nonblind DH problems.* Under the average distortion constraints (1) and (3), we obtain

$$C = C_G(\sigma^2, D_1, D_2) \triangleq \begin{cases} \frac{1}{2}\log\left(1 + \frac{D_1}{D}\right) : & \text{if } D_1 \leq D_2 < \sigma^2, \\ 0 & : \text{if } D_2 \geq \sigma^2 \end{cases} \tag{12}$$

where $D \triangleq \frac{\sigma^2(D_2 - D_1)}{\sigma^2 - D_2}$. When $D_2 < \sigma^2$, the optimal distributions turn out to be Gaussian test channels [6,14,15], see Fig. 3.

Closely related to this result is one derived by Costa [8] in 1983 for communications on an additive white Gaussian noise channel (with power D_2) in the presence of an i.i.d. (independent and identically distributed) Gaussian interference (with power σ^2) that is known at the encoder but not at the decoder. When the channel input power is constrained not to exceed D_1, Costa showed that the capacity of the channel is exactly the same as if the interference was also known to the decoder: $C = \frac{1}{2}\log\left(1 + \frac{D_1}{D_2}\right)$. The analogy to the DH problem is remarkable: the host signal S^N plays the role of the known interference. Capacity in the DH problem is slightly lower than in the Costa problem because the optimal Gaussian attack is not additive; however, the gap vanishes in the low-distortion limit ($D_1/\sigma^2 \to 0$ and $D_2/\sigma^2 \to 0$). Remarkably, this result holds even if the interferer is non-Gaussian [5].

More extensions of Costa's result have appeared last year [12,16,17]. In particular, the capacity formula $C = \frac{1}{2}\log\left(1 + \frac{D_1}{D_2}\right)$ is still valid if the interference

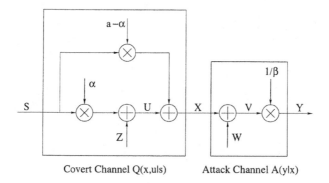

Fig. 3. Optimal data–hiding and attack strategies for Gaussian host data $S \sim \mathcal{N}(0, \sigma^2)$. Here $Z \sim \mathcal{N}(0, aD_1)$ and $W \sim \mathcal{N}(0, \beta(D_2 - D_1))$ are mutually independent random variables, where $a = 1 - D_1/\sigma^2$ and $\beta = \frac{\sigma^2}{\sigma^2 - D_2}$. The optimal channels $p(x|s)$ and $A(y|x)$ are Gaussian test channels with distortion levels D_1 and $D_2 - D_1$, respectively. For public DH, $\alpha = \frac{aD_1}{aD_1 + D}$; for public DH, one may choose $\alpha = a$.

is *any finite-power sequence*, for *any* values of D_1 and D_2. Moreover, the capacity for the following two DH games are identical: (i) the game with average distortion constraint (3) and memoryless attack channel, known to the decoder, and (ii) the game subject to the a.s. distortion constraint (4) with a decoder uninformed about the attack channel.

The optimal decoding rule for Fig. 3 is a minimum-distance decoding rule:

$$\hat{u}^N = \underset{u^N \in \mathcal{C}}{\arg\max}\, p\left(u^N | y^N\right) = \underset{u^N \in \mathcal{C}}{\arg\min} \|u^N - \gamma y^N\|^2 \qquad (13)$$

where $\gamma \sim \alpha$ as D_1/σ^2 and $D_2/\sigma^2 \to 0$. For large N, we have $\|u^N\|^2 \sim N\sigma_u^2$, and (13) is asymptotically equivalent to the following correlation rule:

$$\hat{u}^N \sim \underset{u^N \in \mathcal{C}}{\arg\max} < u^N, y^N > . \qquad (14)$$

This rule is remarkable in its simplicity and robustness. For instance (14) is also optimal if the attacker is allowed to scale the output of the Gaussian channel by an arbitrary factor, because all correlations are scaled by the same factor. More strikingly, (14) turns out to be the optimal universal rule in Cohen and Lapidoth's setup [16].

The property that capacity is the same whether or not S^N is known at the decoder can be illustrated using sphere-packing arguments, see Fig. 4. Assume that $D_1, D_2 << \sigma^2$. The encoder in the random binning construction selects a scaled codeword $\frac{1}{\alpha} U^N$ inside the medium-size sphere of radius $\sqrt{ND_1/\alpha^2}$ centered at S^N. There are approximately 2^{NC} codewords (one for each possible message m) within this medium-size sphere. The received data vector Y^N lies within a small sphere of radius $\sqrt{N\sigma_v^2}$ centered at $\frac{1}{\alpha} U^N$. Decoding by joint typicality means decoding Y^N to the center of the closest small sphere. To yield a vanishing probability of error, the small spheres should not overlap.

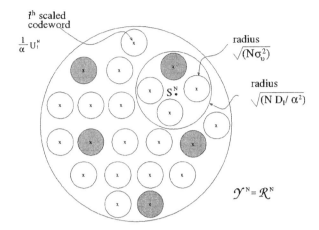

Fig. 4. Sphere-packing interpretation of blind Gaussian information hiding. Shaded spheres are indexed by the same message m.

3.3   Parallel Gaussian Channels

Assume S^N is the union of K independent sources S_k, $1 \leq k \leq K$, each producing N_k i.i.d. Gaussian random variables from the distribution $\mathcal{N}\left(0, \sigma_k^2\right)$, where $\sum_{k=1}^{K} N_k = N$. Thus, we have K parallel Gaussian channels, with samples $\{S_k(n)\}$, and rates $r_k = N_k/N$, $1 \leq k \leq K$. The distortion metric is squared error. Let

$$d_{1k} = \frac{1}{N_k} \sum_{n=1}^{N_k} \mathbb{E}\left[X_k(n) - S_k(n)\right]^2 \quad \text{and} \quad d_{2k} = \frac{1}{N_k} \sum_{n=1}^{N_k} \mathbb{E}\left[Y_k(n) - S_k(n)\right]^2 \tag{15}$$

be the distortions introduced by the embedder and the attacker in channel k, respectively. We have distortion constraints

$$\sum_{k=1}^{K} r_k d_{1k} \leq D_1 \quad \text{and} \quad \sum_{k=1}^{K} r_k d_{2k} \leq D_2. \tag{16}$$

As in the Gaussian case, capacity is the same for both blind and nonblind DH [14,15] :

$$C = \max_{\{d_{1k}\}} \min_{\{d_{2k}\}} \sum_{k=1}^{K} r_k C_G(\sigma_k^2, d_{1k}, d_{2k}) \tag{17}$$

where the maximization and minimization are subject to the distortion constraints (16). The capacity-achieving distributions are product distributions, i.e., the K channels are decoupled.

4   Data-Hiding Codes

The papers [11,12] present a general approach for constructing structured binning schemes to approach capacity in the low quadratic distortion case (for any host signal distribution). This approach is in fact applicable to various communication problems with side information [12]. The goal is to generate U^N, Z^N, X^N whose distribution approximates the ideal distributions shown in Fig. 3.

Step 1: Construct a good vector quantizer with distortion D_1. Define a N-dimensional lattice $\mathbf{L}$ whose Voronoi cells have normalized second moment equal to D_1 and are, loosely speaking, nearly spherical. The distribution of quantization errors in $\mathbf{L}$ may then be approximated as $\mathcal{N}(0, D_1 I_N)$ in the Kullback-Leibler sense.

Step 2: For each $m \in \mathcal{M}$, define a translated lattice $\mathbf{L}_m$ with coset leader $c_m \in \mathbb{R}^N$, i.e., $\mathbf{L}_m = c_m + \mathbf{L}$. Assume $c_1 = 0$. The minimum distance between the translated lattices should be as large as possible. The vectors $c_m, m \in \mathcal{M}$, then form the generator matrix for a good channel code.

The union of the lattices $\mathbf{L}_m$ forms a nested lattice code. Given m and s^N, the encoder obtains $u^N(m)$ by quantizing αs^N to the nearest point in $\mathbf{L}_m$. The difference $z^N = u^N(m) - \alpha s^N$ represents a quantization error, as discussed above. Finally, $x^N = s^N + z^N$.

The decoder quantizes γy^N to the nearest point in $\cup_{m \in \mathcal{M}} \mathbf{L}_m$ and outputs the corresponding index $\hat{m}$. This implements (13).

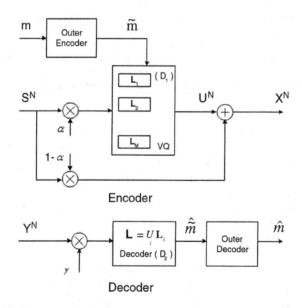

Fig. 5. Lattice-based encoder and decoder for data hiding.

This construction contains Chen and Wornell's scalar Quantization Index Modulation (QIM) technique as a special case [3,10]. In practice, one may not afford a complex high-dimensional lattice, and instead use products of low-dimensional lattices, or even a simple cubic lattice. In order to improve channel coding performance, one can also use an outer code, in which m is encoded into a longer (redundant) sequence $\tilde{m}$, which is used as an input to the nested lattice code (inner code). Chou and Ramchandran [18] recently proposed the use of an outer erasure code; their scheme is intended to resist erasures, insertions and deletions, in addition to the Gaussian-type attacks that the inner code is designed to survive.

5   Data Hiding in Images

Several papers, including [18,19], have recently studied quantization-based codes for embedding data in images. The paper [19] directly illustrates the parallel-Gaussian channel theory, as described below.

Table 1. Quantization-Based Embedding Algorithm.

Step 1	Apply a discrete wavelet transform to the host image.
Step 2	Estimate the variances of the wavelet coefficients at each scale and location.
Step 3	Group wavelet coefficients with similar variances, and treat each group as a channel.
Step 4	Solve the power allocation problem (17), obtaining $\{d_{1k}\}$ and $\{d_{2k}\}$.
Step 5	Choose a target bit rate R_k below $C_k = C_G(\sigma_k^2, d_{1k}, d_{2k})$ for each channel k. For instance, $R_k = 0.1 C_k$.
Step 6	Embed data in each channel using a Gaussian code from Sec. 4.
Step 7	Apply the inverse wavelet transform to the modified wavelet coefficients. This yields the watermarked image.

Wavelet image coefficients are assumed to be Gaussian with zero means and location-dependent variances. The coefficients are conditionally independent, given the variance field. They are grouped into channels containing coefficients with similar variances. This yields a parallel Gaussian model [15,19].

The embedding algorithm is outlined in Table 1. The attacker and decoder are assumed to know the variances of the wavelet coefficients of the host data. [1] The optimal attack is Gaussian, with power allocation $\{d_{2k}\}$ derived in Step 4 of Table 1. The decoder performs MAP decoding in each channel, according to (13).

Results are given for the 512×512 image Lena, using Daubechies' length-8 orthogonal wavelets and 64 parallel Gaussian channels. A value of $D_1 = 10$ is

---

[1] Hence this scheme is *semi-blind*; at the decoder S^N is unknown, but the corresponding variances are known. In practice, the variances would be estimated from the received data.

chosen such that the embedding distortion is just noticeable. For $D_2 = 5D_1$, the operational probability of bit error, P_{be}, is equal to 0.05. This is vastly better than $P_{be} \approx 0.5$ obtained using uniform bit allocation over the channels, and $P_{be} \approx 0.5$ obtained using Chen and Wornell's original QIM (using $\alpha_k = a_k = 1$ instead of the optimal $\alpha_k = \frac{d_{1k}}{d_{1k}+d_{2k}}$). The total bit rate is 398 bits, 10% of NC.

6   Discussion

This paper has reviewed the role of information theory and game theory in the analysis of data-hiding systems. Recent research (2001 and 2002) has revealed that identical or similar results can be obtained under widely different assumptions. For instance, the same capacity may be achievable whether or not the decoder knows the attack channel; and whether or not the attack is allowed to have memory. Related aspects of these problems may be found in recent papers on the characterization of error exponents [20], on optimal design of the key distribution [21], and on optimal estimation of attack channel parameters [22].

Closely related problems include watermarking with a low payload (perhaps as low as one bit of information, for authentication applications). Recent information-theoretic developments in this area include [23,24,25,26]. Also see [27,28] for extensions to the fingerprinting problem.

Acknowledgements. I would like to thank my collaborators: J. A. O'Sullivan, R. Koetter, and M. K. Mıhçak, for contributing to all aspects of this work.

References

1. A. Lapidoth and P. Narayan, "Reliable Communication Under Channel Uncertainty," *IEEE Trans. Info. Thy*, Vol. 44, No. 6, pp. 2148–2177, Oct. 1998.
2. I. J. Cox, J. Killian, F. T. Leighton and T. Shamoon, "Secure Spread Spectrum Watermarking for Multimedia," *IEEE Trans. Image Proc.*, Vol. 6, No. 12, pp. 1673–1687, Dec. 1997.
3. B. Chen and G. W. Wornell, "Quantization Index Modulation Methods: A Class of Provably Good Methods for Digital Watermarking and Information Embedding," *IEEE Trans. Info. Thy*, Vol. 47, No. 4, pp. 1423–1443, May 2001.
4. I. J. Cox, M. L. Miller and A. L. McKellips, "Watermarking as Communications with Side Information," *Proceedings IEEE*, Special Issue on Identification and Protection of Multimedia Information, Vol. 87, No. 7, pp. 1127–1141, July 1999.
5. P. Moulin and J. A. O'Sullivan, "Information-Theoretic Analysis of Information Hiding," Oct. 1999; revised, Sep. 2002. To appear in *IEEE Trans. on Information Theory*, 2003. Available from www.ifp.uiuc.edu/~moulin.
6. T. M. Cover and J. A. Thomas, *Elements of Information Theory*, Wiley, 1991.
7. S. I. Gel'fand and M. S. Pinsker, "Coding for Channel with Random Parameters," *Problems of Control and Information Theory*, Vol. 9, No. 1, pp. 19–31, 1980.
8. M. Costa, "Writing on Dirty Paper," *IEEE Trans. Info. Thy*, Vol. 29, No. 3, pp. 439–441, May 1983.

9. J. Chou, S. Pradhan, L. El Ghaoui and K. Ramchandran, "A Robust Optimization Solution to the Data Hiding Problem using Distributed Source Coding Principles," *Proc. SPIE*, Vol. 3971, San Jose, CA, Jan. 2000.

10. J. J. Eggers, J. K. Su and B. Girod, "A Blind Watermarking Scheme Based on Structured Codebooks," *Proc. IEE Secure Images and Image Authentication*, London, UK, Apr. 2000.

11. M. Kesal, K. M. Mıhçak, R. Kötter and P. Moulin, "Iteratively Decodable Codes for Watermarking Applications," *Proc. 2nd Symposium on Turbo Codes and Related Topics*, Brest, France, Sep. 2000.

12. R. Zamir, S. Shamai (Shitz), and U. Erez, "Nested Linear/Lattice Codes for Structured Multiterminal Binning," *IEEE Trans. Info. Thy*, Vol. 48, No. 6, pp. 1250–1276, June 2002.

13. A. Somekh-Baruch and N. Merhav, "On the Capacity Game of Public Watermarking Systems," *preprint*, Apr. 2002. Available from tiger.technion.ac.il/users/merhav.

14. P. Moulin and M. K. Mıhçak, "The Parallel-Gaussian Watermarking Game," *UIUC TR UIUC-ENG-01-2214*, 2001. Available from www.ifp.uiuc.edu/~moulin.

15. P. Moulin and M. K. Mıhçak, "A Framework for Evaluating the Data-Hiding Capacity of Image Sources," *IEEE Trans. on Image Processing*, Vol. 11, No. 9, pp. 1029–1042, Sep. 2002.

16. A. S. Cohen and A. Lapidoth, "The Gaussian Watermarking Game," *IEEE Trans. Info. Thy*, Vol. 48, No. 6, pp. 1639–1667, June 2002.

17. W. Yu *et al.*, "Writing on Colored Paper," *Proc. IEEE Int. Symp. on Info. Thy*, p. 302, Washington, D.C., 2001.

18. J. Chou and K. Ramchandran, "Robust turbo-based data hiding for image and video sources," *Proc. IEEE Int. Conf. on Image Processing*, Rochester, NY, 2002.

19. M. K. Mıhçak and P. Moulin, "Information-Embedding Codes Matched to Local Gaussian Image Models," *Proc. IEEE Int. Conf. on Im. Proc.*, Rochester, NY, 2002.

20. N. Merhav, "On Random Coding Error Exponents of Watermarking Codes," *IEEE Trans. Info Thy*, Vol. 46, No. 2, pp. 420–430, Mar. 2000.

21. P. Moulin and J. A. O'Sullivan, "Optimal Key Design in Information-Embedding Systems," *Proc. CISS'02*, Princeton, NJ, March 2002.

22. P. Moulin and A. Ivanović, "The Fisher Information Game for Optimal Design of Synchronization Patterns in Blind Watermarking," *Proc. IEEE Int. Conf. on Image Processing*, Thessaloniki, Greece, Oct. 2001.

23. Y. Steinberg and N. Merhav, "Identification in the Presence of Side Information with Application to Watermarking," *IEEE Trans. Info. Thy*, Vol. 47, No. 4, pp. 1410–1422, May 2001.

24. E. Martinian and G. W. Wornell, "Authentication with Distortion Constraints", *Proc. IEEE Int. Conf. on Image Processing*, pp. II.17–20, Rochester, NY, 2002.

25. A. Ivanović and P. Moulin, "Game-Theoretic Performance Analysis of Image Watermark Detectors," *Proc. IEEE Int. Conf. on Im. Proc.*, Rochester, NY, 2002.

26. P. Moulin and A. Ivanović, "The Zero-Rate Spread-Spectrum Watermarking Game," to appear in *IEEE Transactions on Signal Processing*, Apr. 2003.

27. D. Boneh and J. Shaw, "Collusion–Secure Fingerprinting for Digital Data," *IEEE Trans. Info. Thy*, Vol. 44, No. 5, pp. 1897–1905, 1998.

28. P. Moulin and A. Briassouli, "The Gaussian Fingerprinting Game," *Proc. CISS'02*, Princeton, NJ, March 2002.

Informed Embedding for Multi-bit Watermarks

Matt L. Miller[1], Gwenaël J. Doërr[2], and Ingemar J. Cox[1]

[1] NEC Research Institute, Princeton NJ 08540, USA,
[2] Eurécom Institute, Sophia-Antipolis, France

Abstract. Informed embedding is the practice of tailoring each watermarking pattern according to the cover Work in which it is to be embedded. The objective is to attain an optimal trade-off between estimates of perceptual fidelity and robustness. To date, our own studies of informed embedding have been limited to watermarks with very small data payloads. Our purpose in the present paper is to develop a method of informed embedding that is suitable for watermarks with large data payloads.

The method we develop employs an estimate of robustness based on the amount of white noise that can be added before a message error becomes likely. We present an iterative, Monte-Carlo algorithm that tries to ensure watermarks are embedded with a specified value of this robustness estimate. This algorithm is tested in an image watermarking system, and is found to successfully embed robust, 129-bit watermarks in 368 × 240 images.

1 Introduction

In recent years, several researchers [5,1,2] have recognized that watermarking with blind detection can be modeled as communication with side-information at the transmitter [10]. This realization has led to the design of algorithms for *informed coding* and *informed embedding*. In informed coding, a watermark is represented with a pattern that is dependent on the cover Work. In informed embedding, each watermark pattern is tailored according to the cover Work, attempting to attain an optimal trade-off between estimates of perceptual fidelity and robustness. The reader is directed to [4] for a detailed discussion of these concepts.

To date, our own studies of informed embedding have been limited to watermarks with very small data payloads [4,7,5]. Other researchers [1,2,9,6] have employed informed coding to embed large data payloads in images – on the order of 1000 or more bits – but their methods involve only simple forms of informed embedding. Our purpose in the present paper is to develop a more sophisticated method of informed embedding that is suitable for watermarks with large data payloads. This method attempts to explicitly control the probability of obtaining message errors after the addition of white noise.

F. Petitcolas and H.J. Kim (Eds.): IWDW 2002, LNCS 2613, pp. 13–21, 2003.
© Springer-Verlag Berlin Heidelberg 2003

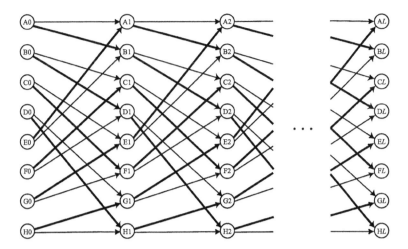

Fig. 1. Simple, 8-state trellis.

Our basic approach to designing a watermarking system with an informed embedder is as follows:

1. Define the watermark detector.
2. Specify a numerical estimate of robustness.
3. Specify a numerical estimate of fidelity.
4. Design an embedder that solves an optimization problem posed in terms of fidelity and robustness.

The following three sections of this paper address the definition of an image watermark detector, a method for estimating robustness, and the design of an embedder. We do not focus on developing a sophisticated estimate of fidelity, using simple mean-squared-error instead. Next, Section 5 presents some experimental results. Finally, Section 6 draws some conclusions.

2   Detector Design

Our watermarking system is built around a trellis-code, as illustrated in Figure 1. This code is similar to that used in the E_TRELLIS8/D_TRELLIS8 watermarking system of [4]. Each possible message corresponds to a path through the trellis from node A0 (state A at time 0) to one of the nodes at the right (any state at time L). We refer to the transition from one column of nodes to the next column of nodes as a *step*, and each such step corresponds to one bit in the coded message. A bold arc is traversed if the corresponding bit is a 1, a non-bold arc is traversed if the corresponding bit is a 0.

Each arc in the trellis is labelled with a randomly-generated, length N reference vector. Each path, and thus each message, is coded with a length $L \times N$ vector that is the concatenation of the labels for the arcs it contains.

The detection algorithm proceeds as follows:

1. Convert the image into the 8×8 block-DCT domain.
2. Place low-frequency AC terms of the blocks into a single, length $L \times N$ vector, in random order. We refer to this as the *extracted vector*.
3. Use a Viterbi decoder [11] to identify the path through the trellis whose $L \times N$ vector has the highest correlation with the extracted vector.
4. Identify the message that is represented by the highest-correlation path.

Note that this detection algorithm does not attempt to determine whether or not the image contains a watermark. It simply maps every possible image into an L-bit message, regardless of whether the image has had a watermark embedded. In large payload applications it is usually not important for the detector to determine whether a watermark is present, since most combinations of bit values are not meaningful. If we need the detector to determine presence of watermarks, we can use some number of bits to contain an error detection checksum or signature of the message.

3   Estimate of Robustness

In [7,5], we defined an estimate of robustness suitable for small-payload watermark systems that use correlation coefficient to test whether or not a mark is present. Since the present detector neither uses correlation coefficient, nor tests for the presence of a watermark, this measure of robustness is not applicable. Instead of estimating the likelihood that a watermarked image will be detected as *unwatermarked*, we need to estimate the likelihood that it will be detected as containing the *wrong message*.

To develop our new robustness measure, consider a simple system in which there are only two possible messages, represented by two different vectors. Denote one of the vectors $\mathbf{g}$, and the other $\mathbf{b}$. When presented with an image, $\mathbf{c}$, the detector returns the message associated with $\mathbf{g}$ if $\mathbf{g} \cdot \mathbf{c} > \mathbf{b} \cdot \mathbf{c}$, where $\mathbf{g} \cdot \mathbf{c} = \sum_i \mathbf{g}[i]\mathbf{c}[i]$ is the correlation between $\mathbf{g}$ and $\mathbf{c}$.

Suppose we wish to embed $\mathbf{g}$ into an image, $\mathbf{c_o}$ (so $\mathbf{g}$ is the "good" vector – the one we want to embed – and $\mathbf{b}$ is the "bad" vector – one we do not want the watermarked image to be confused with). Our task is to estimate the chances that a proposed watermarked image, $\mathbf{c_w}$, will, after corruption by subsequent processing, be detected as containing the message $\mathbf{g}$ rather than the message $\mathbf{b}$. More precisely, we need a value that is monotonically related to the probability that message $\mathbf{g}$ will be correctly detected in a corrupted version of the watermarked Work, $\mathbf{c_w}$.

As in [7,5], we proceed by assuming that the distortions applied to the Work after watermark embedding can be modeled as the addition of white Gaussian noise[1]. Thus, we assume that the detector will receive $\mathbf{c_{wn}} = \mathbf{c_w} + \mathbf{n}$, where $\mathbf{n}$ is a length $L \times N$ vector whose elements are drawn independently from a Gaussian distribution with variance σ_n^2. The probability that $\mathbf{g}$ will be detected in $\mathbf{c_{wn}}$ is

$$P\{\mathbf{g} \cdot \mathbf{c_{wn}} > \mathbf{b} \cdot \mathbf{c_{wn}}\} = P\left\{\frac{(\mathbf{g} - \mathbf{b}) \cdot \mathbf{c_w}}{|\mathbf{g} - \mathbf{b}|} > \sigma_n r\right\} \tag{1}$$

---

[1] See [4] for a justification of this assumption.

where r is a random scalar value drawn from a unit-variance, Gaussian distribution. Clearly, the larger the value of

$$R_0\left(\mathbf{c_w}, \mathbf{g}, \mathbf{b}\right) = \frac{(\mathbf{g} - \mathbf{b}) \cdot \mathbf{c_w}}{|\mathbf{g} - \mathbf{b}|} \tag{2}$$

the higher the probability that it will be greater than $\sigma_n r$, and the greater the chances that the watermark $\mathbf{g}$ will be correctly detected in $\mathbf{c_{wn}}$. $R_0()$, then, can serve as our robustness measure for a simple, two-message watermarking system.

To extend this measure to larger payloads, we take the minimum of R_0 over *all* possible erroneous message vectors, $\mathbf{b_1}$ ... $\mathbf{b_{2^L-1}}$. Thus,

$$R\left(\mathbf{c_w}, \mathbf{g}\right) = \min_{i=1}^{2^L-1} R_0\left(\mathbf{c_w}, \mathbf{g}, \mathbf{b}_i\right). \tag{3}$$

Figure 2 illustrates a geometric interpretation of the embedding region that results when we specify that $R(\mathbf{c_w}, \mathbf{g})$ must be greater than or equal to a given value. The figure shows a Voronoi diagram representing the detection regions for various messages. By specifying a minimum value for $R(\mathbf{c_w}, \mathbf{g})$, we are insisting that $\mathbf{c_w}$ must lie a certain distance from the edge of the detection region for $\mathbf{g}$. The figure also illustrates the behavior of an ideal embedder using this robustness measure. The open circle indicates an unwatermarked cover image, and the filled circle shows the closest possible watermarked image with acceptable robustness.

4   Embedding Algorithm

In practice, it is difficult to implement an algorithm to find the optimal watermarked image, as illustrated in Figure 2. Instead, we use a suboptimal, iterative algorithm. This algorithm is very general, and can be used with a wide variety of watermark coding schemes.

We assume that we have a black-box watermark encoder, $W(m)$, that maps a sequence of bits, m, into a watermark signal, $\mathbf{w}_m$. We futher have a black-box watermark detector, $D(\mathbf{c})$, that maps an image, $\mathbf{c}$, into the sequence of bits corresponding to the watermark signal with which the image has the highest correlation. We make no further assumptions about how these two functions work internally.

We now give the basic outline of the iterative embedding algorithm. Given a cover image, $\mathbf{c_o}$, a message to embed, m, and a target robustness value, R_t, the algorithm proceeds as follows:

1. Let $\mathbf{g} = W(m)$ and $\mathbf{c_w} = \mathbf{c_o}$.
2. Find the signal, $\mathbf{b} \neq \mathbf{g}$ that minimizes $R_0(\mathbf{c_w}, \mathbf{g}, \mathbf{b})$.
3. If $R_0(\mathbf{c_w}, \mathbf{g}, \mathbf{b}) \geq R_t$, then terminate.
4. Otherwise, modify $\mathbf{c_w}$ so that $R_0(\mathbf{c_w}, \mathbf{g}, \mathbf{b}) = R_t$, and go to step 2.

The modification of $\mathbf{c_w}$ in step 4 is performed as follows:

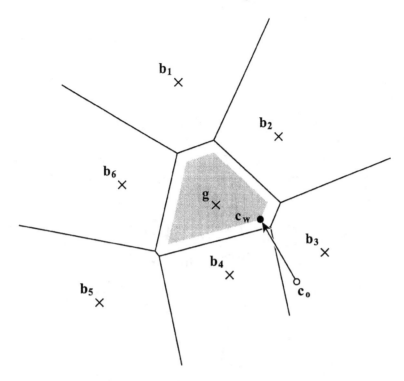

Fig. 2. Geometric interpretation of embedding region defined by placing a lower limit on $R(c_w, g)$.

$$d = \frac{g - b}{|g - b|}$$
$$\alpha = R_t - R_0(c_w, g, b)$$
$$c_w \leftarrow c_w + \alpha d. \tag{4}$$

The new c_w yields $R_0(c_w, g, b)$ exactly equal to R_t, while having a minimum Euclidian distance from the previous c_w.

The operation of this algorithm is shown geometrically in Figure 3. In the first iteration, c_w lies in the detection region for b_3, so $b = b_3$ in step 2, and c_w is moved to a point beyond the boundary between g and b_3. In the second iteration, $b = b_4$, and g is moved into the detection region for g. In the final iteration, the closest bad vector is still b_4, but $R_0(c_w, g, b_4)$ is already satisfactory, so the algorithm terminates. The figure clearly illustrates that this algorithm is suboptimal, since it does not yield the optimal point identified in Figure 2. Nevertheless, it is practical to implement.

The identification of b in step 2 depends on the method of coding. For most codes, it is not easy. We therefore apply a simple, Monte Carlo approach by letting

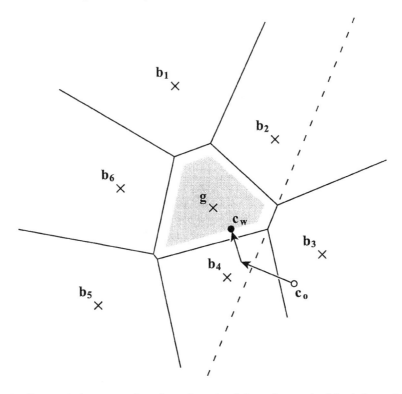

Fig. 3. Geometric interpretation of a sub-optimal, iterative method for informed embedding.

$$b = W\left(D\left(c_w + n\right)\right),\tag{5}$$

where n is some random noise. If a small amount of noise is added to c_w, and the detector returns a message other than m, then b is likely to yield a low value of $R_0()$. If there exist any vectors that yield values of $R_0()$ below the target value, R_t, then b is likely to be one of them.

The best amount of noise to add changes as the embedding process progresses. In the first iteration, when $c_w = c_o$, it is unlikely that $D(c_w) = m$, so we need not add any noise at all to find the nearest bad vector. In later iterations, if too little noise is added, $W(D(c_w + n))$ will equal g. If too much noise is added, $W(D(c_w + n))$ has a high chance of producing a vector for which $R_0()$ is much larger than the minimum available value. We therefore dynamically adjust the amount of noise added in each iteration.

Since the Monte Carlo approach does not guarantee that we find the b that minimizes $R_0(c_w, g, b)$ in each iteration, we cannot terminate the algorithm the first time that $R_0(c_w, g, b)$ is greater than or equal to the target value – there might still be some other b for which $R_0(c_w, g, b) < R_t$. We therefore maintain a count of the number of consecutive **b**'s found for which $R_0(\mathbf{c_w}, \mathbf{g}, \mathbf{b}) \geq R_t$. The algorithm terminates when this count reaches a specified limit.

Thus, the complete, general version of our informed embedding algorithm proceeds as follows:

1. Let $\mathbf{g} = W(m)$, $\mathbf{c_w} = \mathbf{c_o}$, $\sigma_{\mathbf{n}} = 0$, and $j = 0$.
2. Let $\mathbf{b} = W(D(\mathbf{c_w} + \mathbf{n}))$, where $\mathbf{n}$ is a random vector with each element drawn independently from a Gaussian distribution with variance $\sigma_{\mathbf{n}}^2$.
3. If $\mathbf{b} = \mathbf{g}$, let $\sigma_{\mathbf{n}} \leftarrow \sigma_{\mathbf{n}} + \delta$ and go back to step 2.
4. If $R_0(\mathbf{c_w}, \mathbf{g}, \mathbf{b}) < R_t$, then modify $\mathbf{c_w}$ according to Equation 4, reset j to 0, and go back to step 2.
5. If $R_0(\mathbf{c_w}, \mathbf{g}, \mathbf{b}) \geq R_t$, then increment j. If $j < 100$, then let $\sigma_{\mathbf{n}} \leftarrow \sigma_{\mathbf{n}} - \delta$ and go back to step 2. Otherwise, terminate.

5   Experimental Results

To test this algorithm, we implemented a system for embedding and detecting $N = 129$ bits in images of size 368×240. We used the 12 lowest-frequency AC coefficients from each 8×8 block, and discarded 48 randomly-chosen coefficients, giving us an extracted vector of length $L \times N = 16512$, with $L = 128$. Our trellis code had 64 states. Each 0 arc (i.e. non-bold arc in Figure 1) was labeled with a vector drawn from a white, Gaussian distribution, and normalized to have exactly zero mean and unit variance. The 1 arcs (i.e. bold arcs) were labeled with the negations of the 0-arc labels. The step size for adjusting $\sigma_{\mathbf{n}}$ during embedding was $\delta = 0.1$.

We used this implementation to embed random watermarks into 2000 images from the Corel image library [3], with several values of R_t. The average resulting MSE between original and watermarked images ranged from 5, at the lowest strength of $R_t = 10$, to 5.3, at the highest strength of $R_t = 100$.

We then ran the detector after no subsequent distortions, and after simulated JPEG with a quality factor of 75%, recording the resulting message error rate (the frequency with which not all bits were correctly decoded). The results are shown in Figure 4.

In theory, we should always be able to detect all bits correctly after no distortion, since the embedding process does not terminate before the image is within the detection region for the desired message. However, there were round-off and clipping errors in our implementation, which caused a small fraction of images to yield message errors after no distortion, primarily at lower embedding strengths. At the highest embedding strength, the embedder succeeded in embedding error-free messages in over 99% of the images.

The results after simulated JPEG show that watermark robustness is clearly a monotonic function of embedding strength. At the highest embedding strength, all bits of the watermark were correctly detected in over 98% of the images. This implies that, although our estimate of robustness, R, is defined in terms of additive white noise, it is also a reasonable predictor of robustness to quantization.

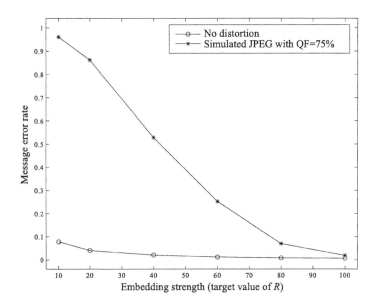

Fig. 4. Results of test on 2000 images.

For comparison, we implemented a blind embedder as well, and applied it to each image with an embedding strength chosen to obtain exactly the same MSE as obtained with the informed embedder. The blind embedder failed to embed error-free messages in well over 95% of the images.

6   Conclusions

We have presented a new method of informed embedding that is suitable for multi-bit watermarks, and tested its performance on a watermark with moderately large payload. The performance was substantially better than blind embedding.

However, by itself, this method does not allow for payloads much larger than that we tested. For larger payloads – on the order of 1000 bits in our 368 × 240 images – the method must be combined with methods for informed coding and perceptual shaping. In another paper, we report results obtained with such a combined system [8]. There, we succeed in embedding 1380 bits into these images in a manner that is robust to substantial valumetric distortions. The present informed embedding method is critical to achieving that result.

References

1. Chen, B., Wornell, G. W.: An information-theoretic approach to the design of robust digital watermarking systems. *IEEE Transactions on Acoustics, Speech, and Signal Processing* (1999)

2. Chou, J., Pradhan, S. S., Ramchandran, K.: On the duality between distributed source coding and data hiding. *Thirty-third Asilomar Conference on Signals, Systems, and Computers* 2 (1999) 1503–1507
3. Corel Stock Photo Library 3. Corel Corporation, Ontario, Canada
4. Cox, I. J., Miller, M. L., Bloom, J. A.: *Digital Watermarking.* Morgan Kaufmann (2001)
5. Cox, I. J., Miller, M. L., McKellips, A.: Watermarking as communications with side information. *Proceedings of the IEEE* 87(7) (1999) 1127–1141
6. Eggers, J. J., Su, J. K., Girod, B.: A blind watermarking scheme based on structured codebooks. *IEE Seminar on Secure Images and Image Authetication* (2000) 4/1-4/21
7. Miller, M. L., Cox, I. J., Bloom, J. A.: Informed embedding: exploiting image and detector information during watermark insertion. *IEEE International Conference on Image Processing* (2000)
8. Miller, M. L., Doërr, G. J., Cox, I. J.: Applying informed coding and embedding to design a robust, high capacity watermark. *IEEE Transactions on Image Processing* (to appear)
9. Ramkumar, M.: *Data Hiding in Multimedia: Theory and Applications.* PhD thesis, New Jersey Institute of Technology (1999)
10. Shannon, C. E.: Channels with side information at the transmitter. *IBM Journal of Research and Development* (1958) 289–293
11. Viterbi, A. J.: CDMA: principles of spread spectrum communications. *Addison Wesley Longman Inc.* (1995)

The Design and Application of DWT-Domain Optimum Decoders

Yongjian Hu[1,2,3], Sam Kwong[1], and Y.K. Chan[1]

[1] Dept. of Computer Science, City University of Hong Kong,
Kowloon, Hong Kong, PRC
cssamk@cityu.edu.hk,
[2] Dept. of Automatic Control Engg., South China University of Tech.,
Guangzhou 510641, PRC
eeyjhu@scut.edu.cn,
[3] School of Info. Sci. and Tech., Sun Yat-Sen University,
Guangzhou 510275, PRC

Abstract. Based on Bayes theory of hypothesis testing, a new DWT-domain decoder structure for image watermarking has been proposed in this work. The statistical distribution of wavelet coefficients is deliberately described with the Laplacian model so that the decoding algorithm could couple effectiveness and simplicity. Under the Neyman-Pearson criterion, the decision rule is optimized by minimizing the probability of missing the watermark for a given false detection rate. Compared with other domain decoders, the proposed DWT-domain decoder has more flexibility in constructing new watermarking algorithms by using visual models that have varying spatial support.

1 Introduction

Correlation-based watermark detection has been extensively used in current watermarking techniques and widely discussed in the literature. Under the assumption that the watermarked feature coefficients follow a Gaussian distribution, this correlation-based detection structure would be optimal in that it permits to minimize the error probability. However, as many authors have pointed out [1]-[3], when the host feature coefficients do not follow a Gaussian pdf (probability density function), correlation-based decoding is not the optimum choice. Hernandez *et al.* [1] proposed an optimum maximum likelihood decoder structure for additive watermarking in DCT-domain, where mid-frequency DCT coefficients are modeled as GGD (generalized Gaussian distribution) random variables. In many cases, though, the non-additive embedding rule is adopted to achieve better image-dependent watermarking. Barni *et al.* [2] constructed a DFT-domain non-additive watermarking decoder and made it optimal. But the Weibull distribution which they used to model the magnitude of DFT coefficients can not be applied to the commonly used transforms such as DCT and DWT. In this work, we propose a method to design DWT-domain multiplicative optimum decoders for image watermarking. We also present a multiresolution watermarking algorithm to exhibit the good performance of the new decoder.

F. Petitcolas and H.J. Kim (Eds.): IWDW 2002, LNCS 2613, pp. 22–30, 2003.
© Springer-Verlag Berlin Heidelberg 2003

Wavelet transform has the advantages of both locality and frequency extraction. Compared with other image transforms (e.g. DFT), more sophisticated perceptual models can be found in the wavelet framework. It endows the DWT-domain decoder structure with more flexibility in constructing new algorithms robust to different attacks. For example, most of current watermark decoders have poor performance under low-pass filtering. By using the visual model based on the low-pass features of the DWT transform image, we can construct the watermark component with wide spatial support and make the decoder robust against such image processing. Early researchers (e.g. [4]) have found that both watermark structure and embedding strategy affect the robustness of image watermarks. In this paper, we further demonstrate that the design of decoders also involves the reliability of watermark recovery.

2   Optimum Decoder Structure

Our proposed decoder structure is based on Bayes statistical detection theory. The wavelet coefficient to be watermarked is modeled as a realization from a Laplacian distribution, whose standard deviation is to be estimated. To achieve adaptive watermarking, the multiplicative embedding rule is adopted, i.e., larger coefficients are superimposed with more strength of the watermark. We give a brief review of coefficient modeling and the multiplicative rule before introducing the optimum decoder structure.

2.1   Coefficient Modeling and Multiplicative Rule

For most natural images, the statistical distribution of subband coefficients can be well described by the zero-mean GGD:

$$f_x(x) = Ae^{-|\beta x|^c}, \quad -\infty < x < +\infty \tag{1}$$

where A and β can be expressed as a function of shape parameter c and the standard deviation σ:

$$\beta = \sigma^{-1} \left[\frac{\Gamma(3/c)}{\Gamma(1/c)} \right]^{1/2}, A = \frac{\beta c}{2\Gamma(1/c)} \tag{2}$$

The special cases of GGD include the Laplacian distribution with $c = 1$ and the Gaussian distribution with $c = 2$. Although GGD random variables can well model wavelet coefficients, the estimation of parameters c and σ for each GGD variable usually incurs great computational complexity. It has been observed in several work [5] that the shape parameter c typically falls within the range $[0.5, 1]$. Thus, we use the Laplacian model to approximate the statistical distribution of a subband coefficient in this work. As will be seen, this approximation is reasonable and efficient. The unknown standard deviation σ can be calculated by using a method called context modeling in [6].

To achieve image-dependent watermark embedding, the multiplicative rule $\mathbf{y} = \mathbf{x} + \gamma \mathbf{m} \mathbf{x}$ is often used, where vectors $\mathbf{x}$, $\mathbf{m}$ and $\mathbf{y}$ refer to the host coefficients, the watermark and the marked coefficients, respectively. The parameter γ is used to control the watermark embedding strength and varies pixel by pixel. Usually, adaptive γ is determined by taking into account spatial masking. For simplicity of description, we do not consider the effect of visual masking while deriving the optimum decoder. We only assume that γ is much less than 1. In fact, the proposed decoder can be flexibly used by determining γ with different masking models.

2.2   Optimum Decoder

Generally, the detection of a certain watermark can be regarded as a hypothesis test. According to the Bayes theory of hypothesis testing, the likelihood function $\ell(\mathbf{y})$ can be described as follows:

$$\ell(\mathbf{y}) = \frac{f_{\mathbf{y}}(\mathbf{y}|M_1)}{f_{\mathbf{y}}(\mathbf{y}|M_0)} \tag{3}$$

where $f_{\mathbf{y}}(\mathbf{y}|M)$ represents the pdf of the random vector $\mathbf{y}$ conditioned to the event M. We assume that $\mathbf{y} = \{y_1, y_2, ..., y_N\}$ is one observation of the possibly watermarked wavelet coefficients and $\mathbf{m}^* = \{m_1^*, m_2^*, ..., m_N^*\}$ a given watermark. The parameter space can be defined as $M = M_0 \bigcup M_1$, where $M_1 = \{\mathbf{m}^*\}$ and $M_0 = \{\mathbf{m_j} \neq \mathbf{m}^*\}$. M_0 contains an infinite number of watermarks. The goal of watermark detection is to verify whether a given watermark $\mathbf{m}^*$ is present in the test image (hypothesis H_1) or not (hypothesis H_0). The decision rule can be concisely described as follows:

$$\ell(\mathbf{y}) > \lambda \tag{4}$$

where λ represents the decision threshold. If (4) is true, H_1 is accepted, otherwise H_0 is accepted. Therefore, the key problem is to find a reasonable solution for the decision threshold.

Assuming that a marked coefficient y_i depends only on the corresponding watermark component m_i. When the Laplacian model is used to approximate the distribution of y_i, the pdf of y_i subject to m_i can be described as follows:

$$f_{y_i}(y_i|m_i) = \frac{\beta_i}{2(1 + \gamma m_i)} e^{-\frac{\beta_i}{1+\gamma m_i}|y_i|} \tag{5}$$

where $\beta_i = \sqrt{2}/\sigma_i$. We further assume the uncorrelated wavelet coefficients as independent random variables. $f_{\mathbf{y}}(\mathbf{y}|\mathbf{m})$ can be directly expressed as follows:

$$f_{\mathbf{y}}(\mathbf{y}|\mathbf{m}) = \prod_{i=1}^{N} f_{y_i}(y_i|m_i) = \prod_{i=1}^{N} \frac{\beta_i}{2(1 + \gamma m_i)} e^{-\frac{\beta_i}{1+\gamma m_i}|y_i|} \tag{6}$$

In the spread spectrum watermarking scheme, the watermark components are chosen to be uniformly distributed in $[-1, 1]$. Since the watermark strength

γ is kept much lower than 1 to satisfy the requirement of invisibility, $f_{\mathbf{y}}(\mathbf{y}|M_0)$ can be reasonably approximated by $f_{\mathbf{y}}(\mathbf{y}|\mathbf{0})$ [2], where $\mathbf{0}$ represents the null watermark. By inserting $f_{\mathbf{y}}(\mathbf{y}|M_0) \simeq f_{\mathbf{y}}(\mathbf{y}|\mathbf{0})$ in (3) and using (6), the likelihood ratio $\ell(\mathbf{y})$ can be further expressed as

$$\ell(\mathbf{y}) = \prod_{i=1}^{N} \frac{1}{1 + \gamma m_i^*} exp \left[\frac{\gamma m_i^* \beta_i}{1 + \gamma m_i^*} |y_i| \right] \tag{7}$$

For simplicity, the log likelihood ratio $\mathcal{L}(\mathbf{y}) = \ln \ell(\mathbf{y})$ is used instead of $\ell(\mathbf{y})$. Then the decision rule has the following form:

$$\mathcal{L}(\mathbf{y}) > \ln \lambda \tag{8}$$

In this paper, the threshold $\ln \lambda$ is decided by means of minimizing the missed detection rate subject to a fixed false positive probability. We insert (7) in (8)

$$\sum_{i=1}^{N} \frac{\gamma m_i^* \beta_i}{1 + \gamma m_i^*} |y_i| > \ln \lambda + \sum_{i=1}^{N} \ln(1 + \gamma m_i^*) \tag{9}$$

The term on the left is the sufficient statistic for detection. Thus, the decision rule can be equivalently given the form:

$$z > \lambda_1 \tag{10}$$

where

$$z = \sum_{i=1}^{N} v_i, \quad v_i = \frac{\gamma m_i^* \beta_i}{1 + \gamma m_i^*} |y_i| \tag{11}$$

$$\lambda_1 = \ln \lambda + \sum_{i=1}^{N} \ln(1 + \gamma m_i^*) \tag{12}$$

Because x_i follows the Laplacian distribution, $|x_i|$ can be regarded as a random variable with the exponential pdf:

$$f_{x_i}(x_i) = \beta_i e^{-\beta_i x_i}, \quad x_i \geq 0 \tag{13}$$

Taking into account the probability of missing the watermark under attacks, we apply the Neyman-Pearson criterion to the log likelihood ratio test in a manner similar to [2]. By fixing the false positive probability on a certain level (for example, 10^{-6}), we finally obtain the optimum threshold $\ln \lambda$:

$$\ln \lambda = 3.3 \sqrt{2\sigma_z^2} + \mu_z - \sum_{i=1}^{N} \ln(1 + \gamma m_i^*) \tag{14}$$

where

$$\mu_z = \sum_{i=1}^{N} \mu_{v_i} = \sum_{i=1}^{N} \frac{\gamma m_i^*}{1 + \gamma m_i^*} \tag{15}$$

Fig. 1. Four-level wavelet decomposition.

$$\sigma_z^2 = \sum_{i=1}^{N} \sigma_{v_i}^2 = \sum_{i=1}^{N} (\frac{\gamma m_i^*}{1 + \gamma m_i^*})^2 \qquad (16)$$

3   Using the Optimum Decoder

The embedding strength parameter γ not only satisfies the perceptual constraints, but also improves the detectability as well as the information embedding rate. As stated earlier, adaptive γ is totally determined by visual models. Therefore, the optimum decoder structure proposed in this paper can be used with different visual models to design watermarking algorithms for varied purposes. Below we give an example to show how to design a watermarking algorithm robust against common attacks, especially low-pass filtering. We note that most of current watermark decoders have poor performance under the attack of low-pass filtering which often results in slight visual distortion.

The low-pass nature of most content-preserving image processing motivates us to use visual models based on the low-pass features of the transform image. It has been observed that the human eye can perceive small differences in luminance. Thus, we use the luminance masking in [6] and change the form to suit invisible watermarking.

$$\mathcal{L}_{mask}(i, j) = (\frac{C_{ij} - C_m}{C_{max}})^2 \qquad (17)$$

where C_{ij} is a coefficient in the low-pass subband with coordinates i and j. C_m and C_{max} are the mean and maximum of the coefficients, respectively.

As to watermark insertion, the multiresolution structure of wavelet decomposition provides us with multiple choices of embedding regions. We avoid embedding the watermark in the highest frequency subbands that contain outstanding edges since this operation could raise visual distortion similar to ringing effect in DWT-based image coding. Instead, we choose subbands that mainly correspond to texture regions with mid-frequency spectrum. The effect of visual masking, i.e., luminance masking, on these high-pass subbands can be estimated by using the quadtree structure of wavelet decomposition [6].

The steps for watermark insertion are described in detail as follows:

1. Perform DWT and decompose the host image into four-level multiresolution structures (Fig.1).
2. Calculate $\mathcal{L}_{mask}$ and scale its value to the range [0.1,0.3]. Let pixelwise γ equal the scaled $\mathcal{L}_{mask}$ in the three high-pass subbands at resolution $r = 3$.
3. By adopting the multiplicative rule, embed the watermark. Perform inverse DWT to obtain the reconstructed image.

In the detection stage, no additional information about the original image is required. The needed parameter γ can be estimated *a-posteriori* on the watermarked image. The log likelihood ratio $\mathcal{L}(\mathbf{y})$ and the threshold $\ln \lambda$ can be calculated respectively as follows:

$$\mathcal{L}(\mathbf{y}) = \sum_{s=1}^{3} \sum_{i=1}^{N_s} \frac{\gamma m_i^* \beta_i}{1 + \gamma m_i^*} |y_i| - \sum_{s=1}^{3} \sum_{i=1}^{N_s} \ln(1 + \gamma m_i^*) \tag{18}$$

$$\ln \lambda = 3.3 \sqrt{2 \sum_{s=1}^{3} \sum_{i=1}^{N_s} \left(\frac{\gamma m_i^*}{1 + \gamma m_i^*}\right)^2 + \sum_{s=1}^{3} \sum_{i=1}^{N_s} \frac{\gamma m_i^*}{1 + \gamma m_i^*}}$$
$$- \sum_{s=1}^{3} \sum_{i=1}^{N_s} \ln(1 + \gamma m_i^*) \tag{19}$$

where $s = 1, 2, 3$ denote frequency orientation LH, HL and HH, respectively. N_s is the number of coefficients in one particular subband. The decision is made after comparing the value of $\mathcal{L}(\mathbf{y})$ with the corresponding threshold $\ln \lambda$.

The watermark embedded in the mid-frequency subbands of wavelet decomposition best protects visual fidelity of the original image, and meanwhile, ensures a large amount of security against attacks.

4 Results

The proposed decoder structure and embedding strategy have been applied to several standard images to validate the theoretical analysis in the paper. The results presented here refer to *lena, F − 16* and *peppers*. Similar results have been obtained on the other images.

It can be seen that the watermarked images (Fig.2) have high visual quality. During the derivation of the optimum decoder, we have assumed that the watermark embedding strength parameter γ is much less than 1. Here we give the Table 1 to exhibit that the assumption has been well satisfied. The mean of γ determined by the HVS model during watermark embedding is far less than 1. The estimation of γ from the original image and the watermarked image is also shown in the Table 1. Because the masking model we used is only related to the lowest frequency subband, the two means are same in value. Generally, they are very close in value with each other for other visual models. It implies that the method of estimating γ *a-posteriori* on the watermarked image is reasonable.

Fig. 2. Watermarked *lena* (PNSR=50.05dB)(left), $F - 16$ (PNSR=49.54dB)(center) and *peppers* (PNSR=50.45dB)(right)

Table 1. Mean of scaling factors (MSF) and its *a-posteriori* estimated one (MASF)

Image	MSF	MASF
lena	0.1309	0.1309
$F - 16$	0.1113	0.1113
peppers	0.1211	0.1211

The attacks we used in this work include median filtering, JPEG compression, noise addition and cropping. For each attack, the detection space contains 1000 randomly generated watermarks, including the one embedded within the test image. The detector response to the true watermark and the highest response among those to the other watermarks are plotted along with the corresponding detection threshold. From Fig.3-Fig.5, we can observe that the new decoder has demonstrated good performance. Even when the response to the true watermark is lower than the corresponding threshold, it is often larger than the highest response of other watermarks. This means that the new decoder has good performance in both false positive and false negative detection.

We can roughly compare the results obtained by the proposed optimum decoder with those achieved by the DFT-domain optimum decoder in [2]. An amount of 12288 DWT coefficients are watermarked in this work while a total of 16046 DFT coefficients have been watermarked in [2]. In either case, the threshold has been achieved at the same false detection rate, i.e., 10^{-6}. Under median filtering, the robustness of the proposed decoder is better than that of the DFT-domain decoder while under Gaussian noise addition and JPEG compression the DFT-domain decoder has slightly better performance than the proposed one. In real-world applications, however, the Gaussian noise with variance of 150 already raises obvious distortion in the image. The compressed image with JPEG quality factor less than 40 also has apparent block artifacts. Thus, the new decoder can well satisfy the practical purposes.

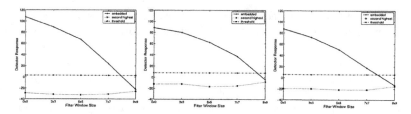

Fig. 3. Responses of the DWT-domain optimum decoder under median filtering. Results refer to the *lena* (left), $F - 16$ (center) and *peppers* (right).

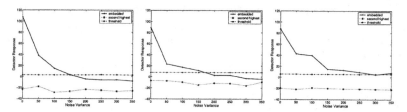

Fig. 4. Responses of the DWT-domain optimum decoder under Gaussian noise addition. Results refer to the *lena* (left), $F - 16$ (center) and *peppers* (right).

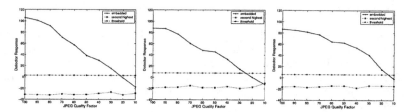

Fig. 5. Responses of the DWT-domain optimum decoder under JPEG compression. Results refer to the *lena* (left), $F - 16$ (center) and *peppers* (right).

As to image cropping, the DFT-domain decoder is better than the proposed decoder. The performance of the new decoder has been affected by calculating the adopted visual model since cropping operations could impact image values in the lower frequency levels more than in the higher levels. This problem can be solved by using other visual models with local spatial support.

5   Conclusions

Due to the hierarchical decomposition, the wavelet domain watermarking approach has the advantage of constructing watermark components that have varying spatial support. DWT-based watermarking schemes have attracted much attention. As a matter of fact, many well-established watermarking algorithms in the literature are based on DWT-domain. Therefore, the exploration of designing

DWT-domain optimum decoders is very significant. In this work, we address the problem of deriving and using the DWT-domain optimum watermark decoder. Unlike classical correlation-based watermark detection, the proposed decoder is based on Bayes theory of hypothesis testing and is made optimal under the Neyman-Pearson criterion. We deliberately describe the statistical distribution of wavelet coefficients with the Laplacian model so that the decoding algorithm could couple effectiveness and simplicity. In order to verify the validity of the proposed decoder, we also present a complete watermarking algorithm which relies on the luminance masking model. This algorithm could be further refined by adding local spatial support components. The watermark component with local spatial support is robust to signal processing such as cropping. However, even this simple visual model yields very good results. The hierarchical framework provides fine control of watermark embedding as well as robust watermark detection.

Acknowledgement. This work was supported by City University research grant 7001181. The first author would like to thank Grace Chang and Bin Yu for providing image denoising code of their work.

References

1. Hernandez, J.R., Amado, M., and Perez-Gonzalez, F. : DCT-Domain watermarking techniques for still images: detector performance analysis and a new structure. IEEE Trans. Image Processing. vol. 9, pp. 55–68, Jan. 2000.
2. Barni, M., Bartolini, F., De Rosa, A., and Piva, A. : A new decoder for the optimum recovery of nonadditive watermarks. IEEE Trans. Image Processing. vol. 10, pp. 755–766, May 2001.
3. Cheng, Q. and Huang, T.S. : An additive approach to transform-domain information hiding and optimum detection structure. IEEE Trans. Multimedia. vol.3, pp. 273–284, Sep. 2001.
4. Huang, J., Shi, Y.Q. and Shi, Y. : Embedding image watermarks in dc components. IEEE Trans. Circuits and Systems for Video Technology. Vol. 10, pp. 974–979, Sept. 2000.
5. Chang, S.G., Yu, B. and Vetterli, M. : Spatially adaptive wavelet thresholding with context modeling for image denoising. IEEE Trans. Image Processing. vol. 9, pp. 1522–1531, Sep. 2000.
6. Hu, Y. and Kwong, S. : Wavelet domain adaptive visible watermarking. Electronics Letters. vol. 37, pp. 1219–1220, Sep. 2001.

Enhanced Watermarking Scheme Based on Removal of Local Means

Hyun Soo Kang[1], Jin Woo Hong[2], and Kwang Yong Kim[2]

[1] Graduate School of AIM, Chung-Ang University,
221, Heuksuk-dong, Dongjak-ku, Seoul, 156-070, Korea
hskang@cau.ac.kr
[2] Broadcasting Media Research Department, ETRI,
161 Gajeong-Dong, Yuseong-Gu, Daejeon, 305-350, Korea
{jwhong, kwangyk}@etri.re.kr

Abstract. This paper presents a new watermarking scheme to reduce the detection error probability through removal of local mean values of an original signal. It will be analytically proven that the removal process plays role in reducing the interference between an original signal and a watermark to be embedded. This is simply based on the orthogonality of the DC signal and the AC signal. As a result, the process improves the ability of the right detection. The proposed method is analytically and empirically evaluated with no attack as well as JPEG compression attacks.

1 Introduction

Recently, networked multimedia systems have undergone rapid development and expansion, so that more and more information is transmitted digitally. When compared with conventional analog data, these digital multimedia data facilitate efficient and easy distribution, reproduction, and manipulation over networked information systems. Therefore, a watermarking of multimedia contents has been essential for copyright protection [1][2][3]. A digital watermark is a perceptually unobtrusive signal embedded in some multimedia asset such as images for copyright protection. The watermarking must be both robust and perceptually invisible [4]. A watermark should be large enough so that it cannot be removed easily by incidental and intended attacks including compression and common signal processing. On the other hand, it should be small enough to be perceptually invisible. In many cases watermark detection amounts to thresholding a correlation value between an input test signal and a watermark. If this value is larger than a given threshold, the watermark is said to be present. Otherwise the watermark is said to be absent.

As well-known, watermarking schemes can be classified into the non-blind and the blind methods by using or not using an original image. In general, the non-blind method such as Cox's scheme [5] is based on a correlation process that is applied to a difference signal between an original image and an input image to be tested. Meanwhile, the blind method such as Dugad's scheme [6] is based on

F. Petitcolas and H.J. Kim (Eds.): IWDW 2002, LNCS 2613, pp. 31–39, 2003.
© Springer-Verlag Berlin Heidelberg 2003

a correlation process that is directly applied to an input image. It is here noted that the non-blind methods fail to prove the rightful ownership as reported in [7]. On the other hand, though the blind methods have an advantage of rightful ownership compared with the non-blind methods, they suffer from relatively low detection reliability, which is caused by the interference between a watermark and an original signal [8].

The interference can be reduced by filtering an input test signal before correlation [9]. However, the filtering operation is not effective in the frequency domain because there is little correlation between the frequency components. Many watermark schemes have been devised to work in the frequency domain due to convenience of Rotation, Scaling, and Translation (RST) invariant realization. Accordingly, the methods to effectively reduce the interference in the frequency domain as well as the spatial domain (or time domain) are required, which is the goal of this paper.

2   Error Probability of Conventional Method

In general, watermark detection is realized by thresholding the correlator's output value, z, represented by

$$z = \sum_{n=0}^{N-1} r(n)w(n) \tag{1}$$

where $r(n)$ and $w(n)$ are an input test signal and a watermark. In case of no attack, if the watermark is present, then $r(n) = x(n) + w(n)$ where $x(n)$ is an original signal which will be considered as a deterministic signal unlike in [9]. By central limit theorem, z has Gaussian distribution of the mean and the variance,

$$\mu_z = E\left[\sum_{n=0}^{N-1}(x(n)+w(n))w(n)\right] = N\sigma_w^2 \tag{2}$$

$$\sigma_z^2 = E\left[\left(\sum_{n=0}^{N-1}x(n)w(n)\right)^2\right] = \sum_{n=0}^{N-1}\sum_{m=0}^{N-1}x(n)x(m)E\left[w(n)w(m)\right]$$

$$= \sum_{n=0}^{N-1}\sum_{m=0}^{N-1}x(n)x(m)\sigma_w^2\delta(n-m) = \sigma_w^2\sum_{n=0}^{N-1}x^2(n) = \sigma_w^2 E_x \tag{3}$$

where E_x are the energy values of $x(n)$. If the watermark is not present, we have $r(n) = x(n)$ with no attack. Similarly above, z has Gaussian distribution of $\mu_z = 0$ and $\sigma_z^2 = \sigma_w^2 E_x$. As a result, the error probability of positive false, P_+, and negative false, P_-, are as follows,

$$P_+ = P_- = \frac{1}{2}Q\left(\frac{T}{\sigma_z}\right)\bigg|_{T=E_w/2} = \frac{1}{2}Q\left(\frac{1}{2}\sqrt{\frac{N\sigma_w^2}{m_x^2 + \gamma_x^2}}\right) \tag{4}$$

where T, m_x, and γ_x^2 are a threshold, the time average value and the variance value of $x(n)$, i.e. $m_x = N^{-1} \sum_{n=0}^{N-1} x(n)$, $\gamma_x^2 = N^{-1} \sum_{n=0}^{N-1} (x(n) - m_x)^2$, respectively. Even though $x(n)$ is considered as a deterministic signal, the result is similar to that of [9]. The m_x in Eq. (4) is easily removed if the time average of $w(n)$ is zero, $\sum_{n=0}^{N-1} w(n) = 0$. That is,

$$\sum_{n=0}^{N-1} x(n)w(n) = \sum_{n=0}^{N-1} (m_x + x_{ac}(n))w(n) = \sum_{n=0}^{N-1} x_{ac}(n)w(n) \qquad (5)$$

where $x_{ac}(n)$ denotes the A.C. term of $x(n)$, while m_x corresponds to its D.C. term. Note that the energy of $x_{ac}(n)$ is $N\gamma_x^2$. Substituting Eq. (5) into Eq. (3), we have a reduced variance, which gives significant improvement in the error probability,

$$\sigma_z^2 = N\sigma_w^2 \gamma_x^2 \qquad (6)$$

Eq. (6) shows that when the time average value of the watermark is zero, the output of correlator has smaller variance. There is little possibility that the watermark that actually generated with the length N has the zero time average value, statistically zero possibility. Thus, in general, the time average value is forced to be zero, subtracted from the generated watermark, which is called DC removal process. The process for a watermark is recommended in embedding. In this paper, the conventional method means the method applying the D.C. removal technique.

3   Proposed Method

The principle that the DC free watermark results in the mean value removal of the original signal as shown in Eq. (6) is generalized in the proposed method. We can consider all positions at which the time average of a watermark with the length of N is zero. Suppose that the zero time average constraint is satisfied at T_i, $i = 0, 1, \cdots, M - 1$, i.e. $\sum_{n=0}^{T_i - 1} w(n) = 0$, where $T_{M-1} = N - 1$. We will call the position *the critical points*. Then we also see that $\sum_{n=T_i}^{T_{i+1}-1} w(n) = 0$. The watermark signal between two adjacent critical points can be considered as a new DC free watermark, which is called a sub-watermark. The sub-watermark is defined as follows.

$$w_i(n) = w(n + T_{i-1})[u(n) - u(n - N_i)] \qquad (7)$$

where $u(n)$ is the unit step function and $N_i = T_i - T_{i-1}$. Now we investigate again the variance of the correlator shown in Eq. (3). With the critical points, we have the following relationship.

$$\sum_{n=0}^{N-1} x(n)w(n) = \sum_{i=0}^{M-1} \sum_{n=0}^{N_i-1} x(n + T_{i-1})w_i(n), \quad T_{-1} = 0 \qquad (8)$$

For convenience, we define $x_i(n) = x(n + T_{i-1})[u(n) - u(n - N_i)]$, like the definition in Eq. (7). Then, the D.C. component of $x_i(n)$ is removed due to the zero time average value of $w_i(n)$, as seen in Eq. (5). That is, defining $x_{i,ac}(n)$ as the A.C. component of $x_i(n)$, we have

$$\sum_{i=0}^{M-1} \sum_{n=0}^{N_i-1} x_i(n) w_i(n) = \sum_{i=0}^{M-1} \sum_{n=0}^{N_i-1} x_{i,ac}(n) w_i(n) \tag{9}$$

$$\sigma_z^2 = E\left[\left(\sum_{i=0}^{M-1} \sum_{n=0}^{N_i-1} x_{i,ac}(n) w_i(n)\right)^2\right] = \sum_{i=0}^{M-1} E\left[\left(\sum_{n=0}^{N_i-1} x_{i,ac}(n) w_i(n)\right)^2\right]$$
$$= \sum_{i=0}^{M-1} \sum_{n=0}^{N_i-1} x_{i,ac}^2(n) \sigma_w^2 = \sigma_w^2 \sum_{i=0}^{M-1} N_i \gamma_{x_i}^2 \tag{10}$$

At this point, let's compare the results of Eq. (6) and Eq. (10). In view of the error probability, Eq. (10) is superior to Eq. (6), if $\sum_{i=0}^{M-1} N_i \gamma_{x_i}^2 \leq N \gamma_x^2$. To prove this, we consider the following equations:

$$E_x = \sum_{n=0}^{N-1} x^2(n) = \sum_{n=0}^{N-1} (x_{ac}(n) + m_x)^2 = N(\gamma_x^2 + m_x^2) \tag{11}$$

and

$$E_x = \sum_{i=0}^{M-1} \sum_{n=0}^{N_i-1} (x_{i,ac}(n) + m_{x_i})^2 = \sum_{i=0}^{M-1} N_i(\gamma_{x_i}^2 + m_{x_i}^2) \tag{12}$$

Now that Eq. (11) equals to Eq. (12), we can conclude that $\sum_{i=0}^{M-1} N_i \gamma_{x_i}^2 \leq N \gamma_x^2$ when $\sum_{i=0}^{M-1} N_i m_{x_i}^2 \geq N m_x^2$, which is easily proved by

$$\sum_{i=0}^{M-1} N_i(m_{x_i} - m_x)^2 \geq 0 \tag{13}$$

By the relations of $N m_x = \sum_{i=0}^{M-1} N_i m_{x_i}$ and $N = \sum_{i=0}^{M-1} N_i$, Eq. (13) is rewritten by

$$\left(\sum_{i=0}^{M-1} N_i m_{x_i}^2\right) - N m_x^2 \geq 0 \tag{14}$$

Eq. (14) say that the D.C. energy value of a signal, $N m_x^2$, is always smaller than the sum of piece-wise D.C. energy values of the signal, $\sum_{i=0}^{M-1} N_i m_{x_i}^2$, which lead to the fact that the A.C. energy value of the signal, $N \gamma_x^2$, is larger than the sum of piece-wise A.C. energy values of the signal, $\sum_{i=0}^{M-1} N_i \gamma_{x_i}^2$, because $N(\gamma_x^2 +$

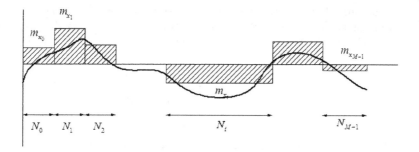

Fig. 1. D.C. values of each partition

$m_x^2) = \sum_{i=0}^{M-1} N_i(\gamma_{x_i}^2 + m_{x_i}^2)$ by Eq. (11) and Eq. (12). This fact becomes obvious more in Fig.1, where each of the shaded regions represents D.C. component of each partition. As shown in this figure, $\sum_{i=0}^{M-1} N_i m_{x_i}^2 \neq 0$ although $N m_x^2 = 0$, which means that the sum of the piece-wise D.C. energy values is always larger than the overall D.C. energy value. Finally, we have

$$Q\left(\frac{1}{2}\sqrt{N\sigma_w^2 / \sum_{i=0}^{M-1} \frac{N_i}{N}\gamma_{x_i}^2}\right) = Q\left(\frac{1}{2}\sqrt{\frac{N\sigma_w^2}{\gamma_x^2}}\right) \tag{15}$$

In Eq. (14), the property is observed that the error probability trends to decrease as the number of the critical points increases. Our proposed scheme is based on the property. For its implementation, the watermark is partitioned into M sub-watermarks and then the time average value of each sub-watermark is removed.

The proposed method is conceptually performed as follows: (1) Generate a random sequence, $w(n)$, with a target variance σ_w^2 and the length of N, (2) Partition $w(n)$ into M sub-watermarks, $w_i(n)$, $i = 0, 1, \cdots, M-1$, where $w_i(n)$ has the length of N_i, having the relationship that $N = \sum_{i=0}^{M-1} N_i$. (3) Obtain $w_i'(n)$ whose time average value is zero, removing the time average of $w_i(n)$, $w_i'(n) = w_i(n) - m_{w_i}$, where m_{w_i} denotes the time average value of $w_i(n)$, (4) Finally, combining $w_i'(n)$ for all i, we have a new watermark, $w'(n) = \cup_{i=0}^{M-1} w_i'(n)$, and then $w'(n)$ is scaled to meet with a target variance σ_w^2 in Eq. (3). Note that the D.C. removal process reduces the energy of the watermark. In step (4), the watermark resulted from scaling of $w'(n)$ is denoted by $w''(n)$, i.e. $w''(n) = \lambda w'(n)$, where $\lambda = \sigma_w/\sigma_{w'}$. After all, the sub-watermark to be embedded is $w_i''(n)$.

4   Realization of Proposed Method

First of all, we assume that a blind and frequency domain watermarking scheme is used and a watermark is embedded into the magnitude components in the middle band of $I(u,v)$, which denotes DFT of an original image $I(x,y)$. We choose an embedding band with a diamond shape, i.e. $a \leq |u| + |v| < b$. Then, one-dimensional sequence $x(n)$ can be constructed by disposing the magnitude values in the middle band of $I(u, v)$ according to a prefixed scanning rule.

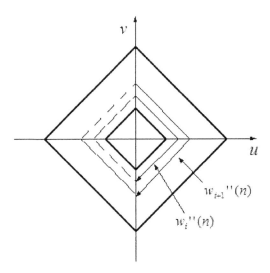

Fig. 2. Algorithm 1: embedding of a watermark

Algorithm 1: As a straightforward method, we choose that $M = b - a$, and M sub-watermarks are embedded in the size-increasing order of the diamond shape of $|u| + |v| = c$, $a \leq c < b$, that is, $w''_0(n), w''_1(n), \cdots, w''_{M-1}(n)$ for $c = a$, $a + 1$, $\cdots$, $b - 1$. Fig.2 explains this algorithm.

Algorithm 2: The analysis in the previous section showed that the error probability can be smaller as the M increases. Then, to maximize the performance of the proposed method, we consider the case of the maximum value of M, i.e. $M = N/2$, where N is assumed as an even number. The maximum value is resulted from $N_i \geq 2$. The D.C. removal process makes a sub-watermark signal disappear for $N_i = 1$ because sub-watermark signal value itself corresponds to the D.C value. In case of $N_i = 2$ for all i, an averaging attack can be very effective to remove the watermark. Fig.3 shows this case where the watermark appears as the sample values at the odd indices are repeated in the form of anti-pole of the sample values at the even indices, which is because the time average of each sub-watermark with $N_i = 2$ has to be zero. To be robust against the attack, therefore, the watermark is disposed sample by sample such that the image quality is seriously impaired by the attack. As in Fig.4, a solution of avoiding the attack is to embed $w''(2n)$ into the first and the third quadrant planes of $|I(u, v)|$, and $w''(2n + 1)$ into the second and the forth quadrant planes, where the symmetric property of $|I(u, v)|$ should be considered. This can protect the watermark from the attack of averaging the frequency components conveying $w''(2n)$ and $w''(2n+1)$. The attack can make image quality degraded seriously because it results in the symmetric in embedding band for all of the four quadrant planes.

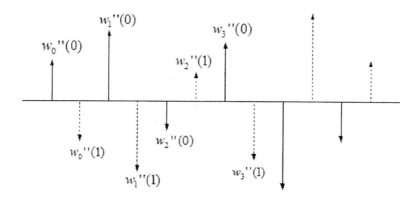

Fig. 3. An example of the watermark accommodating anti-pole

By the zero mean condition, $w''(2n+1)$ is simply in the form of anti-pole of $w''(2n)$, i.e. $w''(2n+1) = -w''(2n)$. Accordingly, we can implement as followings: (1) Obtain a random sequence, $w''(n)$, with a seed, (2) Embed $w''(n)$ according to a predetermined scanning order into the first and the third quadrant planes of $|I(u,v)|$, which is to satisfy the symmetry property of DFT, (3) Embed $-w''(n)$ according to the same scanning order in step (2) into the second and the forth quadrant planes of $|I(u,v)|$.

Though the above procedure does not include the D.C. removal process, it has an effect of applying the D.C. removal process because of accommodating the anti-pole watermark.

5   Experimental Results

For performance evaluation, we measure empirically the normalized correlation value defined as

$$\rho = \sum_{n=0}^{N-1} r(n)w(n)/N\sigma_w^2 \tag{16}$$

It is natural that the closer the normalized correlation value is to 1, the more the watermark is to be detected correctly. That is, it is ideal that the average value of ρ's (μ_ρ) is 1 and the variance of ρ's (σ_ρ^2) is 0. Thus, μ_{rho} and σ_ρ^2 can be good measures for performance evaluation, seeing how close μ_ρ is to 1 and how small σ_ρ^2 is. Also we can consider the right detection ratio (RDR) as another measure, assuming that the detector correctly detected the watermark when $\rho \geq 0.5$,

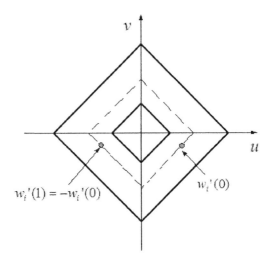

Fig. 4. Algorithm 2: embedding of a watermark

where 0.5 is the optimal decision threshold in case of the equal probability event of zero and one. Conclusively, based on the normalized correlation value, we adopt three measures for performance evaluation, the RDR, the μ_ρ, and the σ_ρ^2.

For 256×256 Lena image, we tried 1000 experiments using the 1000 different seed values for each of the two proposed algorithms and the conventional method. Then we obtained Table 1 which shows that compared with the conventional method, the proposed methods have the following advantages: (1) higher RDR, (2) μ_ρ closer to 1, and (3) smaller σ_ρ^2. As expected, the algorithm 2 is the best, which is resulted from the maximized M.

Table 1. Test results ($a = 16, b = 64$, JPEG QF=50%)

Method	Attack	PSNR	RDR	μ_ρ	σ_ρ^2
Conventional	No	45.00	99.2%	0.963	0.0334
	JPEG	28.75	88.6%	0.723	0.0326
Algorithm 1	No	45.04	99.9%	0.976	0.0214
	JPEG	28.76	94.4%	0.735	0.0207
Algorithm 2	No	45.08	100.0%	0.985	0.0155
	JPEG	28.76	97.5%	0.746	0.0156

In Table 1, the average value of ρ's is less than 1.0, which is because the watermarked signal is clipped to zero when the signal value resulted from adding the watermark signal to the original signal is less than zero. That is, the energy of the watermark signal actually embedded is slightly smaller than that of the watermark signal we intended to embed.

6   Conclusion

In this paper, a new watermarking method was presented to reduce the detection error probability through removal of local mean values of a watermark. The proposed method was realized to the two algorithms. It also was shown that the proposed method is analytically and empirically superior to the conventional method. In particular, the Algorithm 2 with the maximum of M produced the best performance.

Acknowledgement. This work was supported by Ministry of Information and Communication, Korea. The authors would like to thank the related members of MIC and the members of Broadcasting Contents Protection Research Team in ETRI.

References

1. Pitas, I.: A Method for Watermark Casting on Digital Images. vol. 8. no. 6. IEEE Transactions on Circuits and Systems for Video Technology (1998) 775–780
2. Hsu, C.-T., Wu, J.-L.: Hidden Digital Watermarks in Images. vol. 8. no. 1. IEEE Transactions on Image Processing (1999) 58–68
3. Barni, M., Bartolini, F., Cappellini, V., Piva, A.: Copyright protection of digital images by embedded unperceivable marks. vol. 16. Image and Vision Computing (1996) 897–906
4. Podilchuk, C. I., Zeng, W.: Image-Adaptive Watermarking Using Visual Models. vol. 16. no. 4. IEEE Journal on Selected Areas in Communications (1998) 525–539
5. Cox, I. J., Leighton, F. T., Shamoon, T.: Secure spread spectrum watermarking for multimedia. vol. 6. IEEE Transactions on Image Processing (1997) 1673–1687
6. Dugad, R, Ratakonda, K., Ahuja, N.: A New Wavelet-Based Scheme for Watermarking Images. proceeding ICIP'98 (1998) 419–423
7. Ratakonda, K., Dugad, R., Ahuja, N.: Digital Image Watermarking: Issues in Resolving Rightful Ownership. proceeding of ICIP'98 (1998) 414–418
8. Kang, H. S., Choi, J. G., Lee, S. W., Cho, S. J.: Reliable watermark detection method based on analysis of correlation. vol. 39, no. 12. Optical Engineering (2000) 3308–3316
9. Depovere, G., Kalker, T., Linnartz, J.-P.: Improved watermark detection reliability using filtering before correlation. proceeding of ICIP'98 (1998) 430–434

A Multi-user Based Watermarking System with Two-Security-Level Keys

Feng-Hsing Wang[1], Lakhmi Jain[1], and Jeng-Shyang Pan[2]

School of Electrical and Information Eng., University of South Australia
Feng-Hsing.Wang@postgrads.unisa.edu.au
Dept. Electronic Eng., National Kaohsiung University of Applied Sciences,
Kaohsiung, Taiwan, R. O. C.
jspan@cc.kuas.edu.tw

Abstract. A vector quantisation (VQ) based watermarking scheme with shadow watermark extraction ability for multi-users is proposed. One watermark is embedded only in the host image, and only the user with the first-class key can extract the original watermark directly; other users with the second-class keys can only extract the shadow watermarks. The watermark can also be obtained by combining all the shadow watermarks.

1   Introduction

With the ease of getting the digital data through the Internet, the copyright protection and authority identification become an important issue. A variety of schemes for digital watermarking [1] were proposed to provide useful functions to users. In the design of a multi-user based watermarking scheme for images, we are concerned with the security of the system, the quality of the output images, the robustness of the algorithm, etc. Hence, some related works were surveyed and studied. In sharing secret with multi-users, Noar and Shamir [2], and Stinson [3] proposed visual cryptography schemes to hide secret image into several shadow images. Huang et al. [4] introduced an efficient and robust VQ based watermarking technique by hiding the watermark into secret keys, which provides better quality of watermarked images. Huang et al. [5] also proposed a multiple watermarking scheme for embedding multiple watermarks. Pan et al. [6] proposed a modified visual secret sharing scheme based on shape gain VQ to separate a watermark into several shadow watermarks for embedding into an image.

Based on these proposed techniques, we will introduce a new multi-user based watermarking scheme in this paper. Instead of embedding and extracting several shadow watermarks in [6], the proposed scheme only embeds one watermark but have the ability to extract out shadow watermarks.

The content of this paper will begin with the introduction of the VQ-based watermarking scheme in Sect. 2, and follow with the proposed scheme in Sect. 3. The concept of using different secure-level keys to enhance the system with

F. Petitcolas and H.J. Kim (Eds.): IWDW 2002, LNCS 2613, pp. 40–50, 2003.
© Springer-Verlag Berlin Heidelberg 2003

the ability of sharing secret with multi-users will be mentioned in this section also. Simulation results will be presented in Sect. 4, and end with the conclusion section.

2   Vector Quantisation Based Watermarking Scheme

Vector quantisation (VQ) is a well-known and easily implemented method, which has been successfully applied on a variety of fields and subjects. In image vector quantisation, the image to be coded is first divided into a set of sub-images, which are called vectors. For each vector, the search procedure for obtaining a nearest codeword from the input codebook is carried out. The index of the obtained codeword will be assigned to the vector and delivered to the receiver. The encoding procedure is repeated until all the vectors have been handled. On the receiver side, after receiving one index, the codeword that corresponds to the index will be used to reconstruct the decoded image. The decoding procedure is also repeated until all the received indices have been handled. The amount of transmitted data can be reduced because instead of delivering the sub-images, a VQ system merely delivers the indices. For example, assume the size of each vector is 4×4 pixels (in gray-scale that means $4 \times 4 \times 8 = 128$ bits), and the size of the codebook is 256, which means the length of each index is 8 bits. For each vector, instead of transmitting the 128 bits, the VQ system in this case only transmits 8 bits.

To describe the watermarking scheme based on VQ, we define the symbols that used in this paper first. Let X denote a gray-valued image of size $M \times N$ pixels, W denote a binary-valued watermark of size $M_W \times N_W$ pixels, C denote a codebook with size L in D dimension, and the codewords therein, c_k, $k \in [0, L-1]$, can be represented by $C = \{c_0, c_1, \ldots, c_{L-1}\}$. The steps for embedding and extraction procedures are described below, and the block diagrams for the VQ-based embedding and extraction are depicted in Fig. 3(a) and (b), respectively.

Embedding steps:

1. Permute the original watermark to disperse its spatial-domain relationship.
2. Perform the VQ operation on the host image to obtain the indices.
3. Transform the VQ indices into binary format, called 'Polarity'.
4. Generate the secret key for watermark extraction.

Extraction steps:

1. Perform the VQ operation on the received image to obtain the indices.
2. Transform the VQ indices into binary format.
3. Extract the embedded watermark with the secret key.
4. Execute the inverse permutation upon the extracted watermark to recover the original watermark.

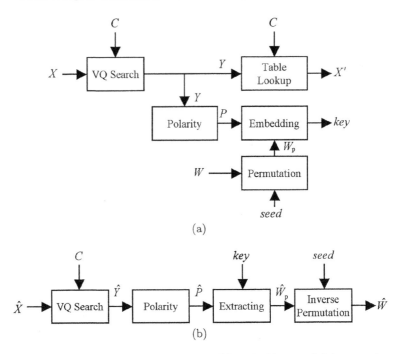

Fig. 1. The block diagrams for the VQ-based (a) embedding and (b) extraction procedures

2.1   Embedding Procedure

To decrease the effect of the picture-cropping attacks, a pseudo-random number traversing method with a user-selected seed is carried out first, which permutes the watermark to disperse its spatial-domain relationships.

$$W_\text{P} = \text{Permute}(W, seed) \,. \tag{1}$$

Then, we divide the host image into many sub-images, which are also called vectors. The VQ operation is performed to get the indices of the nearest codewords for each vector. Assume the vector at the position (m, n) of the original source X is $x(m, n)$. After performing VQ, the indices Y and $y(m, n)$ can be expressed with

$$Y = \text{VQ}(X) \,, \tag{2}$$

$$y(m, n) = \text{VQ}(x(m, n)) \in C \,. \tag{3}$$

In order to embed the binary watermark into the original source, we need to introduce some relationships to transform the VQ indices into binary formats for further embedding. Hence, we bring up the *polarities*, P, of the VQ indices to embed the watermark. For natural images, the VQ indices among the neighboring blocks tend to be very similar, and we can make use of this characteristic to generate P. To begin with, we calculate the mean value of $y(m, n)$ and the indices of its surrounding vectors with

$$\mu(m, n) = \frac{1}{9} \sum_{i=m-1}^{m+1} \sum_{j=n-1}^{n+1} y(i, j) , \tag{4}$$

where (m, n) is the vector position of the original source, and $0 \leq m < M_{\mathrm{W}}, 0 \leq n < N_{\mathrm{W}}$. The polarities that based on the mean value can be decided by

$$P = \bigcup_{m=0}^{\frac{M}{M_{\mathrm{W}}}-1} \bigcup_{n=0}^{\frac{N}{N_{\mathrm{W}}}-1} \{p(m, n)\} , \tag{5}$$

$$p(m, n) = \begin{cases} 1, \text{ if } y(m, n) \geq \mu(m, n) ; \\ 0, \text{ otherwise.} \end{cases} \tag{6}$$

Then, we are able to embed W_{P} with P by using the exclusive-or operation

$$key = W_{\mathrm{P}} \oplus P . \tag{7}$$

After the inverse-VQ operation, the reconstructed image, X', along with the secret key, work together to protect the ownership of the original image. The image quality of X' is good because only the error by the VQ operation is introduced, and it would not be influenced by the information conveyed in the watermarks because the information is hiding into the secret key.

From another point of view, the algorithm is efficient for implementation with the conventional VQ compression algorithms. Once the codeword of each vector is chosen, we are able to determine the polarity of each vector; consequently, we get the secret key. The secret key and X' are assigned to the user. The block diagram for embedding is illustrated in Fig. 1(a).

2.2   Extraction Procedure

To extract the watermark information is not difficult. First the VQ operation is performed on the received image $\hat{X}$ to obtain the indices $\hat{Y}$, and then the polarities $\hat{P}$ from the mean value of $\hat{Y}$ is calculated and estimated. With the obtained $\hat{P}$ and the existed key, the embedded watermark can be extracted by

$$\hat{W}_{\mathrm{P}} = \hat{P} \oplus key . \tag{8}$$

Finally, we perform the inverse permutation to recover the watermark

$$\hat{W} = \mathrm{InversePermute}(\hat{W}_{\mathrm{P}}, seed) . \tag{9}$$

The block diagram for describing the extraction procedure is shown in Fig. 1(b).

3   Proposed Watermarking Scheme

To enhance the watermarking system with the ability of sharing the hidden information with multi-users, and to ensure the quality of the host image does not degrade, the concept of using different keys at different levels is introduced. The proposed scheme includes four parts: embedding, key generating, extraction, and watermark recovery. The steps of the proposed scheme are listed below. The block diagrams are shown in Fig. 2.

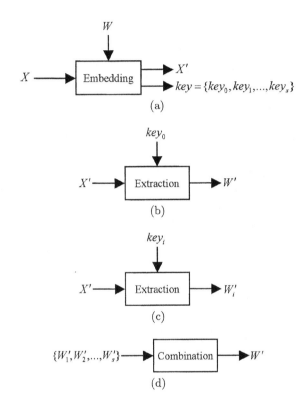

Fig. 2. The block diagrams for proposed watermarking scheme. (a) Embedding and generating keys, (b) extracting the original watermark directly with the first-class key, key_0, (c) a shadow watermark can be extracted out only while using a second-class key, key_i ($i \in [1, s]$), (d) combining all extracted shadow watermarks to obtain the original watermark

Embedding steps:

1. Perform the VQ operation on the host image to obtain the indices by using formulas (2) and (3).
2. Transform the VQ indices into binary format by using formulas (4)~(6).

3. Generate the first-class key using formula (7).
4. Generate the second-class keys.

Extraction steps:

1. Perform the VQ operation on the received image to obtain the indices by using formulas (2) and (3).
2. Transform the VQ indices into binary format by using formulas (4)~(6).
3. Extract the original watermark with the first-class key directly using formula (8).
4. Or extract a shadow watermark with either of the second-class keys using formula (8).
5. Combine all the extracted shadow watermarks to recover the original watermark.

3.1 Key Generating Procedure

In the VQ-based watermarking embedding procedure, which is described in Sect. 2.1, a secret key will be generated. Here, we use this key as the first-class key, and use it to generate the second-class keys. The algorithm in generating these keys is described below.

1. Generate the first $(s-1)$ second-class keys randomly.
2. Generate the last second-class key by controlling the amount of bit-0 or bit-1 of all the obtained keys in each bit as odd or even. For example, in a three second-class keys case, assume the i-th bit of the first-class key and the two second-class keys is 0, 1, and 1 respectively. The total amount of bit-1 is even, hence the i-th bit of the last second-class key is set as 1 to keep the total amount of bit-1 as odd; otherwise set the bit as 0.

The C/C++ source codes for this algorithm are shown below.

```
for(int i=0; i<KEY_LEN; i++)
{
  // 1. Generate the first s-1 second-class keys.
  int count=key[0][i]; //key[0] is the first-class key.
  for(j=1; j<s; j++)
  {
    key[j][i]=random(2);
    count+=key[j][i];
  }

  // 2. Generate the last second-class key.
  key[s][i]=count%2==0? 1:0;
}
```

The output image and the generated keys (one first-class key, and s second-class keys) can then be assigned to the related users for sharing the hidden secret.

3.2   Watermark Recovery Procedure

In the extraction procedure, the steps for extracting a watermark with either key are the same as the steps in Sect. 2.2. Only an extra step for recovering the original watermark has to be done. The algorithm is defined as: if the total amount of bit-1 in the i-th bit of all the shadow watermarks is odd, the bit of the real watermark is 0; otherwise, the bit is 1. The C/C++ source codes for this algorithm are shown below.

```
for(int i=0; i<WATERMARK_LEN; i++)
{
  // 1. Count the total amount of bit-1 for current watermark bit.
  int count=0;
  for(int j=0; j<s; j++)
    count+= shadow_watermark[j][i];

  // 2. Recover the watermark bit.
  watermark[i]=count%2==0? 1:0;
}
```

An example of the proposed algorithm with three second-class keys is shown in Fig. 3. In this example, Fig. 3(a)~(c) are the shadow watermarks that was extracted from the watermarked image with the second-class keys, $key_1 \sim key_3$, respectively. Fig. 3(d) is the watermark obtained by combining all the extracted shadow watermarks. In this algorithm, the extracted watermark using the first-class key is the same as the combined one.

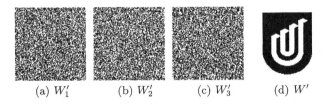

(a) W_1' (b) W_2' (c) W_3' (d) W'

Fig. 3. An example of three second-class keys case. (a)~(c) Extracted shadow watermarks and (d) combined result

4   Simulation Results

The used host image of the experiment is LENA with size 512×512. The watermark to be embedded within the host image is a binary logo, whose size is 128×128 and is shown in Fig. 3(d). The codebook with 256 codewords therein was trained from LENA image by using LBG algorithm.

For testing the robustness of our system, some different attacking functions are employed upon the system. The attacking functions are JPEG compression with different quality factors (QF), low-pass filtering, median filtering, cropping with different proportion, and replacing the surroundings with PEPPERS image. We applied the peak signal-to-noise ratio (PSNR) and normalized cross-correction (NC) as the benchmark to evaluate the quality of the output images and the robustness of our algorithm, respectively.

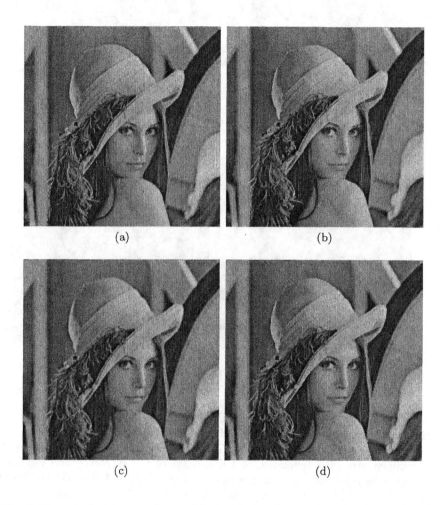

Fig. 4. The attacked images generated by employing the attacking functions upon the watermarked image: (a) JPEG compression with quality factor (QF) =60%, (b) JPEG compression with QF =70%, (c) low-pass filtering with window size =3, (d) median filtering with window size =3, (e) cropping 20% of the surroundings, (f) cropping 25% in the lower-left quarter, (g) replacing the surroundings of Fig. 4(e) with PEPPERS image, and (h) replacing the surroundings of Fig. 4(b) with PEPPERS image

(e)   (f)

(g)   (h)

Fig. 4. (continued)

When no attack introduced, the PSNR value between the host image and the output image is 31.83 dB. The NC value between the original watermark and the final combined result is 1.0. Fig. 4 shows the attacked images under the mentioned attacking functions, and Fig. 5 shows the extracted and recovered watermarks from these attacked images in Fig. 4. Table 1 displays the PSNR values between the output image and the attacked images, and the NC values between the original watermark and the recovered results.

5   Conclusion

The main contribution of this paper is to introduce the use of different secure-level of keys into the watermarking system, which provides a useful function for sharing information with different users at different levels. The user at the first-

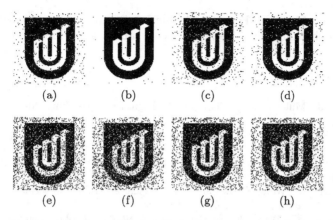

(a)	(b)	(c)	(d)
(e)	(f)	(g)	(h)

Fig. 5. Combined results after extracting all the shadow watermarks from the attacked images in Fig. 4: (a) JPEG compression with QF=60%, (b) JPEG compression with QF=70%, (c) low-pass filtering with window size =3, (d) median filtering with window size =3, (e) cropping 20% of the surroundings, (f) cropping 25% in the lower-left quarter, (g) replacing the surroundings of Fig. 4(e) with PEPPERS image, and (h) replacing the surroundings of Fig. 4(b) with PEPPERS image

Table 1. The PSNR values between the output image and the attacked images, and the NC values between the original watermark and the combined results

Attacks	PSNR (dB)	NC
JPEG (QF=60%)	38.66	0.9742
JPEG (QF=70%)	39.74	0.9965
Low-pass Filtering	34.34	0.9624
Median Filtering	36.44	0.9743
Cropping (20%)	12.10	0.8803
Cropping (25%)	9.82	0.8684
Replacing Surroundings (20%)	18.28	0.8911
JPEG (QF=70%) + Replacing Surroundings (20%)	18.26	0.8886

class level can extract out the genuine watermark directly with his first-class key, and the users at the second-class level can only extract out shadow watermarks. Comparing with [6] and [2], instead of embedding all the shadow watermarks into the host image in [6] and assigning the shadow images to the users directly in [2], the proposed scheme embeds one watermark only and assigns the secret keys to users. That means our scheme has better effectiveness and security. In additional, although the proposed scheme is based on VQ, it is very easy to implement and to be employed in other watermarking schemes. As for the key-assign problem, the known and proposed schemes that have been used in other watermarking systems could be used. From the simulation results and the provided functions, it is clear that our method is novel, useful, robust, and effective.

References

1. Cox, I. J., Miller, M. L., Bloom, J. A.: Digital watermarking. Morgan Kaufmann (2000)
2. Noar, M., Shamir, A.: Visual cryptography. Lecture Notes in Computer Science. Springer-Verlag, Perugia Italy (1994) 1–12
3. Stinson, D.: Visual cryptography and threshold schemes. Vol. 18. IEEE Potentials (1999) 13–16
4. Huang, H. -C., Wang, F. H., Pan, J. S.: Efficient and robust watermarking algorithm with vector quantisation. Vol. 37. Electronics Letters (2001) 826–828
5. Huang, H. -C., Wang, F. H., Pan, J. S.: A VQ-based robust multi-watermarking algorithm. IEICE Transactions on Fundamentals of Electronics, Communication and Computer Sciences (2002) 1719–1726
6. Pan J. S., Wang, F. H., Yang, T. C., Jain, L. C.: A gain-shape VQ based watermarking technique with modified visual secret sharing scheme. International Conference on Knowledge-Based Intelligent Information and Engineering Systems, IEE, Italy (2002) 402–406

A New Blind Watermarking Technique Based on Independent Component Analysis

Dan Yu and Farook Sattar

Division of Information Engineering, School of Electrical and Electronic Engineering
Nanyang Technological University, Nanyang Avenue, Singapore 639798.
{p141450770,efsattar}@ntu.edu.sg

Abstract. In this paper, we propose a new blind watermarking scheme by embedding a digital image signature/watermark in the wavelet domain and using Independent Component Analysis (ICA) technique for blind watermark extraction. The watermark is inserted in the middle frequency sub-bands. A visual masking function is used to modify the digital signature to assure the perceptual quality of the watermarked image. Independent Component Analysis (ICA) method is employed for blind watermark extraction without requiring the original image. The presented technique has been successfully evaluated and compared with other wavelet-based blind watermarking techniques against the most prominent attacks, such as JPEG and JPEG2000 compression and quantization.

1 Introduction

With the rapid growth of digital networks, digital libraries, and World Wide Web services, the convenient broadcasting or exposition of digital products on the global network leads easily to illegal copying, modifying and retransmission. Digital watermarking offers a way to counter copyright piracy on the global networks. This paper proposes a new efficient watermarking technique using ICA method, for protecting intellectual propriety rights on digital multimedia content.

In general, digital watermarking can be classified into according to embedding domain, i.e. the spatial-domain and the frequency-domain watermarking. The spatial-domain watermarking is comparatively easy to implement, but less robust against compression and filtering. Frequency domain watermarking shows better robustness under most of the signal processing attacks. The wavelet-based watermarking technique satisfies the requirement for Internet distribution – the progressive transmission property. Some existing blind wavelet-domain watermarking techniques are summarized in the following.

Wang *et al.* [1] proposes an adaptive watermarking method to embed watermarks into selected significant sub-band wavelet coefficients. A blind watermark retrieval technique is proposed by truncating selected significant coefficients to some specific value. Inoue *et al.* [2] classify wavelet coefficients as insignificant and significant by zerotree which is defined in the embedded zerotree wavelet

F. Petitcolas and H.J. Kim (Eds.): IWDW 2002, LNCS 2613, pp. 51–63, 2003.
© Springer-Verlag Berlin Heidelberg 2003

(EZW) algorithm. Information data embedding algorithms in the locations of significant and insignificant coefficients are developed. Information data are detected using the position of the zerotree's root and the threshold value after decomposition of the watermarked image. Dugad *et al.* [3] add the watermark in selected coefficients with significant image energy in the transform domain in order to ensure non-erasability of the watermark. During watermark detection, all the high pass coefficients above the threshold are chosen and correlated with the original copy of the watermark. Kundur *et al.* [4] presents a novel technique for the digital watermarking of still images based on the concept of multiresolution wavelet fusion, which is robust to a variety of signal distortions. In [5], Xie *et al.* develop a blind watermarking digital signature for the purpose of authentication. The signature algorithm is first implemented in wavelet transform domain and is coupled within the SPIHT compression algorithm.

Most of the existing watermarking schemes are always based on some assumptions for watermark detection and extraction. Some schemes require the previous knowledge of watermark location, strength or some threshold. In some algorithms, the watermark is estimated with the help of the original watermark information. Firstly, to ensure the robustness and invisibility of a watermark, the optimum embedding location are generally different for different images. For a large image database, it could be a disadvantage if requiring watermark location and strength information for detection and extraction, since a large amount of information are needed to be stored. In the Internet distribution application, the owner can always distribute the multimedia data by assigning different watermarks to different users in order to prevent illegal redistribution of data by a legal user. In such scenario, the watermark detection/extraction algorithms requiring the information of watermark location and strength, or the original watermark should fail, since the users do not know exactly which watermark is embedded in this copy of the watermarked image.

Thus a new blind watermarking scheme which overcomes the problems discussed above is proposed in this paper. The advantages of the proposed watermarking scheme with ICA-based watermark extraction, are the followings:

(a) The proposed method has a general framework for copyright protection and ownership identification, since extraction algorithm does not require any information on watermark locations and strengths. Only requiring an owner's copy of the original image and the key, the present method can extract the watermark embedded in different copies of the watermarked image for ownership identification.

(b) Instead of random sequences, some readable signature or pattern image is used as watermark. By using such a watermark, it is more robust against attacks, because the signature or image pattern can always preserve a certain degree of structural information, which are meaningful and recognizable, can be more easy to be verified by human eyes rather than some objective similarity measurements.

(c) A visual masking – Noise Visibility Function (NVF) is used during watermark insertion to ensure the perceptual quality of the watermarked image.

2   Proposed Watermark Embedding Scheme

This section presents the watermark embedding scheme in the wavelet domain. Watermark embedding locations are selected. The watermark generation and embedding procedure are presented in detail.

Fig. 1 shows a second level wavelet decomposition of Lena image into four bands – low frequency band (LL), high frequency band (HH), low-high frequency band (LH), and high-low frequency band (HL). Sub-bands LL and HH are not suitable for watermark embedding among these four sub-band components. The image quality can be degraded if watermark is embedding in LL sub-band, since it contains most important information of an image. Sub-band HH is insignificant compared to LH and HL sub-bands, and watermark embedding in such sub-band is difficult to survive against lossy JPEG compression attacks. In this paper, watermark embedding in the two sub-bands (e.g. LH2, HL2 of the second level wavelet decomposition) consisting the middle frequency pair are demonstrated.

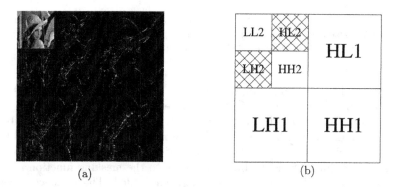

(a)   (b)

Fig. 1. Second level wavelet decomposition of Lena image.

Some digital signature/pattern or company logo (**S**), for example, a text image in Fig. 2(a), can be used to generate the watermark (**W**) to be embedded. As pointed out earlier, such watermarks are more robust against attacks. They are very unique to identify the ownership, and can be more easier to be verified by human eyes rather than some objective similarity measurements. A masking function – Noise Visibility Function [6] is obtained to characterize the local image properties, identifying the textured and edge regions where the information can be more strongly embedded. Such high activity regions are generally highly insensitive to distortion. With the visual mask, the watermark strength can be reasonably increased without visually degrading the image quality.

Fig. 3 illustrates the watermark embedding procedure using second level decomposed middle frequency pair (LH2 and HL2):

[**Step 1.**] Perform the second level discrete wavelet decomposition of the original image, **I**. Sub-bands LH2 and HL2 are selected for the watermark insertion.

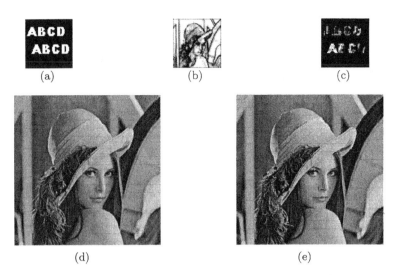

(a)   (b)   (c)

(d)   (e)

Fig. 2. (a) A text signature (64×64), (b) a NVF masking function, (c) modified text watermark based on the visual mask in (b), (d) original Lena image (256×256), and (e) a watermarked Lena image (PSNR=45.5dB).

[**Step 2.**] The NVF masking function [6], $\mathbf{M}$, of the original image is generated. Fig. 2(b) shows a NVF mask of the Lena image. For the homogeneous region, NVF approaches 1 (white color), and the strength of the embedded watermark approaches to zero. The watermark should embed in highly textured regions containing edges instead of homogeneous regions. The original signature image $\mathbf{S}$, is modified according to the masking function to assure the imperceptibility of the watermark embedded. The final watermark is quantized into [0-7] gray levels. The expression for watermark generation is given as

$$\mathbf{W} = \mathbf{Q_8}[(\mathbf{1} - \mathbf{M}).\mathbf{S}], \tag{1}$$

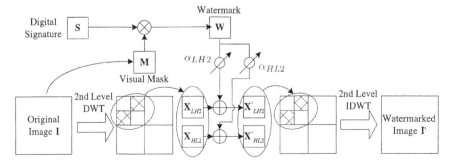

Fig. 3. Watermark embedding scheme (for the second level wavelet decomposition).

where $\mathbf{Q_8}$ denotes the quantization operator with 8 gray levels. Fig. 2(c) shows a text watermark generated using the NVF masking function shown in Fig. 2(b).

[**Step 3.**] The watermark $\mathbf{W}$ is embedded in the following way:

$$\mathbf{X}'_{LH2} = \mathbf{X}_{LH2} + \alpha_{LH2} \cdot \mathbf{W} = \mathbf{X}_{LH2} + \alpha_{\mathbf{X}} \cdot \mu(|\mathbf{X}_{LH2}|) \cdot \mathbf{W};$$
$$\mathbf{X}'_{HL2} = \mathbf{X}_{HL2} + \alpha_{HL2} \cdot \mathbf{W} = \mathbf{X}_{HL2} + \alpha_{\mathbf{X}} \cdot \mu(|\mathbf{X}_{HL2}|) \cdot \mathbf{W}, \qquad (2)$$

where $\mathbf{X}$ and $\mathbf{X}'$ are respectively the wavelet transform coefficients of the original image and the watermarked image, α_{LH2} and α_{HL2} denote respectively the weighting coefficients of the watermark embedding in sub-bands LH2 and HL2, $\mu(|\cdot|)$ denotes the operation of mean of the absolute value, and a common control parameter α_X is used to adjust the watermark embedding strength to maintain the quality of the watermarked image within 40-50dB in terms of PSNR (*Peak-Signal-to-Noise-Ratio*) [7].

[**Step 4.**] The watermarked image, $\mathbf{I}'$, is obtained by the inverse discrete wavelet transform. Fig. 2(e) gives a watermarked Lena image with PSNR 45.5dB. Table 1 lists the quality of watermarked image (PSNR in dB) with respect to the control parameter α_X.

Table 1. PSNR (in dB) of the watermarked image with respect to α_X.

α_X	0.01	0.05	0.10	0.15	0.20	0.25	0.30
PSNR(dB)	67.50	53.52	47.50	43.98	41.48	39.54	37.96

For the security purpose in multimedia, the original data are always kept in secret and should not be known to the users during their watermark detection/extraction. The technique used in this paper to solve the problem is that the user can keep a copy of the dataset embedding with an owner's watermark following the same procedure shown in Fig. 3. The owner's watermark is also known as the *key* of the watermarking system, which is used for watermark extraction. Using only the owner's copy, $\mathbf{I}'_0$, and the key, $\mathbf{K}$, the owner is able to identify the ownership of any copy of a watermarked image. This will be elaborated in the following Section 3 in detail.

Fig. 4(a) is an owner's copy of the Lena image, embedded with an owner's watermark (a gold-like sequence image [8], and shown in Fig. Fig. 4(b)). The owner's copy is obtained similarly by embedding $\mathbf{K}$ in the wavelet domain using the following equations,

$$\mathbf{X}'_{0LH2} = \mathbf{X}_{LH2} + \alpha_{LH2} \cdot \mathbf{K} = \mathbf{X}_{LH2} + \alpha_{\mathbf{X_0}} \cdot \mu(|\mathbf{X_0}_{LH2}|) \cdot \mathbf{K};$$
$$\mathbf{X}'_{0HL2} = \mathbf{X}_{HL2} + \alpha_{HL2} \cdot \mathbf{K} = \mathbf{X}_{HL2} + \alpha_{\mathbf{X_0}} \cdot \mu(|\mathbf{X_0}_{HL2}|) \cdot \mathbf{K}, \qquad (3)$$

where $\mathbf{X}_0$ and $\mathbf{X}'_0$ are respectively the wavelet transform coefficients of the original image and the owner's watermarked image, $\alpha_{\mathbf{X_0}}$ is a control parameter for the visual quality of the watermarked image $\mathbf{I}'_0$.

(b)

(a)

Fig. 4. (a) The owner's copy of the original Lena image (PSNR=47.6dB and 256×256), (b) the owner's watermark or the key (64×64).

3   Proposed Watermark Extraction Scheme Using ICA Method

In this section, the concept of ICA is firstly introduced briefly. A blind watermark extraction scheme is then proposed, where ICA is employed for watermark extraction successfully.

3.1   Independent Component Analysis

Independent Component Analysis (ICA) is one of the most widely used method for performing Blind Source Separation (BSS). It is a very general-purpose statistical technique to recover the independent sources given only sensor observations that are linear mixtures of independent source signals [9,10,11]. ICA has widely applied in many areas such as audio processing, biomedical signal processing, telecommunications. In this paper, ICA is further applied in blind watermarking for ownership identification.

ICA model consists of two parts: the mixing process and unmixing process. In the mixing process [9,10,11], the observed linear mixtures $x_1, \cdots, x_m$ of n number of independent components are defined as

$$x_j = a_{j1}s_1 + a_{j2}s_2 + ... + a_{jn}s_n;\, 1 \leq j \leq m, \tag{4}$$

where $\{s_k, k = 1, \cdots, n\}$ denote the source variables, i.e., the independent components, and $\{a_{jk}, j = 1, \cdots, m; k = 1, \cdots, n\}$ are the mixing coefficients. In vector-matrix form, the above mixing model can be expressed as

$$\mathbf{x} = \mathbf{As}, \tag{5}$$

where $\mathbf{A} = \begin{pmatrix} a_{11} & a_{12} & \cdots & a_{1n} \\ a_{21} & a_{22} & \cdots & a_{2n} \\ \vdots & \vdots & \ddots & \vdots \\ a_{m1} & a_{m2} & \cdots & a_{mn} \end{pmatrix}$ is the mixing matrix [9,10,11], $\mathbf{x} = [x_1 x_2 \cdots x_m]^T$, $\mathbf{s} = [s_1 s_2 \cdots s_n]^T$, and T is the transpose operator. For unmixing process [9,10,11], after estimating the matrix $\mathbf{A}$, one can compute its inverse – the unmixing matrix, $\mathbf{B}$, and the independent components are obtained as:

$$\mathbf{s} = \mathbf{Bx}. \tag{6}$$

To assure the identifiability of the ICA model, following fundamental restrictions are imposed [9,10]:

- The source signals in the mixing process should be principally statistically independent.
- All the independent components $\mathbf{s}_k$, with the possible exception of one component, must be non-Gaussian.
- The number of observed linear mixtures m must be at least as large as the number of independent components n, i.e., m$\geq$n.
- The matrix $\mathbf{A}$ must be of full column rank.

There are many various ICA algorithms which have been proposed recently. Some popular ICA methods include Hyvärinen and Oja's FastICA [12], Bell and Sejnowski's Infomax [13], Cardoso's JADE [14] and Cichocki and Barro's RICA [15] and so on. In this paper, Cichocki and Barro's RICA [15] is exploited in the watermark extraction process. The robust batch algorithm models the signal as an autoregressive (AR) process [15], therefore, it is an effective blind separation approach particularly for the temporally correlated sources.

3.2   Proposed Blind Watermark Extraction Scheme

This section proposes an ICA-based blind watermark extraction scheme. Instead of using the original image, only an owner's copy of the original image is required for watermark extraction. The new useful features of the proposed scheme are that the present method does not require the previous knowledge of watermark locations and watermark strength information for watermark extraction. The main idea is to consider two sub-bands ($\mathbf{X}'_{\mathbf{R}}$) of the watermarked image to have a mixture image of the wavelet transformed image ($\mathbf{X_R}$) of the original image $\mathbf{I}$ and the watermark image ($\mathbf{W}$). Fig. 5 shows the above blind watermark extraction scheme.

[**Step 1.**] Perform the second level discrete wavelet decomposition of the watermarked image $\mathbf{I}'$ in order to obtain the wavelet coefficients, $\mathbf{X}'_{LH2}$ and $\mathbf{X}'_{HL2}$ for the two selected sub-bands of LH2 and HL2.
[**Step 2.**] The first mixture signal, $\mathbf{Y}_1$, is obtained by

$$\mathbf{Y}_1 = \mathbf{X}'_{LH2} + \mathbf{X}'_{HL2}. \tag{7}$$

From (2), $\mathbf{X}'_{\mathbf{R}}$ ($\mathbf{R} \in [LH2, HL2]$) are the mixture observations of the wavelet transform of the original image ($\mathbf{X_R}$) and the watermark ($\mathbf{W}$), therefore, (7) can be rewritten as

$$\mathbf{Y}_1 = \mathbf{X} + \alpha_1 \mathbf{W}, \tag{8}$$

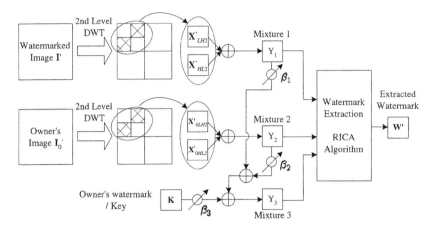

Fig. 5. The proposed blind watermark extraction scheme (using the second level decomposed images).

where $\mathbf{X} = \mathbf{X}_{LH2} + \mathbf{X}_{HL2}$ and $\alpha_1 = \alpha_X \cdot [\mu(|\mathbf{X}_{LH2}|) + \mu(|\mathbf{X}_{HL2}|)]$. It is found that the first mixture image is a linear mixture of the two independent source images, i.e., $\mathbf{X}$ and $\mathbf{W}$.

[**Step 3.**] Repeat the same procedure in Step 1 and 2 for the owner's image $\mathbf{I}_0'$. The second mixture, $\mathbf{Y}_2$, is obtained by

$$\mathbf{Y}_2 = \mathbf{X}'_{0_{LH2}} + \mathbf{X}'_{0_{HL2}}. \tag{9}$$

Similarly $\mathbf{Y}_2$ is also a linear mixture of the wavelet transform of the original image ($\mathbf{X_R}, \mathbf{R} \in [LH2, HL2]$) and the key/owner's watermark ($\mathbf{K}$). It can be written as

$$\mathbf{Y}_2 = \mathbf{X} + \alpha_2 \mathbf{K}, \tag{10}$$

where $\alpha_2 = \alpha_{\mathbf{X}_0} \cdot [\mu(|\mathbf{X}_{0LH2}|) + \mu(|\mathbf{X}_{0HL2}|)]$.

[**Step 4.**] From (7) and (9), two mixture images can be obtained containing three source images or independent components in the observations – $\mathbf{X}$, key $\mathbf{K}$ and the watermark $\mathbf{W}$. As pointed out earlier, to exploit ICA methods for watermark extraction, it is required that the number of observed linear mixture inputs is at least equal to or larger than the number of independent sources, in order to assure the identifiability of ICA model [9,10, 11]. Therefore, another linear mixture of the three independent sources is needed. The third mixture $\mathbf{Y}_3$ can be generated by linear superposition of $\mathbf{Y}_1$, $\mathbf{Y}_2$ and $\mathbf{K}$:

$$\mathbf{Y}_3 = \beta_1 \mathbf{Y}_1 + \beta_2 \mathbf{Y}_2 + \beta_3 \mathbf{K}, \tag{11}$$

where β_1, β_2 and β_3 are arbitrary real numbers. The coefficient β_3 should be non-zero. Either β_1 or β_2 can be set to zero to efficiently reduce the computational load of ICA.

[**Step 5.**] The three mixtures input into the RICA algorithm [8,15], and the watermark image, $\mathbf{W}'$, is extracted. The ownership is able to be verified directly from the extracted signature. Fig. 6 shows the extracted watermark from the watermarked image shown in Fig. 2(e).

Fig. 6. The extracted watermark image using ICA method (normalized correlation coefficient, $r \approx 1.0000$).

4   Experimental Results

The results for robustness of the proposed watermarking scheme are shown in the section by using the original lena image of size (256×256) where the simulations are performed in the MATLAB 5.3 software environment. A watermarked image (PSNR=45.5dB) in Fig. 2(e) is generated by inserting 389 bits information (with $\alpha_{\mathbf{X}}=0.125$). In the experiments of watermark extraction, the parameters β_1, β_2 and β_3 are set as 0, 1, 1, respectively, to simplify the computational load of ICA; Daubechies-1 (Haar) orthogonal filters are employed for wavelet decomposition. In order to investigate the robustness of the watermark, the watermarked image is attacked by various signal processing techniques, such as JPEG and JPEG2000 compression, color quantization. The watermark extraction is performed against those attacks to the watermarked image and compared the extracted watermark with the original watermark. For a robust watermark scheme, it should be able to survive against various attacks before the quality of the watermarked image would be degraded drastically.

4.1   The Performance Index

The performance of the blind watermark extraction result is evaluated in term of *normalized correlation coefficient, r,* of the extracted watermark $\mathbf{W}'$ and the original watermark $\mathbf{W}$ as:

$$r = \frac{\mathbf{W} \cdot \mathbf{W}'}{\sqrt{\mathbf{W}^2 \cdot \mathbf{W}'^2}}. \tag{12}$$

The magnitude range of r is [-1, 1], and the unity holds if the extracted image perfectly matches its original image.

4.2   Results and Performance Comparison

In the following, the robustness of the proposed watermarking scheme is compared with some other blind wavelet-domain watermarking techniques [7] in terms of *normalized correlation coefficient r* as shown by (12). These techniques include Wang's algorithm [1], Inoue's blind algorithm (based on manipulating insignificant coefficients) [2], Dugad's algorithm [3], Kundur's algorithm [4] and Xie's algorithm [5].

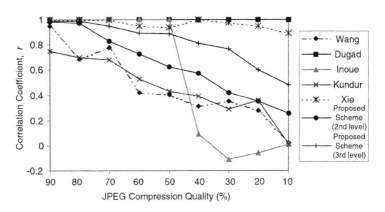

Fig. 7. Comparisons of results against JPEG compression attacks.

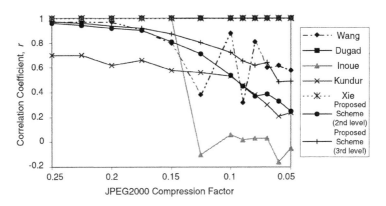

Fig. 8. Comparisons of results against JPEG2000 compression attacks.

Fig. 7 shows the comparison results in terms of performance index against JPEG compression. For the proposed scheme, the extracted watermark's correlation decreases gradually as with the compression quality factor. The image quality has degraded significantly to 27dB PSNR when the compression quality becomes quite low to 10%. In this difficult case, the watermark can be still

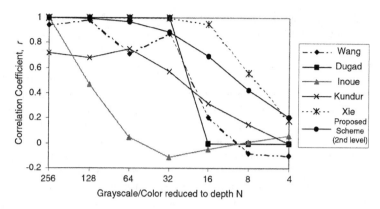

Fig. 9. Comparisons of results against color quantization.

extracted with the value of the performance index of 0.2553 for watermark embedding in second level wavelet decomposition. According to Fig. 7, the present scheme performs better than Wang's and Kundur's methods, and much better than Inoue's method in terms of robustness against JPEG compression attack when the compression quality factor is very low.

Fig. 8 is the extraction comparison against the JPEG2000 compression attacks. The robustness of the proposed scheme is demonstrated up to the compression factor 0.05 or compression rate 0.4 bpp (bit per pixel). The proposed scheme has better result than Kundur's method, and comparable result to Wang's method. The extraction performance of Inoue's method drops sharply when the JPEG2000 compression factor goes to 0.125. Embedding in the sub-bands of higher level wavelet decomposition (see curves for extraction performance of third level decomposition in Figs. 7 and 8), can improve the robustness of the proposed scheme against compression attacks. The possible reason for higher robustness against compression attack is that the energy spectrum becomes more flat (less compact) as the decomposition level increases.

Fig. 9 shows extraction results against color quantization from gray level 256 to 4 per pixel. The proposed scheme has very good robustness result against color quantization. The performance of the proposed scheme can be comparable to that of the Xie's method, and much better than the other methods.

From Figs. 7 and 8, it is found that Xie's and Dugad's methods have excellent robustness against JPEG and JPEG2000 compression. In Xie's algorithm, the watermark is embedded solely in the approximation image (LL sub-band) of the host image [5]. Although LL sub-band embedding is robust against compression attacks, the image quality could be degraded visually because the coefficients of this portion always contain the most important information of an image [7] . It is claimed that the robustness of Xie's method is determined by the number of decomposition steps. Very good robustness result can be obtained by employing a five-level wavelet decomposition using Daubechies-7/9 bi-orthogonal filters [5, 7]. Dugad's method embeds the watermark in the significant coefficients of all the detail sub-bands [3], therefore it is more resistant to compression. During the watermark detection in Dugad's method, the original watermark is required to compute the correlation with the high pass coefficients above a threshold [3]. The presence of a watermark is determined by comparing this correlation with a threshold setting. It is not as general as our proposed scheme in the case when the watermark embedded in a watermarked image is previously unknown.

The experimental results show that the proposed scheme has good robustness against the most prominent attacks – JPEG and JPEG2000 compression, color quantization, and can be comparable to the existing blind wavelet-domain watermarking schemes. The new watermarking scheme shows its main advantage in terms of generality. No previous knowledge of watermark strength and location are required for watermark extraction. Experiments also show that the type of wavelet transform used is not critical for the robustness of the proposed watermarking scheme (the corresponding results are not included), which is crucial for Xie's method from robustness point of view [5,7]. Moreover, most of the existing algorithms need to set a threshold for watermark detection while using the correlation method. The another advantage of the proposed ICA-based method is that without using a threshold, the extracted watermark could simply be verified from visually rather than by using some objective measures or some thresholds, since the embedded watermark is a readable digital signature image or logo image.

5   Discussion and Conclusion

In this paper, a new blind image watermarking technique based on Independent Component Analysis (ICA) is presented. Watermark is obtained by modifying the signature image with a visual mask to prevent perceptual quality degradation of the watermarked image. The watermark is inserted in the two middle frequency sub-band pair for the higher decomposition level (say second/third decomposition level) for the DWT of the original image. Without requiring any information on watermark location and strength, the proposed scheme can extract the watermark by using an owner's copy of the image and the owner's watermark/key. Experimental results show that the proposed watermarking scheme can provide good resistance under attacks of image compression and color quantization.

The advantage of using ICA algorithm for this blind watermark scheme is that, unlike other methods, no *a priori* information about watermark location and strength as well as threshold, are needed for our blind watermark extraction scheme. Therefore, it is possible to extract the watermark from any copy of the watermarked image, where the embedded watermark is previously unknown. The generality of the proposed scheme implicates the method to be a quite useful tool for the ownership identification and copyright protection in the application of Internet distribution. The only disadvantage to achieve the generality using ICA-based technique could be the complexity of the ICA itself. In this paper, this has been compromised by exploiting the second-order RICA method, which is simple and efficient. In the future work, more experiments will be carried out in order to evaluate the resistance of the scheme against other types of attacks, and to improve the robustness of the system further.

Acknowledgement. The authors would like to thank Prof. N. G. Kingsbury for his valuable suggestions and comments that help to improve this paper. They are also thankful to Prof. K.-K. Ma for contributing useful discussion regarding the use of ICA in image watermarking.

References

1. Wang H.-J. M., Su P.-C., Kuo C.-C. J.: Wavelet-Based Digital Image Watermarking. Optics Express, Vol. 3, No. 12 (1998) 491–496
2. Inoue H., Miyazaki A., Yamamoto A., Katsura T.: A Digital Watermark Based on the Wavelet Transform and Its Robustness on Image Compression. Proc. of IEEE ICIP (1998)
3. Dugad R., Ratakonda K., Ahuja N.: A New Wavelet-Based Scheme for Watermarking Images. Proc. of IEEE ICIP (1998)
4. Kundur D., Hatzinakos D.: Digital Watermarking Using Multiresolution Wavelet Decomposition. Proc. of IEEE ICASSP, Vol. 5 (1998) 2969–2972
5. Xie L., Arce G. R.: Joint Wavelet Compression and Authentication Watermarking. Proc. of IEEE ICIP (1998)
6. Voloshynovskiy S., Herrigel A., Baumgaertner N., Pun T.: A Stochastic Approach to Content Adaptive Digital Image Watermarking. Proc. of International Workshop on Information Hiding. Dresden. Germany (1999)
7. Peter P.: Digital Image Watermarking in the Wavelet Transform Domain (Master's Thesis). (2001)
8. Yu D., Sattar F. and Ma K.-K., Watermark Detection and Extraction using Independent Component Analysis Method. EURASIP Jounal on Applied Signal Processing – Special Issue on Nonlinear Signal and Image Processing (Part II), Vol. 2002, No. 1 (2002)
9. Hyvärinen A.: Survey on Independent Component Analysis. Neural Computing Surveys, Vol. 2 (1999) 94–128
10. Hyvärinen A., Oja E.: Independent Component Analysis: a Tutorial. http://www.cis.hut.fi/projects/ica/ (1999)
11. Lee T.-W.: Independent Component Analysis: Theory and Applications. Kluwer Academic Publishers (1998)
12. Hyvärinen A.: Fast and Robust Fixed-Point Algorithms for Independent Component Analysis. IEEE Trans. Neural Networks, Vol. 10 (1999) 626–634
13. Bell A., Sejnowski T.: An Information-Maximization Approach to Blind Separation and Blind Deconvolution. Neural Compt., Vol. 7 (1995) 1129–1159
14. Cardoso J.-F.: High-Order Contrasts for Independent Component Analysis. Neural Comput., Vol. 11 (1999) 157–192
15. Cichocki A., Barros A. K.: Robust Batch Algorithm for Sequential Blind Extraction of Noisy Biomedical Signals. Proc. ISSPA'99, Vol. 1 (1999) 363–366

A New Collusion Attack and Its Performance Evaluation

Viktor Wahadaniah, Yong Liang Guan, and Hock Chuan Chua

Nanyang Technological University, School of EEE, Nanyang Avenue, Singapore 639798.
{pf438001, eylguan, ehchua}@ntu.edu.sg

Abstract. Digital watermarking is a technology proposed to help address the concern of copyright protection for digital content. To facilitate tracing of copyright violators, different watermarks carrying information about the transaction or content recipient can be embedded into multimedia content before distribution. Such form of "personalised" watermark is called "fingerprint". A powerful attack against digital fingerprinting is the collusion attack, in which different fingerprinted copies of same host data are jointly processed to remove the fingerprints or hinder their detection. This paper first studies a number of existing collusion attack schemes against image fingerprinting. A new collusion attack scheme is then proposed and evaluated, both analytically and empirically. Attack performance in terms of fingerprint detectability and visual quality degradation after attack is assessed. Results obtained from spread spectrum fingerprinting experiments show that the proposed attack can impede fingerprint detection using as few as three fingerprinted images without introducing noticeable visual degradation, hence it is more powerful than those reported in literature. It is also found that increasing the fingerprint embedding strength and spreading factor do not help resist such malicious attacks.

1 Introduction

Recent advances in signal processing and communication networking technologies have fuelled the growth and electronic distribution of digital multimedia content such as audio, image and video. However, the same technological advances have also raised growing concern over how to control unauthorized duplication and redistribution of such content. Digital watermarking technology is one of the technologies proposed to tackle this concern. A digital watermark is a secret hidden code irremovably, imperceptibly, and robustly embedded in the host data so as to facilitate copyright protection of the host data. It typically contains information about the origin, ownership, status, destination or any other transaction information pertaining to the host data. When a watermarked data is copied, the hidden watermark gets copied along too, thus providing means for appropriate actions to be taken against the copyright violators [1].

Depending on the information they carry and their subsequent usage, watermarks can be classified into two broad categories namely *watermarks* and *fingerprints*. Under this classification, a *watermark* is regarded as containing information about the *ownership* or *origin*, while a *fingerprint* is regarded as containing information specific to each *recipient/user* or *transaction*, of the data under protection. The former provides evidence of copyright violation while the latter helps trace the copyright viola-

F. Petitcolas and H.J. Kim (Eds.): IWDW 2002, LNCS 2613, pp. 64–80, 2003.
© Springer-Verlag Berlin Heidelberg 2003

tors [2]. Clearly, fingerprints can also be regarded as "personalised watermarks". In this paper, we focus on digital fingerprinting techniques for still or moving images. As such, we shall use the terms "fingerprint" and "watermark", as well as "finger-printing" and "watermarking", interchangeably.

In e-commerce applications, typically the same host data is embedded with different fingerprints before distribution or sale. If a coalition of users carrying different fingerprinted versions of the same multimedia content get together, they can collaborate to remove or disable each others' fingerprints using a form of attack known as *collusion attack*. This paper aims to analyze a number of collusion attack techniques [6][7] and study the severity of these attacks in terms of the resultant watermark detectability and visual distortion. It is noted that techniques for collusion-secure watermark construction have been proposed, for example in [3][4]. However, the study of such watermark constructions is beyond the scope of this paper. More emphasis is given to the study of collusion attack techniques, among which only averaging has been widely discussed in the literature.

The rest of this paper is organized as follows. Section 2 defines the performance measures of a watermark attack. A number of different collusion attacks are studied in Section 3. It contains mathematical modelling of the watermark robustness after the attacks. A new variant is also proposed and modelled in this section. Section 4 then presents and discusses the simulation results. Finally, conclusions are drawn in Section 5.

2 Performance Measures of Watermark/Fingerprint Attack

The performance of a watermark/fingerprint attack algorithm can at least be quantified by two measures, namely watermark/fingerprint detectability and imperceptibility. In terms of fingerprint detectability, an attack is considered effective if the original fingerprint cannot be detected from the attacked data. This may not necessarily mean that the original fingerprint is completely removed. It may still be present in the attacked data, but somehow modified to the point that the detector cannot successfully detect it. In terms of imperceptibility, an attack is successful if the perceptual quality of the attacked data does not deteriorate substantially from the original fingerprinted data. For image fingerprinting, this means that the visual quality of the attacked image must not drop too much compared to the fingerprinted image.

In this paper, we use correlation coefficient to measure the fingerprint detectability and weighted PSNR (wPSNR) [5] to measure the visual quality. The notations and formulas for correlation coefficient and weighted PSNR will be presented next.

Let us consider S components of an original image P. These components can be pixel values or any linear transform coefficients, e.g DCT coefficients. Their values are denoted as p_j, $j = 1,2,...,S$. The value S is often referred to as the spreading factor of the watermark/fingerprint. The image owner generates a set $W = \{W_i\}$ of independent and identically distributed fingerprints. The values of each fingerprint W_i are denoted as $w_{i,j}$. After multiplication with appropriate scaling factors $\{\lambda_j\}$, each fingerprint is linearly added to the host image data to produce a fingerprinted image E_i whose values are denoted as:

$$e_{i,j} = p_j + \lambda_j w_{i,j}, \quad j = 1,2,\ldots,S. \tag{1}$$

The scaling factors λ_j can be image-adaptive [9] or constant throughout the image. For simplicity, in the subsequent formulations we will use $\lambda_j = 1 \ \forall j$.

When an unauthorized or a suspicious image $\hat{E}$ of values $\hat{e}_j$ is found, the owner would try to identify the culprit by detecting the embedded fingerprint. To do this, he subtracts the values of P from $\hat{E}$ to obtain the suspected fingerprint sequence $\hat{W}$. The correlation coefficient of $\hat{W}$ with all previously issued fingerprints W_i is then calculated according to the expression:

$$c(\hat{W}, W_i) = \frac{cov(\hat{W}, W_i)}{\sqrt{var(\hat{W}) \cdot var(W_i)}} = \frac{\dfrac{1}{S} \sum_{j=1}^{S} \hat{w}_j \cdot w_{i,j} - \dfrac{1}{S^2} \sum_{j=1}^{S} \hat{w}_j \cdot \sum_{j=1}^{S} w_{i,j}}{\sqrt{\left(\dfrac{1}{S}\sum_{j=1}^{S} \hat{w}_j^2 - \dfrac{1}{S^2}\left(\sum_{j=1}^{S} \hat{w}_j\right)^2\right)\left(\dfrac{1}{S}\sum_{j=1}^{S} w_{i,j}^2 - \dfrac{1}{S^2}\left(\sum_{j=1}^{S} w_{i,j}\right)^2\right)}}. \tag{2}$$

If the correlation coefficient is larger than a predetermined threshold for a particular fingerprint, the culprit is correspondingly identified. As discussed in [5], the threshold should be set according to the required detection confidence interval.

For our analysis, two commonly used fingerprint distributions are considered, namely uniform distribution between $[-L, +L]$ and Gaussian distribution with mean zero. Since both distributions have zero means, Equation (2) can be simplified to:

$$c(\hat{W}, W_i) = \frac{\sum_{j=1}^{S} \hat{w}_j \cdot w_{i,j}}{\sqrt{\left(\sum_{j=1}^{S} \hat{w}_j^2 - \dfrac{1}{S}\left(\sum_{j=1}^{S} \hat{w}_j\right)^2\right)\left(\sum_{j=1}^{S} w_{i,j}^2\right)}}. \tag{3}$$

For the following attack descriptions, we assume that collusion attackers have access to K different fingerprinted images, each of which contains S fingerprint values.

The expression for weighted PSNR (wPSNR) is given in [3] to be:

$$wPSNR = 20 \log_{10} \frac{max(p)}{\|NVF(p'-p)\|} \tag{4}$$

$$NVF_{j1,j2} = \frac{1}{1 + \sigma_{L j1,j2}^2}$$

where p denotes the original image pixels, p' denotes pixels of the image under test, $\|\bullet\|$ denotes the root-mean-square value. In the expression of NVF (noise visibility function), $\sigma_{L j1,j2}^2$ denotes the local variance of an image in a window centered on the pixel with coordinates $(j1, j2)$. Compared to the well-known PSNR measure, wPSNR has been claimed to be a better representation of the human visual system (HVS) [3].

3 Variants of Collusion Attack

In this section we first review some existing collusion attack techniques. A new collusion attack will then be introduced and its performance will be assessed.

3.1 Averaging Collusion Attack

The averaging collusion attack was introduced by Cox, *et al.* [6]. The attacked image $\hat{E}$ is created by averaging K fingerprinted images according to the expression:

$$\hat{e}_j = p_j + \hat{w}_j = p_j + \frac{1}{K}\sum_{i=1}^{K} w_{i,j}. \tag{5}$$

Under this attack, each colluding fingerprint has a contribution of strength $1/K$ in the attacked (averaged) sequence $\hat{W}$. The correlation between $\hat{W}$ and a colluding fingerprint W_t, $1 < t < K$, has been derived by Stone [7] to be:

$$c(\hat{w}, W_t) = \frac{\sum_{j}\left(\frac{1}{K}\sum_{i=1}^{K} w_{i,j}\right)\cdot w_{t,j}}{\sqrt{\left(\sum_{j}\left(\frac{1}{K}\sum_{i=1}^{K} w_{i,j}\right)^2 - \frac{1}{S}\left(\sum_{j}\left(\frac{1}{K}\sum_{i=1}^{K} w_{i,j}\right)\right)^2\right)\left(\sum_{j} w_{t,j}^2\right)}} = \frac{1}{\sqrt{K}}. \tag{6}$$

The above expression shows that the attack requires a large number of fingerprinted images in order to reduce the correlation coefficient substantially. For example, 100 fingerprinted images are needed to obtain a correlation coefficient of 0.1. Clearly, this is quite impossible for an attacker to achieve. Earlier experiments by Cox, *et al.*, and Stone confirmed this model and hence it is claimed that collusion attack by averaging is not an effective attack [6][7].

3.2 Maximum-Minimum Collusion Attack

A more powerful collusion attack is the maximum-minimum collusion attack proposed by Stone [7]. The attacked image is created by taking the average of the maximum and minimum values across the component values of the fingerprinted image. The attacked image is given by:

$$\hat{e}_j = p_j + \frac{1}{2}\left(\max_{i=1}^{K}(w_{i,j}) + \min_{i=1}^{K}(w_{i,j})\right) \tag{7}$$

This attack takes into account the possibility that the fingerprint values of a particular position across the fingerprinted images may not be evenly distributed around its mean value. Therefore, instead of using the actual mean value (as in the averaging attack), this attack takes the middle point between the maximum and minimum. Consequently, the attacked sequence contains less original fingerprint and the correlation value becomes lower. The analytical correlation coefficient is given as [7]:

$$C(\hat{W}, W_t) = \sqrt{\frac{6}{(K+1)(K+2)}}. \tag{8}$$

Equation (8) shows that the correlation coefficient approximately decreases in proportion to $1/K$, hence this attack theoretically requires only 23 fingerprinted copies to drive the correlation coefficient down to 0.1. Nonetheless this is still rather difficult to achieve in practice.

3.3   Stone's Negative-Correlation and Zero-Correlation Collusion Attacks

This attack is able to drive the correlation coefficient to a negative value using as few as five fingerprinted images. The algorithm is formulated as [7]:

$$\hat{e}_j = \begin{cases} p_j + \max\limits_{i=1}^{K}(w_{i,j}) & \text{if} \quad \med\limits_{i=1}^{K}(w_{i,j}) \le (1-\alpha)\max\limits_{i=1}^{K}(w_{i,j}) + \alpha\min\limits_{i=1}^{K}(w_{i,j}) \\ p_j + \min\limits_{i=1}^{K}(w_{i,j}) & \text{otherwise} \end{cases} \tag{9}$$

where $\max(\bullet)$, $\min(\bullet)$ and $\med(\bullet)$ denote the maximum, minimum and median values, respectively, and α is a constant between 0 and 1. Typically, α is set to 0.5. From the expression, it can be seen that this attack does not attempt to restore the original unfingerprinted image by removing the fingerprint. Instead, the attacked image takes on the least likely values across the fingerprinted copies as the attacked values. As a result, the polarity of the fingerprints is inverted at a number of locations, therefore negative correlation is achieved.

For uniformly distributed fingerprints, Stone derived an analytical model of this attack for $K = 3$ where each fingerprinted copy corresponds exactly either to the maximum, minimum or median value. For $K = 3$ and $\alpha = 0.5$, the analytical model gives a correlation coefficient of 0.1369. For $K \ge 4$, however, the attack cannot be modelled mathematically. Stone's experiments showed that this attack produces a negative correlation for $K \ge 5$ and $\alpha = 0.5$. Subsequently, to achieve zero-correlation, Stone adjusted α through empirical testing. The results suggest that for $K = 5$ and $\alpha = 0.713$, this attack can successfully produce a correlation coefficient that lies within the range [-0.003, 0.003], i.e. zero-correlation is achieved. Stone did not have an analytical model for these attacks when the fingerprints follow the Gaussian distribution, but his experimental results indicate that Stone's negative-correlation attack could not drive the correlation coefficient of Gaussian fingerprints to zero even when as many as 30 fingerprinted images are used in the attack.

3.4   New Zero-Correlation Collusion Attack

In this section we propose a new attack which is a modification from Stone's negative/zero-correlation collusion attack. We will derive an analytical model for the attack and show that it matches the empirical results.

Stone's negative/zero-correlation attack produces an attacked image by examining the clustering behaviour of the fingerprints in a group of images. We find that the severity of the attack can be increased by targeting a specific fingerprinted image instead of considering a group of them as in Equation (9). Furthermore, the choice of a specific target also makes it possible to derive an analytical model for this attack for any number of colluding parties.

For our proposed attack, we similarly start by establishing a technique that drives the correlation coefficient to a negative value. Thereafter, we moderate the attack to obtain a near-zero correlation coefficient.

First, we arbitrarily select a fingerprinted image from a number of available fingerprinted images. We call this image the attack target E_T, $1 < T < K$, and denote its embedded fingerprint as W_T. The attack is performed according to:

$$\hat{e}_j = \begin{cases} p_j + \max\limits_{i=1}^{K}(w_{i,j}) & \text{if} \quad w_{T,j} \leq \frac{1}{2}\left[\max\limits_{i=1}^{K}(w_{i,j}) + \min\limits_{i=1}^{K}(w_{i,j})\right] \\ p_j + \min\limits_{i=1}^{K}(w_{i,j}) & \text{otherwise} \end{cases} \tag{10}$$

To derive the analytical model of the correlation coefficient after attack, we use the joint probability distribution (jdf) for w_{max}, w_{min}, and w for K independent and identically distributed random variables w, whose maximum is w_{max} and minimum is w_{min}. A closed form of this jdf is given in the Appendix for uniformly distributed w between $-L$ and $+L$. Through algebraic derivations, the covariance of $\hat{W}$ and W_T is found to be:

$$cov(\hat{W}, W_T) = -\frac{K^2 + K - 6}{2(K+1)(K+2)}L^2. \tag{11}$$

Similarly, the variance of $\hat{W}$ is found to be:

$$var(\hat{W}) = \frac{K^2 - K + 2}{(K+1)(K+2)}L^2. \tag{12}$$

The variance of the uniformly distributed W_T is well known:

$$var(W_T) = \frac{L^2}{3}. \tag{13}$$

Substituting the above expressions into Equation (2), we obtain:

$$C(\hat{W}, W_T) = \frac{cov(\hat{W}, W_T)}{\sqrt{var(\hat{W}) \cdot var(W_T)}} = -(K^2 + K - 6)\sqrt{\frac{3/4}{(K+1)(K+2)(K^2 - K + 2)}}. \tag{14}$$

Figure 1 plots the correlation coefficient values calculated using Equation (14) together with the empirical values. It is shown that the analytical model fits perfectly for uniformly distributed fingerprints. Also, the correlation coefficient values become negative when 3 or more fingerprinted images are used in the attack, i.e. $K \geq 3$. Although we do not have an analytical model for Gaussian fingerprints, empirically it can be shown that our attack is also able to drive the correlation coefficient to a negative value when $K \geq 3$. The Gaussian fingerprints are observed to give slightly more positive correlation coefficient values than the uniformly distributed fingerprints.

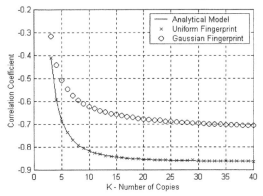

Fig. 1. Negative correlation coefficients obtained after attacking fingerprint data using Equation (10). Each empirical data point is averaged over 1000 runs

Figure 1 shows that the correlation coefficient becomes progressively more negative for $K \geq 3$. However, a negative correlation means that a correlation does exist and the fingerprint is still present in its negative-polarity form. Therefore it is more desirable to drive the correlation coefficient to zero. One way to achieve this is to attack only a portion of the target fingerprint so that the attacked and un-attacked portions contribute roughly equal levels of negative and positive correlation output respectively such that the combined result is close to zero. The question is how can the respective portions be selected. An answer is provided by the analytical model.

Let R be the number of attacked elements. The number of un-attacked elements is hence $(S-R)$ where S is the spreading factor. Let us denote by Ω the new attacked sequence containing R elements of the original target fingerprint W_T and $(S-R)$ elements of the attacked sequence $\hat{W}$ obtained by applying Equation (10). Mathematically, Ω can be expressed as:

$$\Omega = \left\{ \varpi_j \right\} = \left\{ w_{T,1}, w_{T,2}, \dots, w_{T,R}, \hat{w}_{R+1}, \hat{w}_{R+2}, \dots, \hat{w}_S \right\} \quad j = 1, 2, \dots, S. \tag{15}$$

where $w_{T,j}$ denotes the jth element of W_T and $\hat{w}_j$ denotes the jth element of $\hat{W}$. Note that, for simplicity, we have assumed that the first R elements in Ω are un-attacked while the rest are attacked. There is no statistical difference when the R elements are randomly selected. The attack aims to achieve zero correlation coefficient, i.e.:

$$C(\Omega, W_T) = \frac{cov(\Omega, W_T)}{\sqrt{var(\Omega) \cdot var(W_T)}} = 0. \tag{16}$$

Therefore,

$$cov(\Omega, W_T) = \underbrace{\frac{1}{S} \left(\sum_{j=1}^{R} w_{T,j} w_{T,j} + \sum_{j=S-R+1}^{S} \hat{w}_j w_{T,j} \right)}_{T1} - \underbrace{\frac{1}{S^2} \left(\sum_{j=1}^{R} w_{T,j} + \sum_{j=S-R+1}^{S} \hat{w}_j \right) \sum_{j=1}^{S} w_{T,j}}_{T2} = 0. \tag{17}$$

The second term $T2$ reduces to zero because the mean of W_T is zero. Hence we are left with $T1 = 0$. However,

$$\frac{1}{S}\sum_{j=1}^{R} w_{T,j} \; w_{T,j} = \frac{1}{S} \cdot \frac{R}{S}\sum_{j=1}^{S} w_{T,j} \; w_{T,j} = \frac{R}{S}E\!\left(w_T^2\right) = \frac{R}{S}var(W_T). \tag{18}$$

Similarly,

$$\frac{1}{S}\sum_{j=S-R+1}^{S} \hat{w}_j \; w_{T,j} = \frac{1}{S} \cdot \frac{(S-R)}{S}\sum_{j=1}^{S} \hat{w}_j \; w_{T,j} = \left(1-\frac{R}{S}\right)E\!\left(\hat{W} \cdot W_T\right) = \left(1-\frac{R}{S}\right)cov\!\left(\hat{W},W_T\right) \tag{19}$$

since the mean of $\hat{W}$ is zero (see Appendix). Both $var(W_T)$ and $cov(\hat{W}, W_T)$ have been given previously in Equations (13) and (11), respectively. Therefore we have:

$$\frac{R}{S} \cdot \frac{L^2}{3} - \left(1-\frac{R}{S}\right)\frac{K^2+K-6}{2(K+1)(K+2)}L^2 = 0 \quad \text{or} \tag{20}$$

$$x = \frac{R}{S} = \frac{k}{k+\frac{1}{3}} \quad \text{where} \quad k = \frac{K^2+K-6}{2(K+1)(K+2)}.$$

The term $x = R/S$ represents the fraction of attacked sequence Ω that are un-attacked. Figure 2 shows the empirical values of the correlation coefficient between the target fingerprint W_T and the attacked sequence Ω containing xS elements taken randomly from W_T and the remaining $(1-x)S$ elements taken randomly from $\hat{W}$.

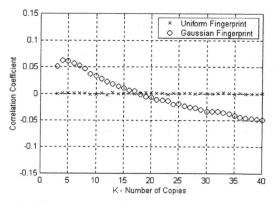

Fig. 2. Correlation coefficient of the proposed zero-correlation collusion attack. Each empirical data point is averaged over 1000 runs

Figure 2 shows that the uniformly distributed fingerprints after attack adhere closely to the attack objective of achieving zero correlation coefficient for $K \geq 3$, while the attacked Gaussian fingerprints show a slight deviation of between ± 0.06 from zero. This is not surprising as the optimum value of x in Equation (20) was derived specifically for the former. Nevertheless, for most practical purposes, the proposed attack can be considered very successful on both types of fingerprint distributions, because as few as 3 fingerprinted images are sufficient to prevent the detection of the embedded fingerprint.

4   Simulation on Image Fingerprints

This section presents the experimental results obtained by applying different collusion attacks on image fingerprints. The first part examines the effectiveness of the collusion attacks when performed on different image domains and different fingerprint distributions, while the second part examines the image visual quality after collusion attack.

The images used in our simulation are in the portable greymap (.pgm) format. The fingerprints are randomly drawn from a continuous distribution. To ensure invisibility, they are scaled using the 3×3-based TMF (texture masking function) [5] prior to linear addition to the host image pixels. Further distortion on the fingerprints comes from its discretization and clipping to [0, 255]. As a result, it is expected that the correlation coefficient values obtained in these experiments will be slightly different from those obtained previously without digitization.

4.1   Effects of Watermark/Attack Domains and Fingerprint Distributions

For this section, since we are interested in the detectability of fingerprints after attack, our simulation is conducted using the two most effective attacks, i.e. Stone's zero-correlation attack and our proposed zero-correlation attack. The image used is *baboon.pgm* of size 512×512.

The watermark and attack domains examined are the spatial and DCT (discrete cosine transform) domains. Four domain combinations are observed:

- *s-s* : Spatial-domain fingerprint attacked in the spatial domain
- *d-d* : DCT-domain fingerprint attacked in the DCT domain
- *s-d* : Spatial-domain fingerprint attacked in the DCT domain
- *d-s* : DCT-domain fingerprint attacked in the spatial domain

Table 1 shows the results obtained for uniformly distributed fingerprints with varying dynamic ranges [-L, +L] and spreading factor S. For each attack variant, we use the corresponding minimum number of colluding fingerprinted images required to obtain near-zero correlation coefficients ($K = 5$ and $\alpha = 0.713$ for Stone's zero-correlation attack and $K = 3$ for our proposed zero-correlation attack).

Corresponding results for zero-mean Gaussian fingerprints with variance σ_w^2 are tabulated in Table 2. For comparison purpose, we use the same number of colluding images as used previously for the uniformly distributed fingerprints.

In general, the results obtained are found to agree with analytical expectations discussed in Section 3 of this paper. Some discrepancies occur due to loss of the fingerprints introduced during the embedding and image coding process, as explained earlier.

Table 1. Effect of varying L and S of uniformly distributed fingerprints for Stone's and our proposed attacks. Each correlation coefficient value is averaged over 1000 runs. Spatial-domain and DCT-domain fingerprints are denoted by s and d, respectively

attack variant	L	S	correlation coefficient					
			before attack		after attack			
			s	d	s-s	d-d	d-s	d-s
Stone's	5		0.9320	0.9285	-0.0010	0.0399	0.1501	0.1468
	10	5000	0.9411	0.9386	-0.0019	0.0359	0.1512	0.1491
	15		0.9428	0.9403	-0.0021	0.0356	0.1519	0.1496
		1000	0.9411	0.9388	-0.0018	0.0351	0.1511	0.1486
	10	5000	0.9411	0.9386	-0.0019	0.0359	0.1512	0.1491
		10000	0.9410	0.9386	-0.0021	0.0360	0.1497	0.1471
proposed	5		0.9319	0.9285	0.0044	0.0067	0.0463	0.0508
	10	5000	0.9411	0.9386	0.0012	0.0066	0.0470	0.0481
	15		0.9428	0.9404	0.0016	0.0073	0.0480	0.0484
		1000	0.9410	0.9387	0.0009	0.0059	0.0474	0.0491
	10	5000	0.9411	0.9386	0.0012	0.0066	0.0470	0.0481
		10000	0.9410	0.9386	0.0012	0.0065	0.0476	0.0487

The Gaussian fingerprints appear to have higher resistance against both types of collusion attack compared to the uniformly distributed fingerprints. The proposed zero-correlation attack seems to be more successful compared to Stone's zero-correlation attack in defeating the Gaussian fingerprints. On the average, it achieves correlation coefficient of around 0.05 which is smaller than Stone's 0.16.

Another notable observation is that the attacks are less effective when performed in a domain different from the fingerprint domain. Such "performance drop" is observed to be more pronounced in Stone's zero-correlation attack than in the proposed zero-correlation attack.

It can also be observed that increasing the power of the fingerprints and/or the spreading factor does not improve the fingerprint resistance against both attacks. In some cases, the correlation coefficient after attack even shifts slightly closer to zero when the strength of the fingerprint increases. This is a bad news to the watermark/fingerprint designer, because the traditional techniques for enhancing watermark robustness, i.e. increasing the watermark embedding strength and/or the spreading factor, are no longer useful.

Table 2. Effect of varying σ_w^2 and S of Gaussian fingerprints for Stone's and our proposed attacks. Each correlation coefficient value is averaged over 1000 runs

attack variant	σ_w^2	S	correlation coefficient					
			before attack		after attack			
			s	d	s-s	d-d	s-d	d-s
Stone's	5		0.9247	0.9192	0.1486	0.1509	0.1489	0.1474
	10	5000	0.9342	0.9308	0.1481	0.1522	0.1503	0.1470
	15		0.9374	0.9345	0.1483	0.1533	0.1503	0.1478
		1000	0.9341	0.9306	0.1491	0.1535	0.1537	0.1488
	10	5000	0.9342	0.9308	0.1481	0.1522	0.1503	0.1470
		10000	0.9340	0.9307	0.1480	0.1523	0.1484	0.1454
proposed	5		0.9247	0.9192	0.0522	0.0468	0.0462	0.0535
	10	5000	0.9341	0.9308	0.0508	0.0478	0.0465	0.0499
	15		0.9375	0.9344	0.0501	0.0475	0.0474	0.0504
		1000	0.9342	0.9306	0.0489	0.0480	0.0486	0.0499
	10	5000	0.9341	0.9308	0.0508	0.0478	0.0465	0.0499
		10000	0.9340	0.9307	0.0506	0.0473	0.0467	0.0511

4.2   Visual Quality of Collusion Attacks

In this section, we study the image visual quality resulting from applying 3 different collusion attacks, namely the maximum-minimum attack, Stone's zero-correlation attack, and the proposed zero-correlation attack. The averaging attack is excluded because it is too weak for practical purposes. Two 512×512 images are used for study, i.e. *Baboon.pgm* and *Peppers.pgm*, chosen because *Baboon* contains a lot of textures while *Peppers* is made up mostly of flat regions. Similar to the previous section, the number of fingerprinted images used is the minimum number required to drive the fingerprint correlation coefficient to zero. For the maximum-minimum attack, we consider that a correlation coefficient of 0.1 is low enough, therefore $K = 23$ is used. On the other hand, $K = 5$ and $\alpha = 0.713$ are used for Stone's zero-correlation attack and $K = 3$ is used the proposed zero-correlation attack.

Figure 3 shows the wPSNR values of fingerprinted *Baboon* before and after attacks with respect to the original un-fingerprinted *Baboon*. It is observed from the simulation results that *Peppers* behaves very similarly to *Baboon*. For the sake of brevity, results for *Peppers* are not shown.

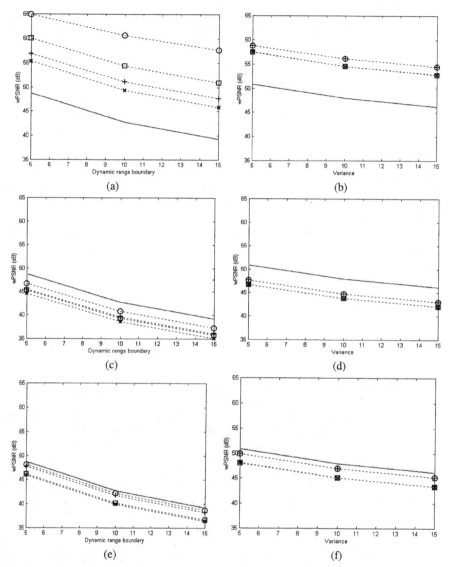

Fig. 3. Image visual quality after collusion attacks for *Baboon*. Each wPSNR value is averaged over 5 runs

(a) Maximum-minimum attack, uniform fingerprints
(b) Maximum-minimum attack, Gaussian fingerprints
(c) Stone's zero-correlation attack, uniform fingerprints
(d) Stone's zero-correlation attack, Gaussian fingerprints
(e) Proposed zero-correlation attack, uniform fingerprints
(f) Proposed zero-correlation attack, Gaussian fingerprints

Legend

⣿⣿⣿	before attack (spatial fingerprints)
——	before attack (DCT fingerprints)
- ◇ -	*s-s*
- ⊟ -	*s-d*
- ✳ -	*d-d*
- + -	*d-s*

The results in Figure 3 suggest that collusion attacks generally does not introduce substantial visual degradation. The maximum-minimum attack even improves the visual quality of the attacked image, since it restores the original un-fingerprinted pixel values to some extent. On the other hand, Stone's zero-correlation attack appears to introduce the most distortion (wPSNR decreases by up to 5 dB).

When the fingerprint is uniformly distributed, the image quality resulting from all attacks is lower when the attack is applied in a domain different from the fingerprinting domain. However, for Gaussian fingerprints, the visual degradation seems to be independent of the domain of the fingerprints and is affected only by the domain of attack.

It can be observed that spatial-domain attack always brings about less visual degradation compared to the DCT-domain attack. Therefore, it can be reasoned that when information regarding the domain of fingerprints is unavailable, an attacker should perform the attack in the spatial domain for optimum compromise between detectability and visual quality.

Finally, comparing the results for *Baboon* and *Peppers*, we conclude that visual degradation due to collusion attack is unaffected by differences in the host image texture properties.

5   Conclusion

In this paper, we have conducted a comprehensive study of the vulnerability of digital fingerprinting (personalised watermarking) schemes against a number of collusion attacks. We first review some existing collusion attacks proposed by Cox, *et al.* and Stone. We then propose a new negative-correlation collusion attack algorithm and derive an analytical expression for its performance. When applied globally on the target fingerprint, the proposed attack is capable of producing negative correlation coefficient values. By modifying this attack to attack only a selected portion of the target fingerprint, we develop a powerful zero-correlation collusion attack capable of driving the correlation coefficient of the fingerprint detector to within [-0.0002, 0.0002] using as few as 3 colluding parties (fingerprinted data).

The performance of the existing and proposed collusion attacks is compared in terms of fingerprint detectability and visual quality using representative image data encoded in common digital formats. The proposed zero-correlation collusion attack is found to perform better as it needs fewer colluding parties to achieve near-zero detection correlation and the resultant visual quality of the attacked data is also better. In general, we found that all collusion attacks are more effective when performed in the same domain as the fingerprinting/watermarking domain. Also, Gaussian fingerprints appear to have higher resistance against collusion attacks compared to the uniformly distributed fingerprints. Visually, attacks in the spatial-domain introduce less image degradation compared to the DCT-domain attacks. Another noteworthy observation attained in this study is that the fingerprint robustness against collusion attacks generally cannot be improved by simply increasing the embedding strength of the fingerprint or its spreading factor.

References

1. Hartung, F., Su, J.K., Girod, B., "Spread spectrum watermarking: malicious attacks and counterattacks," *Proceedings SPIE, Security and Watermarking of Multimedia Contents, Electronic Imaging 1999*, vol. 3657, San Jose, CA, 1999.
2. Petitcolas, F., Anderson, R., Kuhn, M., "Attacks on copyright marking systems," *Proceedings of the Second International Workshop in Information Hiding*, Portland, 1998.
3. Boneh, D., Shaw, J., "Collusion-secure fingerprinting for digital data," *IEEE Transactions on Information* Theory, vol. 44, no. 5, 1998.
4. Trappe, W., Wu, M., Liu, K.J.R., "Collusion-resistant fingerprinting for multimedia," *IEEE International Conference on Acoustics, Speech, and Signal Processing*, Orlando, FL, 2002.
5. Voloshynovskiy, S., Pereira, S., Iquise, V., Pun, T., "Attack modelling: towards a second generation watermarking benchmark," *Signal Processing, Special Issue on Information Theoretic Issues in Digital Watermarking*, vol. 81, no. 6, 2001.
6. Cox, I.J., Kilian, J., Leighton, T., Shamoon, T., "Secure spread spectrum watermarking for multimedia," *IEEE Transactions on Image Processing*, vol. 6, no.12, 1997.
7. Stone, H., "Analysis of attacks on image watermarks with randomised coefficients," *NEC Technical Report*, 1996.
8. Brunk, H.D., "An introduction to mathematical statistics," Lexington: Xerox College Publishing, 3rd ed., 1975.
9. Podilchuk, C., Zeng, W., "Image adaptive watermarking using visual models," *IEEE Journal on Selected Areas in Communications*, vol. 16, no. 4, 1998.
10. Devore, J., Peck, R., "Introductory statistics," MN: West Publishing Company, 1990.
11. David, H.A., "Order statistics," NY: John Wiley and Son, 1981.

Appendix: Derivation of Analytical Model for Proposed Attack

In order to derive the analytical model of the proposed attack, we need to find the joint distribution function (jdf) for w_{max}, w_{min}, and w. David [11] has developed the expression for $p_K(w_{max}, w_{min})$, the jdf of w_{max} and w_{min} for K samples of a random variable w whose probability density function (pdf) is $p(x)$. This jdf is given as:

$$p_K(w_{max}, w_{min}) = (K)(K-1)p(w_{max})p(w_{min})F(w_{max}, w_{min})^{K-2} \qquad (21)$$

where $F(b,a)$ is the cumulative distribution function of $p(x)$, defined as:

$$F(b, a) = \int_a^b p(x)dx. \qquad (22)$$

Let the jdf of w_{max}, w_{min}, and w for K samples of $p(x)$ be $p_K(w_{max}, w_{min}, w)$. Equation (21) can be extended to $p_K(w_{max}, w_{min}, w)$ by breaking the jdf into three nonzero regions:

- Region 1, w is a new maximum ($w = w_{max}$, $w_{min} \leq w$);
- Region 2, w is a new minimum ($w = w_{min}$, $w \leq w_{max}$);
- Region 3, w lies between w_{max} and w_{min} ($w_{min} \leq w \leq w_{max}$).

In Region 1, the Kth variate w replaces the former maximum. The probability that this happens can be found by integrating the former maximum over the region from w_{min} to the new maximum w. Therefore in this region,

$$p_K(w_{max}, w_{min}, w) = p(w)\int_{w_{min}}^{w} p_K(w_{max}, w_{min})dw_{max} \tag{23}$$
$$= (K-1)(K-2)p(w)p(w_{min})\int_{w_{min}}^{w} p(w_{max})F(w_{max}, w_{min})^{K-3} dw_{max}.$$

For Region 1, we treat w and w_{max} as the same variable. Hence, $p_K(w_{max}, w_{min}, w)$ $= p_K(w, w_{min}, w) = p_K(w_{max}, w_{min}, w_{max})$. Likewise, we should treat w and w_{min} as the same variable in Region 2. The jdf for Region 2 can be found as:

$$p_K(w_{max}, w_{min}, w) = p(w)\int_{w}^{w_{max}} p_K(w_{max}, w_{min})dw_{min} \tag{24}$$
$$= (K-1)(K-2)p(w)p(w_{max})\int_{w}^{w_{max}} p(w_{min})F(w_{max}, w_{min})^{K-3} dw_{min}.$$

Finally, w is independent of w_{min} and w_{max} in Region 3, hence the jdf can be found as the multiplication:

$$p_K(w_{max}, w_{min}, w) = p(w)p_K(w_{max}, w_{min}) \tag{25}$$
$$= (K-1)(K-2)p(w)p(w_{max})p(w_{min})F(w_{max}, w_{min})^{K-3}.$$

We will now consider w variable as being uniformly distributed from $-L$ to $+L$. For this particular distribution:

$$p(w) = p(w_{max}) = p(w_{min}) = \frac{1}{2L}, \tag{26}$$

$$F(w_{max}, w_{min}) = \int_{w_{min}}^{w_{max}} \frac{1}{2L} dx = \frac{1}{2L}(w_{max} - w_{min}) \quad \text{where } x \text{ is a dummy variable.} \tag{27}$$

Hence the jdf becomes:

$$p_K(w_{max}, w_{min}, w) \tag{28}$$

$$= \frac{(K-1)(K-2)}{(2L)^K} \int_{w_{min}}^{w} (w_{max} - w_{min})^{K-3} dw_{max}$$
$$= \frac{(K-1)}{(2L)^K}(w - w_{min})^{K-2} \qquad \text{(Region 1)}$$

$$= \frac{(K-1)(K-2)}{(2L)^K} \int_{w}^{w_{max}} (w_{max} - w_{min})^{K-3} dw_{min}$$
$$= \frac{(K-1)}{(2L)^K}(w_{max} - w)^{K-2} \qquad \text{(Region 2)}$$

$$= \frac{(K-1)(K-2)}{(2L)^K}(w_{max} - w_{min})^{K-3} \qquad \text{(Region 3)}$$

$$= 0 \qquad \text{(otherwise)}.$$

The expression of the correlation coefficient requires us to find the variance of $\hat{w}$, denoted as $var(\hat{w})$, as well as the covariance of w and $\hat{w}$, denoted as $cov(w, \hat{w})$. Because the mean of w (denoted as $E(w)$) is zero, $cov(w, \hat{w})$ reduces to $E(w \cdot \hat{w})$. To calculate

$var(\hat{w})$, we first assumed that $E(\hat{w}) = 0$. Under this assumption, we have $var(\hat{w}) = E(\hat{w}^2)$. Our empirical results verified that this assumption is true.

In Region 1 the attacks sets $\hat{w} = w_{min}$ because w is always larger than or equal to the average between itself and any smaller value. Similarly, in region 2 the attack sets $\hat{w} = w_{max}$. Region 3 is split into two sub-regions:

- Region 3a, $\dfrac{w_{max} + w_{min}}{2} \le w \le w_{max}$. The attack sets $\hat{w} = w_{min}$.

- Region 3b, $w_{min} \le w \le \dfrac{w_{max} + w_{min}}{2}$. The attack sets $\hat{w} = w_{max}$.

We will now calculate the contribution to $E(w \cdot \hat{w})$ from each region and sum all the contributions. $E(w \cdot \hat{w})$ can be calculated from:

$$E(w \cdot \hat{w}) = \iint w \cdot \hat{w} \, p(w, \hat{w}) \, d\hat{w} \, dw. \tag{29}$$

In Region 1, $\hat{w} = w_{min}$ and $p_K(w_{max}, w_{min}, w) = p_K(w, w_{min}, w) = p_K(w, w_{min}) = p_K(w, \hat{w})$. Hence Equation (29) becomes:

$$E(w \cdot \hat{w})\Big|_{\text{Region 1}} = \frac{(K-1)}{(2L)^K} \int_{-L}^{L} w \int_{-L}^{w} w_{min} \left(w - w_{min}\right)^{K-2} dw_{min} \, dw \tag{30}$$
$$= \left[-\frac{1}{K} + \frac{4}{K(K+1)} - \frac{4}{K(K+1)(K+2)} \right] L^2 .$$

In Region 2, $\hat{w} = w_{max}$ and $p_K(w_{max}, w_{min}, w) = p_K(w_{max}, w, w) = p_K(w_{max}, w) = p_K(\hat{w}, w)$. Hence Equation (29) becomes:

$$E(w \cdot \hat{w})\Big|_{\text{Region 2}} = \frac{(K-1)}{(2L)^K} \int_{-L}^{L} w \int_{w}^{L} w_{max} \left(w_{max} - w\right)^{K-2} dw_{max} \, dw \tag{31}$$
$$= \left[-\frac{1}{K} + \frac{4}{K(K+1)} - \frac{4}{K(K+1)(K+2)} \right] L^2 .$$

In Region 3a, $\hat{w} = w_{min}$ and $p(w, \hat{w}) = p(w, w_{min}) = \int_{w_{min}}^{L} p_K\left(w_{max}, w_{min}, w\right) dw_{max}$. Thus,

$$E(w \cdot \hat{w})\Big|_{\text{Region 3a}} = \frac{(K-1)(K-2)}{(2L)^K} \int_{-L}^{L} w_{min} \int_{w_{min}}^{L} \int_{\frac{w_{min}+w_{max}}{2}}^{w_{max}} w \left(w_{max} - w_{min}\right)^{K-3} dw \, dw_{max} dw_{min} \tag{32}$$
$$= \left[-\frac{1}{4} + \frac{3}{2K} - \frac{7}{2K(K+1)} + \frac{2}{K(K+1)(K+2)} \right] L^2 .$$

In Region 3b, $\hat{w} = w_{max}$ and $p(w, \hat{w}) = p(w, w_{max}) = \int_{-L}^{w_{max}} p_K\left(w_{max}, w_{min}, w\right) dw_{min}$. Thus,

$$E(w \cdot \hat{w})\Big|_{\text{Region 3b}} = \frac{(K-1)(K-2)}{(2L)^K} \int_{-L}^{L} w_{max} \int_{-L}^{w_{max}} \int_{w_{min}}^{\frac{w_{min}+w_{max}}{2}} w \left(w_{max} - w_{min}\right)^{K-3} dw \, dw_{min} dw_{max} \tag{33}$$
$$= \left[-\frac{1}{4} + \frac{3}{2K} - \frac{7}{2K(K+1)} + \frac{2}{K(K+1)(K+2)} \right] L^2 .$$

Upon summing the contributions from Regions 1, 2, 3a and 3b, we get:

$$cov(w, \hat{w}) = E(w \cdot \hat{w}) = -\frac{K^2 + K - 6}{2(K+1)(K+2)} L^2.$$
(34)

Next, to derive $var(\hat{w})$, we first note that:

$$E(\hat{w}^2) = \int \hat{w}^2 \, p(\hat{w}) d\hat{w} = \int \hat{w}^2 \int p(w, \hat{w}) dw \, d\hat{w}$$
(35)

Subsequently, calculating $E(\hat{w}^2)$ as a sum of 4 contributions, we obtain:

$$var(\hat{w}) = E(\hat{w}^2) = \frac{K^2 - K + 2}{(K+1)(K+2)} L^2$$
(36)

A Multistage VQ Based Watermarking Technique with Fake Watermarks

Jeng-Shyang Pan[1], Feng-Hsing Wang[2], Lakhmi Jain[2], and Nikhil Ichalkaranje[2]

Dept. Electronic Eng., National Kaohsiung University of Applied Sciences,
Kaohsiung, Taiwan, R. O. C.
jspan@cc.kuas.edu.tw
School of Electrical and Information Eng., University of South Australia
Feng-Hsing.Wang@postgrads.unisa.edu.au

Abstract. A multiple watermarks embedding scheme based on multistage vector quantisation (VQ) is proposed. A reference watermark is generated first by referring to all the fake watermarks and the real one. Then all the watermarks except the real one are embedded into each stage of the multistage VQ system. The generated keys can be assigned to the related users to share the hidden information. Combining all the extracted watermarks, the real watermark will appear. With the fake watermarks and the structure of the multistage vector quantisation, the proposed scheme has superior features than traditional VQ-based watermarking schemes not only in security, encoding time, and codebook storage space, but also in secret sharing ability.

1 Introduction

Digital watermark technique [1] is getting more and more attention with the popular of the Internet and the development of technology. A variety of schemes to digital watermarking were proposed, which can be generally classified into three categories: spatial-domain techniques [2], transform-domain techniques (discrete cosine transform, wavelet transform, etc) [3], and vector quantisation (VQ) domain techniques [4].

Vector quantisation has been successfully applied to image and speech processing due to its easy implementation and good compression ratio. In image vector quantisation, the image to be coded is first divided into a set of sub-images, which are called vectors. For each vector, the search procedure for obtaining a nearest codeword from the input codebook is carried out. The index of the nearest codeword will be assigned to the vector and delivered to the receiver. On the receiver side, after receiving one index, the codeword that corresponds to the index will be used to reconstruct the decoded image. Instead of sending the sub-images, a VQ system delivers the indices so that the total amount of transmitted data can be reduced. For example, assume the size of each vector is 4×4 pixels (in gray-scale that means $4 \times 4 \times 8$ bits), and the size of the codebook is 256, i.e., the length of each index is 8 bits. Instead of transmitting the 128 bits, the VQ system in this case only transmits 8 bits. One disadvantage of the traditional VQ

F. Petitcolas and H.J. Kim (Eds.): IWDW 2002, LNCS 2613, pp. 81–90, 2003.
© Springer-Verlag Berlin Heidelberg 2003

system is the computational complexity for searching nearest codewords will increase with the codebook size. An effective way to solve this problem is to divide the VQ system into several subsystems, or in other words, several stages. Hence, a multistage VQ system [5], which has the ability to decrease the searching time and save the storage space of codebooks, was proposed.

For embedding watermarks in VQ domain, Lu et al. [6] [7] proposed a new way to hide information into the VQ indices. Huang et al. [4] [8] introduced an efficient and robust technique by hiding watermarks into secret keys , which provides better quality in watermarked images. In this paper, a multiple watermarks embedding system based on multistage VQ is proposed. This scheme possesses the ability of secret sharing [9] with multi-users. The experimental results will be presented at the end of this paper to show the superiority of the proposed watermarking system.

2   Multistage Vector Quantisation and Watermarking Scheme

In this section, the illustration of the multistage VQ will be introduced firstly then the VQ-based watermarking scheme.

2.1   Multistage Vector Quantisation

Comparing with the traditional VQ system, multistage VQ possesses some advantages, such as faster codeword search time and smaller storage space for codebooks. An illustration of n-stage multistage VQ is shown in Fig. 1, where X is the input image of the multistage VQ system; E_i, C_i, X_i, and I_i are the input image, codebook, output image, and indices set of the i-th stage VQ subsystem, respectively. The definition of E_i is

$$E_i = \begin{cases} X, & \text{if } i = 1 ; \\ E_{i-1} - X_{i-1}, & \text{if } i > 1. \end{cases} \qquad (1)$$

The encoding procedure for each stage is the same as the standard VQ encoding procedure. First, we divide the input image of the current stage into many non-overlap blocks (vectors) with size $m \times m$. Afterward we perform the nearest codeword search to find the nearest codeword from the codebook C_i for each vector. With the obtained indices, which are collected as a set and is termed as I_i, a table lookup procedure is then carried to obtain the reconstructed image X_i. Then formula (1) is used to generate the input image for the next stage. We transmit I_i to the receiver and E_i to the next stage.

When the receiver gets the indices from all the stages, the table lookup process is merely performed to obtain the reconstructed images. We then sum up all of them to get the final reconstructed image $\hat{X}$.

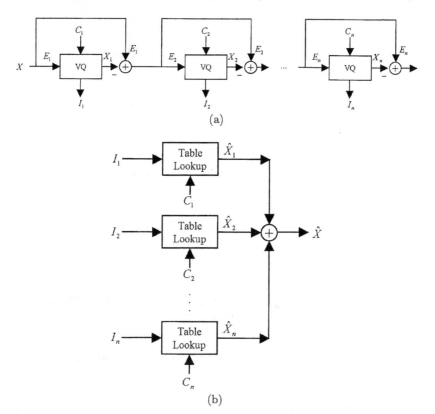

Fig. 1. The block diagrams for multistage VQ based (a) encoding and (b) decoding procedures

2.2 Watermarking Scheme Based on Vector Quantisation

Given a gray-valued image X with size $M \times N$ and a binary-valued watermark W with size $M_W \times N_W$ to be embedded within X. The VQ-based watermarking scheme is illustrated in Fig. 2.

In order to survive the picture-cropping attacks, a pseudo-random number traversing method is suggested. The technique is performed for permuting the watermark to disperse its spatial-domain relationships. With a user-selected seed, we have

$$W_P = \text{Permute}(W, seed) . \tag{2}$$

We then perform the VQ operation to get the indices of the nearest codewords. Assume the vector at the position (r, s) of the original source X is $x(r, s)$. After performing VQ, the indices Y and $y(r, s)$ can be expressed with

$$Y = \text{VQ}(X) , \tag{3}$$

$$y(r, s) = \text{VQ}(x(r, s)) \in C , \tag{4}$$

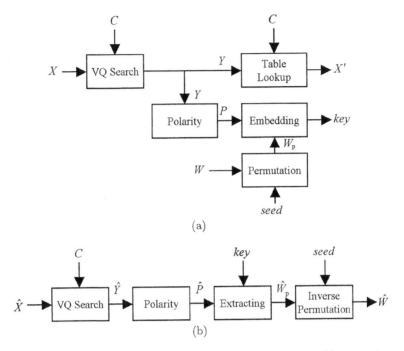

Fig. 2. The block diagrams for the VQ-based (a) embedding and (b) extraction procedures

where C is a codebook with size L, and the codewords therein, c_k, $k \in [0, L-1]$ can be represented by $C = \{c_0, c_1, \ldots, c_{L-1}\}$.

To embed the binary watermarks into the original source, we need to introduce some relationships to transform the VQ indices into binary formats for further embedding. Hence, we bring up the polarities, P, of the VQ indices to embed the watermarks. For natural images, the VQ indices among the neighboring blocks tend to be very similar. We can make use of this characteristic to generate P by calculating the mean value of $y(r, s)$ and the indices of its surrounding vectors:

$$\mu(r, s) = \frac{1}{9} \sum_{i=r-1}^{r+1} \sum_{j=s-1}^{s+1} y(i, j) , \tag{5}$$

where (r, s) is the vector position of the original source, and $0 \le r < M_W$, $0 \le s < N_W$. Based on the mean value, the polarity of $y(r, s)$ can be decided by

$$p(r, s) = \begin{cases} 1, & \text{if } y(r, s) \ge \mu(r, s) ; \\ 0, & \text{otherwise}. \end{cases} \tag{6}$$

$$P = \bigcup_{r=0}^{\frac{M}{M_W}-1} \bigcup_{s=0}^{\frac{N}{N_W}-1} \{p(r, s)\} . \tag{7}$$

Then, we are able to embed W_P with P by the exclusive-or operation

$$key = W_P \oplus P . \tag{8}$$

After the inverse-VQ operation, the reconstructed image, X', along with the secret key, work together to protect the ownership of the original image.

The image quality of X' is good because only the error by the VQ is introduced, and it will not be influenced by the information conveyed in the watermarks because the information is hidden into the secret key. From another point of view, the proposed algorithm is efficient for implementation with the conventional VQ compression algorithms. Once the codeword of each vector is chosen, we are able to determine the polarity of each vector; consequently, we get the secret key. The secret key and X' are transmitted to the receiver. Fig. 2(a) illustrates the embedding procedure.

In the watermark extraction procedure, first the VQ operation has to be performed on the received image $\hat{X}$ to obtain the indices $\hat{Y}$, then the estimated polarities $\hat{P}$ is calculated from the mean value of $\hat{X}$. With the obtained $\hat{P}$ and the existed key, the embedded watermark can be determined by

$$\hat{W}_P = \hat{P} \oplus key . \tag{9}$$

After that, the inverse permutation is performed to recover the extracted watermark

$$\hat{W} = \text{InversePermute}(\hat{W}_P, seed) . \tag{10}$$

Fig. 2(b) shows the block diagrams for illustrating the extraction procedure.

3   Proposed Watermarking Scheme

In this section, the procedures for encrypting and decrypting the fake watermarks with the real watermark will be mentioned first. The proposed watermarking scheme based on multistage VQ will be illustrated next.

3.1   Encryption and Decryption for Watermarks

Let W be the genuine watermark, $W_F = \{W_{F_i}; 1 \leq i \leq n\}$ be a set of recognizable fake watermarks, and W_R be an unrecognizable reference watermark. Our goal here is to mix up the real watermark and fake watermarks to generate an unrecognizable reference watermark with a user-selected seed for future use. The relationship between them is defined as:

$$W_R = \text{Encrypt}(W, W_F, seed) . \tag{11}$$

The encryption process is divided into two sub-processes. First, formula (12) is applied to generate a temporary watermark W_T, then, a pseudo-random number traversing method is carried upon the temporary watermark for dispersing its spatial-domain relationships with a user-selected seed.

$$W_T = W \oplus W_{F_1} \oplus W_{F_2} \oplus \ldots \oplus W_{F_n} , \tag{12}$$

$$W_R = \text{Permute}(W_T, seed) . \tag{13}$$

The decryption procedure for obtaining the hidden real watermark is easy; first the inverse permutation is carried to generate a temporary watermark with the same seed that used in the encryption procedure. Then the exclusive-or operation is executed upon the temporary watermark and the entire fake watermarks.

$$W_T = \text{InversePermute}(W_R, seed) , \tag{14}$$

$$W = W_T \oplus W_{F_1} \oplus W_{F_2} \oplus \ldots \oplus W_{F_n} . \tag{15}$$

We use formula (16) to replace formulas (14) and (15) for expressing the decryption procedure.

$$W = \text{Decrypt}(W_R, W_F, seed) . \tag{16}$$

The block diagrams for illustrating the encryption and decryption procedures are shown in Fig. 3 (a) and (b). An example of the proposed method with three fake watermarks is shown in Fig. 4.

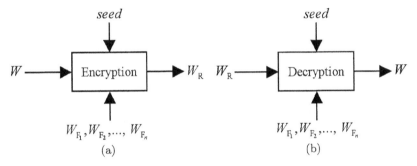

Fig. 3. The block diagrams for (a) encrypting and (b) decrypting the fake watermarks with the real watermark

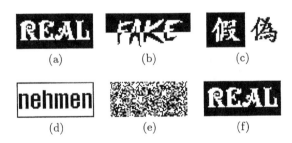

Fig. 4. An example of the proposed encryption and decryption schemes. (a) The real watermark, (b)~(d) three fake watermarks, (e) the generated reference watermark, and (f) the recovered watermark

3.2   Embedding and Extraction Procedures

The goal of our proposed watermarking scheme in this paper is to hide the real watermark with some fake watermarks to make the security of the system superior and safer. Hence, we carry out the encryption procedure upon the watermarks first. Afterward, the n-stage multistage VQ operation is performed upon the input image X to obtain the indices for each stage. With the obtained indices, formulas (5)∼(6) can be used to generate the polarity stream for embedding. The reference watermark is assigned to be embedded in the first stage, the first fake watermark is assigned to be embedded in the second stage, and so on.

In the extraction procedure, the n-stage multistage VQ operation is performed first to obtain the indices. With the indices, formulas (5)∼(6) are used again to generate the polarity stream. With the polarity stream and the secret keys that generated in each stage of the embedding procedure, we can extract the embedded watermarks out stage by stage. Finally, the decryption process is carried out upon all the extracted watermarks to recover the real one. The block diagrams for illustrating the embedding and extraction procedures are shown in Fig. 5.

4   Simulation Results

In our simulation, the well-known test image "Lena" was used as the host image. The image size is 512×512 in gray-level. The images shown in Fig. 6(a), Fig. 6(b) and (c) were used as the genuine watermark image, and the fake watermarks, respectively. All of the watermarks are binary images and the size of them is 128×128. The number of stages in our multistage VQ system is 3. The codebook size in each stage is 8.

For testing the robustness of our system, we applied some attacking functions to our system. The attacking functions are JPEG compression with different quality factors (QF), low-pass filtering, median filtering, cropping, and rotation.

Table 1. The NC values between the original watermarks and the extracted results under the attacking functions

Attacks	$NC(W_{F_1}, \hat{W}_{F_1})$	$NC(W_{F_2}, \hat{W}_{F_2})$	$NC(W, \hat{W})$
JPEG (QF=60%)	0.9998	0.9897	0.9894
JPEG (QF=80%)	0.9999	0.9947	0.9946
Low-pass Filtering	0.9980	0.9725	0.9712
Median Filtering	0.9998	0.9900	0.9899
Cropping (25%)	0.9743	0.9626	0.9453
Rotation (1°)	0.9825	0.9051	0.8930
Rotation (2°)	0.9739	0.8912	0.8715

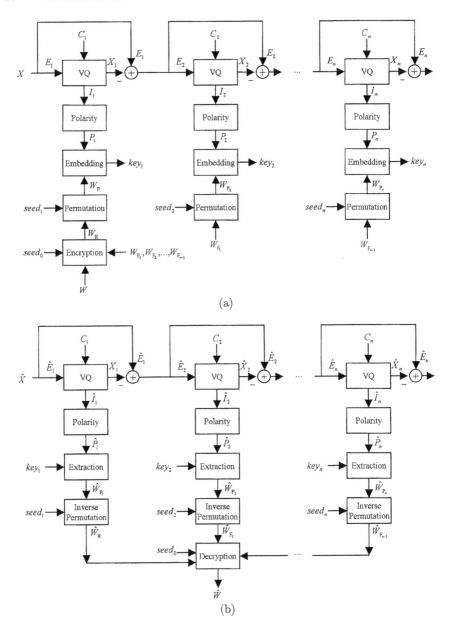

Fig. 5. The block diagrams for proposed multistage VQ based (a) embedding and (b) extraction procedures

We first encrypted the real watermark with the fake watermarks to generate a reference watermark. The PSNR value between the host image and the output image is 30.188 dB. Fig. 7 shows the recovered real watermarks under the men-

Fig. 6. The watermarks that used in the simulation: (a) the real watermark, (b) the 1st fake watermark, (c) the 2nd fake watermark, and (d) the reference watermark generated by the proposed encryption algorithm

tioned attacking functions. Table 1 lists the normalized cross-correction (NC) values between the embedded watermarks and the extracted watermarks under the mentioned attacking functions.

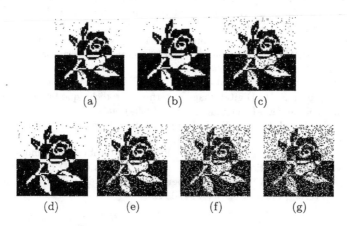

Fig. 7. The recovered watermarks after decrypting all the extracted watermarks under the mentioned attacking functions. (a) JPEG compression with QF=60%, (b) JPEG compression with QF=80%, (c) low-pass filtering with window size =3, (d) median filtering with window size =3, (e) cropping 25% in the lower-left quarter, (f) rotation with 1°, and (g) rotation with 2°

5 Conclusion

Watermarking with fake watermarks based on multistage VQ system is presented in this paper. Our system is easy to implement and robust to some common attacks, especially the most-used JPEG attack. The simulation results confirm the usefulness of the proposed approach. Also, the proposed method not only possesses the advantages of multistage VQ, such as faster encoding time and smaller storage space for codebooks, but also possesses the secret sharing ability, which means our system provides a useful function for sharing the secret information with multi-users. One example of the use of our system is to apply the secure information of the daily bank password. After using the proposed function to hide the secret within the host image, the generated secret keys can then be assigned to the related users for sharing the secret information. The hidden information cannot be extracted if one of the users is absent. With the use of the visible fake watermarks, the security of this system becomes stronger.

From the simulation results and the ability of our system, we are able to claim that our method is robust and is also superior in security.

References

1. Katzenbeisser, S., Petitcolas, F. A.: Information hiding. London, Artech House.
2. Podilchuk, C. I., Zeng, W. J.: Image-adaptive watermarking using visual models. Vol. 16. No. 4. IEEE Journal on Selected Areas in Communications (1998) 525–539
3. Hsu, C. T., Wu, J. L.: Hidden digital watermarks in images. Vol. 8. IEEE Trans. Image Proc. (1999) 58–68
4. Huang, H. -C., Wang, F. H., Pan, J. S.: A VQ-based robust multi-watermarking algorithm. IEICE Transactions on Fundamentals of Electronics, Communication and Computer Sciences (2002) 1719–1726
5. Gray, R. M.: Vector quantization. IEEE ASSP Magazine (1984) 4–29
6. Lu, Z. M., Sun, S. H.: Digital image watermarking technique based on vector quantisation. Vol. 36. IEE Electronics Letters (2000) 303–305
7. Lu, Z. M., Pan, J. S., Sun, S. H.: VQ-based digital watermarking method. Vol. 32. No 14. Electronics Letters (2000) 1201–1202
8. Huang, H. -C., Wang, F. H., Pan, J. S.: Efficient and robust watermarking algorithm with vector quantisation. Vol. 37. Electronics Letters (2001) 826–828
9. Noar, M., Shamir, A.: Visual cryptography. Lecture Notes in Computer Science. Springer-Verlag, Perugia Italy (1994) 1–12

BER Formulation for the Blind Retrieval of MPEG Video Watermark

Sugiri Pranata, Yong Liang Guan, and Hock Chuan Chua

Nanyang Technological University, School of EEE, Nanyang Avenue, Singapore 639798
{pf564811, eylguan, ehchua}@ntu.edu.sg

Abstract. In this paper, we attempt to develop simple but effective formulations for the bit error rate (BER) pertaining to the blind retrieval of spread-spectrum watermarks linearly embedded in compressed video such as MPEG video. Both spatial and discrete cosine transform (DCT) watermarking schemes are considered. A set of formulas is developed to predict the watermark retrieval BER in the presence of distortions due to MPEG encod-ing/decoding operations, cropping attacks, selective DCT-domain embedding, and linear filtering on the watermarked video subject to watermark amplitude and spreading factor variation. The derived formulas are simple to use and they are proven to be successful in reliably predicting the watermark retrieval BER. With the help of such BER formulas, watermark robustness can be more easily fine-tuned without the need for time-consuming simulations.

1 Introduction

Many digital watermarking schemes have been proposed in the literature for the protection of digital still image and video. Caronni [1] suggested adding tags (small geometric patterns) to digitised images at brightness levels that are imperceptible. Cox [2] introduced a method to embed random numbers as watermark in the discrete cosine transform (DCT) or fast Fourier transform (FFT) domain. Herrigel [3] also used modulation of magnitude components in the Fourier space to embed a watermark. In [4], Tanaka introduced one of the earliest examples of video data embedding by modifying quantized DCT coefficients of the video data to the nearest odd or even integers based on the watermark data. In [5] and [6], Hartung and George presented methods for watermarking uncompressed and compressed video using spread spectrum principles. In [7] and [8], Langelaar and Hanjalic proposed a method to embed a watermark data at bitstream level using selected variable length codewords that do not differ significantly in length from the unwatermarked codewords. In [9], Busch developed a watermarking algorithm and applied it to MPEG-2 streaming video.

An important issue in the design of digital watermarking schemes concerns the performance evaluation of watermark robustness in terms of the correlation coefficient, false alarm rates, or watermark retrieval bit error rate (BER) [10-16], particularly when the watermarked data is subjected to distortions caused by signal

F. Petitcolas and H.J. Kim (Eds.): IWDW 2002, LNCS 2613, pp. 91–104, 2003.
© Springer-Verlag Berlin Heidelberg 2003

processing or malicious attacks. Four types of distortion on watermark robustness, namely additive noise, amplitude changes, linear filtering, and lossy compression, are discussed in [10]. The effects of lossy compression or quantization noise on watermarked JPEG images are studied in [17].

In this paper, we aim to analyse the watermark retrieval BER pertaining to the blind retrieval of spread spectrum watermark additively embedded in compressed digital video. We assume that the host video before watermark embedding exists in the compressed MPEG format, and the watermarked video is re-compressed into the MPEG format without changing the compression rate, i.e., MPEG-in-MPEG-out watermarking. As such, the watermarked video needs to be decompressed to some extent before watermark retrieval can be carried out. Both spatial- and frequency-domain watermarks are considered. The goal is to develop useful BER expressions that adequately capture the effects of watermark distortions due to MPEG compression/decompression, cropping attacks, selective DCT-domain embedding, and linear filtering on the watermark retrieval reliability.

2   Spread Spectrum Watermark Embedding and Retrieval

Two generic types of linear watermarks are considered, namely spatial watermark and DCT watermark. In our context, spatial watermark is spread spectrum signal linearly added to the pixel values of the host video, while DCT watermark is spread spectrum signal linearly added to the DCT coefficients of the host video. Perceptually, spatial watermark appears as a pattern of pixel amplitude changes overlaid onto the host video, while DCT watermark appears as a combination of inverse DCT basis functions.

The watermark embedding process based on spread-spectrum modulation can be mathematically expressed as:

$$\hat{v}_i = v_i + Gb_i p_i \tag{1}$$

where v_i is the host video data in the form of pixel brightness values or DCT coefficients, $\hat{v}_i$ is the watermarked data, G is a watermark amplitude scaling factor, p_i is a pseudo-noise (PN) bit sequence ($p_i \in \{-1,1\}$), and b_i is the watermark information bit sequence obtained by repeating a watermark information bit, a_j ($a_j \in \{-1,1\}$), by a factor s such that $b_i = a_j$ for $js \le i < (j+1)s$ [5]. The factor s is a spread spectrum parameter called spreading factor or chip rate.

Blind retrieval of the embedded watermark data without using the original host data can be achieved by de-spreading the watermarked video using the well-known correlation detector. As the de-spreading process operates on the DCT coefficients or pixel values, the watermarked MPEG video bitstream needs first to be partially or fully decompressed.

The PN signal, p_i, used earlier for embedding is now used to multiply the watermarked video data $\hat{v}_i$, followed by a summation over s number of data, yielding a correlation sum S_j:

$$S_j = \sum_{i=js}^{(j+1)s-1} p_i \hat{v}_i = \underbrace{\sum_{i=js}^{(j+1)s-1} p_i v_i}_{S1_j} + G \underbrace{\sum_{i=js}^{(j+1)s-1} p_i^2 b_i}_{S2_j} \tag{2}$$

The terms $S1_j$ and $S2_j$ denote contributions from the host video and the watermark respectively. For large values of s, $S2_j$ is usually much larger than $S1_j$ because the video signal v_i is statistically uncorrelated with the PN sequence p_i. This produces very small $S1_j$ in general. As a result, the sign of the correlation sum S_j is mostly equivalent to the embedded watermark bit a_j, hence blind retrieval of the watermark is deemed successful.

3   BER Formulation of Blind Retrieval of MPEG Video Watermark

Watermark retrieval errors occur when the sign of S_j is not equal to a_j. The probability of occurrence of such events can be estimated based on a BER formula [5]:

$$\text{BER} = Q\left(\sqrt{\frac{\sigma_p^2 \cdot G^2 \cdot s}{\sigma_v^2 + \mu_v^2}} \right) \tag{3}$$

where $Q(x) = \dfrac{1}{\sqrt{2\pi}} \displaystyle\int_x^\infty e^{\frac{-t^2}{2}} dt$, σ_p^2 is the variance of the PN sequence, σ_v^2 and μ_v are the variance and mean of the host video pixel values or DCT coefficients respectively.

In the case of MPEG-in-MPEG-out watermarking, however, Equation (3) has not considered the non-linear distortion effects due to many MPEG processes such as [18] MPEG quantization, MPEG inverse quantization with mismatch control, and rounding and clipping of pixel values and DCT coefficients.

Distortions like those mentioned above have two effects on the watermark embedded, i.e., reducing the effective spreading factor s and altering the effective amplitude G of the embedded watermark.

Likewise, application of watermark attacks or signal processing such as cropping attacks, selective DCT-domain embedding, and linear filtering on the watermarked data is also expected to affect the validity of Equation (3). In this paper, we propose to model some of the above-mentioned distortions by inserting a scaling factor T into the BER equation, as shown below:

$$\text{BER} = Q\left(T\sqrt{\frac{\sigma_p^{2} \cdot G^{2} \cdot s}{\sigma_v^{2} + \mu_v^{2}}}\right) \tag{4}$$

In Equation (4), the values of σ_p^2, σ_v^2 and μ_v can be pre-determined prior to watermark embedding. The value of T, on the other hand, depends on the type of distortions applied on the watermarked data. This will be discussed in separate case studies in the following parts of this paper.

4   Case Studies

Video watermark embedding and retrieval algorithms outlined earlier have been implemented in software. Two MPEG-2 video sequences, namely *flower.m2v* and *table-tennis.m2v*, are used for testing. The total number of frames in both video sequences is 430, which include 35 I-frames. Watermarks are embedded into the Y blocks of the I-frames and each frame consists of 352×240 pixels. After blind watermark retrieval, error bits found are collated to obtain the experimental (measured) BER. Theoretical BER values estimated from Equation (4) are then computed and compared with the measured BER. The resultant video quality in peak-signal-to-noise ratio (PSNR) [19] is also measured.

The parameter values required by Equation (4) are listed separately in Table 1 for spatial watermark and DCT watermark. Since only I-frames are watermarked, the listed video parameters pertain to the I-frames only.

Table 1. Parameters required in the BER Equation (4)

Video Test File	Parameters for spatial watermark			Parameters for DCT watermark		
	σ_v^2	μ_v	σ_p^2	σ_v^2	μ_v	σ_p^2
flower.m2v	3859.2	146.3	1.0	4202.1	2.3	1.0
table-tennis.m2v	2282.2	132.8	1.0	2322.5	0.5	1.0

4.1   MPEG-in-MPEG-out Watermarking

In this section, the BER performance of MPEG-in-MPEG-out watermarking is studied. Spreading factor s is 10000. Several watermark amplitudes G (1,3, and 5) are used to generate different watermarked MPEG files. In order to calculate the theoretical BER, the values of T are empirically obtained and listed in Table 2. The distortions associated to T in this case are MPEG quantization and inverse quantization, rounding, and clipping effects.

Table 2. Empirical values of parameter T for spatial and DCT watermark

Video Test File	T for spatial watermark	T for DCT watermark
flower.m2v	0.71	0.53
table-tennis.m2v	0.44	0.44

BERs (theoretical and experimental) of the retrieved watermark and PSNR values of the watermarked video sequences are shown in Figure 1 and Figure 2.

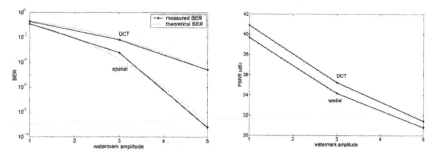

Fig. 1. Watermark retrieval BER and PSNR of *flower.m2v* with constant spreading factor (s=10000) and different watermark amplitudes G

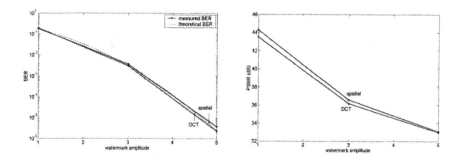

Fig. 2. Watermark retrieval BER and PSNR of *table-tennis.m2v* with constant spreading factor (s=10000) and different watermark amplitudes G

It is observed that the watermark retrieval success rate can be improved by increasing the watermark amplitude. This, understandably, brings about a drop in the video visual quality, as indicated by a lower PSNR. The BERs estimated from Equation (4) are quite close to the measured ones. This shows that our BER formulas are useful for predicting the performance of the watermark retrieval. According to these results, we observe that the watermark amplitude should not exceed 3 while the spreading factor should be at least 10000 in order to achieve acceptable video quality with PSNR above 34dB and good watermark retrieval reliability with BER lower than 10^{-3}.

Next, watermark is embedded using different spreading factors s (1000, 5000, and 10000). The watermark amplitude is maintained at 3 because previous results show that larger watermark amplitude starts to produce noticeable distortion. The BER results are plotted in Figure 3 and Figure 4.

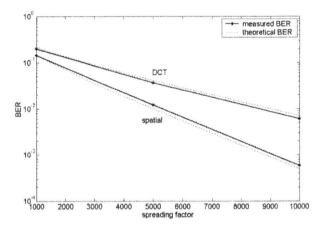

Fig. 3. Watermark retrieval BER of *flower.m2v* with constant watermark amplitude (G=3) and different spreading factors s

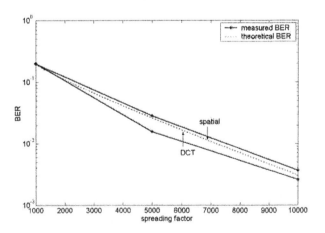

Fig. 4. Watermark retrieval BER of *table-tennis.m2v* with constant watermark amplitude (G=3) and different spreading factors s

From these results, it can be observed that watermark retrieval BER can be improved by increasing the spreading factor. However, fewer bits (payload) can be embedded into the video stream, hence the hiding capacity drops. The BERs estimated from Equation (4) are again close to the measured ones, indicating that our

BER formula is useful for a large range of spreading factors. This gives us confidence to use Equation (4) to estimate the necessary watermarking parameters required to achieve even lower BER that may be of practical interest. For example, assuming that we want to achieve BER=10^{-6} with watermark amplitude $G=3$ and spatial watermarking on *flower.m2v*, then Equation (4) predicts that the spreading factor s should be at least 21500. When verified using simulation, the actual measured BER turns out to be 1.58×10^{-6} which is again an excellent match.

4.2   MPEG-in-MPEG-out Watermarking with Row/Column Cropping Attack

Row/column cropping attack means that some pixel rows/columns of the watermarked video frames are removed in order to induce loss of synchronization in the watermark retrieval, hence disabling its ability to retrieve the watermark. In this case study, watermark data is spread with a spreading factor of s=10000 for embedding as spatial watermark into the I-frames. The watermark amplitude is chosen to be 3. Then column cropping attack is inflicted on every frame of the compressed watermarked video. In order to achieve watermark re-synchronization, a sliding-window correlator [5] is employed. The resultant watermark retrieval BERs of the sliding-window correlator after achieving re-synchronisation are shown in Figure 5 and Figure 6 for *flower.m2v* and *table-tennis.m2v* respectively.

The BER after row/column cropping attack can be predicted from Equation (4) by decreasing the spreading factor s by an appropriate amount. In this case study, since every watermark bit after spreading is embedded into 10000÷352=28.4 rows, cropping one column is equivalent to decreasing the spreading factor s by 28.4. Every other parameter in Equation (4), including T, remains unchanged. These theoretical BERs are plotted in Figure 5 and Figure 6 for comparison with the simulation values.

From the results shown in the figures, it is observed that if a few columns in the watermarked frame are cropped, the watermark can still be retrieved with a high success rate. However, when more columns are cropped, watermark retrieval becomes progressively less reliable. As row/column cropping attack results in an effective decrease in the spreading factor, a countermeasure against this attack is to over-design the spreading factor during watermark embedding. Our BER formula hence provides a useful means for the watermark designer to predict how much additional spreading factor is needed to withstand the maximum anticipated level of row/column cropping attacks without the need for extensive Monte Carlo simulations.

4.3   MPEG-in-MPEG-out Watermarking with Selective DCT-Domain Embedding

In this section, we study the effect of embedding in selected DCT locations of the host video. Embedding in a chosen set of DCT coefficients has been highly advocated for its robustness to common signal processing and low visual distortion. For example,

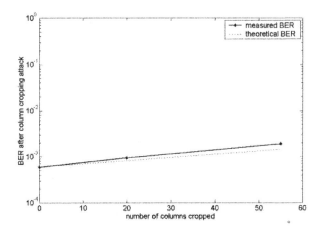

Fig. 5. Watermark retrieval BER of *flower.m2v* with spatial watermark after column cropping attack

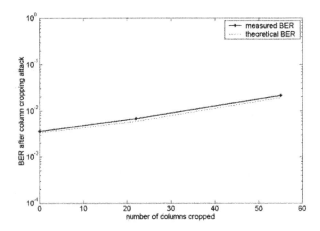

Fig. 6. Watermark retrieval BER of *table-tennis.m2v* with spatial watermark after column cropping attack

Cox [2] suggested embedding in DCT coefficients with high energy content while others suggested embedding in the mid-frequency range [20][21][22]. In this case study, DCT watermark is embedded into all DCT locations except for the 10 lowest and 10 highest frequency locations following the MPEG zig-zag-scan order. This results in only the middle 44 locations in each 8×8 DCT block being embedded with watermarks. The resultant watermark retrieval BER is shown in Figure 7 and Figure 8.

It is not too difficult to see that such selective DCT-domain watermarking is the frequency-domain equivalence of spatial watermarking with spatial cropping. For example, embedding in 44 out of 64 DCT coefficients may be viewed as frequency-domain cropping of watermarks originally embedded in the 10 lowest and highest DCT locations, therefore the resultant watermark retrieval BER can be predicted from Equation (4) by scaling down the spreading factor s by 44/64. Our results in Figure 7 and Figure 8 show that a better scaling factor for s in this case should be 54/64 instead of 44/64. This may appear counter-intuitive initially, but it can be explained as follows. In the case of embedding binary watermarks in all DCT locations, the watermarks originally embedded in the 10 highest DCT locations are nonetheless removed by the MPEG compression process, which normally has large quantization factors at high frequency locations. Therefore, with selective DCT-domain embedding into the 44 mid-frequency locations, the effective loss in embedding locations is only 10.

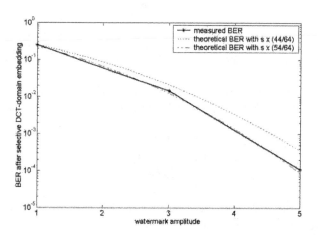

Fig. 7. Watermark retrieval BER of *flower.m2v* with DCT watermark embedded into the 44 mid-frequency locations with $s=10000$

4.4   Linear Filtering

Linear filtering is commonly applied by means of a convolution operation with a filter kernel in the spatial domain. This type of signal processing can be used to enhance the image quality (e.g. smoothing or edge enhancement), but it also distorts the watermark contained in the videos in a deterministic fashion [10]. In this section, we shall show how this type of distortion can be modelled by an appropriate T in Equation (4). To isolate the non-linear effects due to MPEG compression and decompression, we embed a spatial watermark into uncompressed host video frames, perform linear filtering on the watermarked frames, and retrieve the embedded watermark directly from the uncompressed watermarked frames. Both low-pass and high-pass filters are considered.

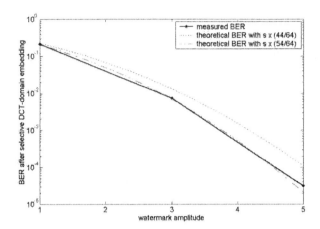

Fig. 8. Watermark retrieval BER of *table-tennis.m2v* with DCT watermark embedded into the 44 mid-frequency locations with $s=10000$

Given a general 3×3 spatial filter kernel/mask as shown in Figure 9, the expression of T to be used for modelling the filtering effect on Equation (4) is given as:

$$T = \frac{f_{22}}{\left(\sum_{i=1}^{3}\sum_{j=1}^{3}f_{ij}\right)\sqrt{q}} \tag{5}$$

where f_{ij} is the filter kernel/mask coefficient and q is a ratio between the video power after filtering and the video power before filtering.

f_{11}	f_{12}	f_{13}
f_{21}	f_{22}	f_{23}
f_{31}	f_{32}	f_{33}

Fig. 9. A general 3×3 spatial filter kernel/mask

Low-pass filtering. Let us consider a Gaussian low-pass filter with spatial mask of [1 2 1; 2 4 2; 1 2 1]. Given that the value of q is pre-determined to be 0.85, the value of T in this case is $\frac{4}{16 \times \sqrt{0.85}} = 0.27$.

The effects of the above low-pass filter on the watermark retrieval BER are shown in Figure 10 and Figure 11. It is shown that the measured and theoretical BERs match closely. By further comparing the theoretical BERs after filtering and without filtering (i.e., $T=1$), we can see that the low-pass filtering distortion is very severe.

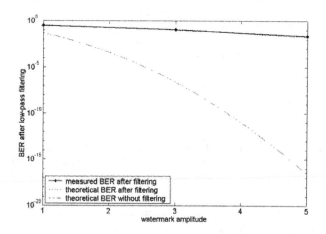

Fig. 10. Watermark retrieval BER of uncompressed frames of *flower.m2v* with spatial watermark ($s=10000$) after low-pass filtering

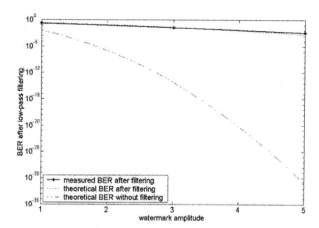

Fig. 11. Watermark retrieval BER of uncompressed frames of *table-tennis.m2v* with spatial watermark ($s=10000$) after low-pass filtering

High-pass filtering. A high-pass filter kernel of [0 -1 0; -1 5 -1; 0 -1 0] is considered here. If the corresponding value of q is pre-determined to be 1.80, $T = \dfrac{5}{1 \times \sqrt{1.80}} = 3.73$.

It is known that PN watermark signal mainly comprises high-frequency components while video signals are mostly low pass in nature. Unlike low-pass filter, high-pass filter turns out to enhance the watermark robustness. Consequently, if the spreading factor s is large, the error bits become very rare and hardly observable. As a result, instead of using BER values, we use signal-power-to-noise-power ratio (SNR) to quantify the watermark robustness in this case. The expression of SNR is as follows:

$$SNR = T^2 \cdot \frac{\sigma_p^{\,2} \cdot G^2 \cdot s}{\sigma_v^2 + \mu_v^2} \qquad (6)$$

The measured and theoretical values of SNRs due to the above high-pass filtering are shown in Figure 12. It can be observed that they match closely. The SNR formula in Equation (6) can hence be substituted into Equation (4) to obtain the corresponding BER.

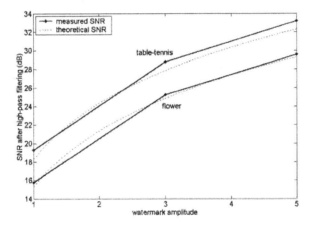

Fig. 12. Watermark retrieval SNR of uncompressed frames of *flower.m2v* and *table-tennis.m2v* with spatial watermark (s=10000) after high-pass filtering

5   Conclusion

In this paper, the robustness of spread spectrum watermark with linear additive embedding and blind retrieval for compressed MPEG video is studied. Both spatial and DCT watermarks are considered. A set of simple but effective formulas is developed to predict the BER of the blind watermark retrieval operation in the presence of distortions due to MPEG encoding/decoding processes, cropping attacks, selective DCT-domain embedding, and linear filtering under watermark amplitude and spreading factor variation. With the help of such BER formulas, watermark robustness can be more easily fine-tuned without the need for time-consuming simulations.

References

1. Caronni, G.: Assuring Ownership Rights for Digital Images. Proceedings of Reliable IT Systems, VIS'95. Vieweg Publishing Company (1995)
2. Cox, I.J., Kilian, J., Leighton, F.T., Shamoon, T.: Secure Spread Spectrum Watermarking for Multimedia. IEEE Transactions on Image Processing, Vol. 6, No. 12 (1997) 1673–1687
3. Herrigel A., Ruanaidh, J.O., Petersen, H., Pereira, S., Pun, T.: Secure Copyright Protection Techniques for Digital Images. In: Auchsmith, D. (ed.): Information Hiding. Lecture Notes in Computer Science, Vol. 1525. Springer-Verlag (1998) 160–190
4. Tanaka, K., Nakamura, Y., Matsui, K.: Embedding Secret Information into a Dithered Multilevel Image. Proceedings of IEEE Military Communications Conference. (1990) 216–220
5. Hartung, F., Girod, B.: Watermarking of Uncompressed and Compressed Video. Signal Processing, Vol. 66, No. 3. (1998) 283–301
6. George, M., Chouinard, J.-V., Georganas, N.: Digital Watermarking of Images and Video Using Direct Sequence Spread Spectrum Techniques. IEEE Canadian Conference on Electrical and Computer Engineering. Edmonton, Canada (1997) 116–121
7. Langelaar, G.C.: Real-Time Watermarking Techniques for Compressed Video Data. Ph.D. thesis, Delft University of Technology. Delft (2000)
8. Hanjalic, A., Langelaar, G.C., Van Roosmalen, P.M.B., Biemond, J.: Image and Video Databases: Restoration, Watermarking And Retrieval. Elsevier Science (2000)
9. Busch, C., Funk, W., Wolthusen, S.: Digital Watermarking: From Concepts to Real-Time Video Applications. IEEE Computer Graphics and Applications, Vol. 19, No. 1 (1999) 25–35
10. Cox, I.J., Miller, M.L., Bloom, J.A.: Digital Watermarking. Morgan Kaufmann (2001)
11. Maes, M., Kalker, T., Linnartz, J.P.M.G., Talstra, J., Depovere, G., Haitsma, J.: Digital Watermarking for DVD Video Copy Protection: What Issues Play a Role in Designing an Effective System? IEEE Signal Processing Magazine (2000) 47–57
12. Hernandez, J.R., Perez-Gonzalez, F., Rodriguez, J.M., Nieto, G.: Performance Analysis of a 2-D Multipulse Amplitude Modulation Scheme for Data Hiding and Watermarking Still Images. IEEE Journal of Selected Areas in Communication, Vol. 16, No. 4 (1998) 510–524
13. Hernandez, J.R., Amado, M., Perez-Gonzalez, F.: DCT-domain Watermarking Techniques for Still Images: Detector Performance Analysis and a New Structure. IEEE Transactions on Image Processing, Vol. 9, No. 1 (2000) 55–68
14. Hernandez, J.R., Amado, M., Perez-Gonzalez, F.: Statistical Analysis of Watermarking Schemes for Copyright Protection of Images. Proceedings of the IEEE, Vol. 87, No. 7 (1999) 1142–1166
15. Kutter, M.: Performance Improvement of Spread-spectrum-based Image Watermarking Schemes through M-ary Modulation. Third International Workshop on Information Hiding. Lecture Notes in Computer Science, Vol. 1768. Springer-Verlag (1999) 237–252

16. Cheng, Q., Huang, T.S.: Blind Digital Watermarking for Images and Videos and Performance Analysis. IEEE International Conference on Multimedia and Expo, Vol. 1 (2000) 389–392

17. Eggers, J.J., Girod, B.: Quantization Effects on Digital Watermarks. Signal Processing, Vol. 81, No. 2 (2001) 239–263

18. BS ISO/IEC 13818-2: Information Technology – Generic Coding of Moving Pictures and Associated Audio Information: Video (1996)

19. Kutter, M., Petitcolas, F.A.P.: A Fair Benchmark for Image Watermarking Systems. Proceedings of SPIE: Security and Watermarking of Multimedia Contents, Vol. 3657 (1999) 226–239

20. Langelaar, G.C., Setyawan, I., Lagendjik, R.L.: Watermarking Digital Image and Video Data: A State-of-the-art Overview. IEEE Signal Processing Magazine (2000) 20–46

21. Bae, K.-H., Jung, S.-H.: A Study on the Robustness of Watermark According to Frequency Band. Proceedings of IEEE International Symposium on Industrial Electronics. Pusan, Korea (2001)

22. Hsu, C.-T., Wu, J.-L.: Hidden Digital Watermarks in Images. IEEE Transactions on Image Processing, Vol. 8, No. 1 (1999)

Optimal Detection of Transform Domain Additive Watermark by Using Low Density Diversity

Yafei Shao, Guowei Wu, and Xinggang Lin

Dept. Electronic Eng., Tsinghua University
100084 Beijing, China
shaoyf98@mails.tsinghua.edu.cn

Abstract. Perceptual based additive watermarking algorithms have good performance in literature, while the optimal detection of such watermarks under attacks remains a problem due to the inaccurate estimation of actual noise distribution. In this paper, a hybrid watermark with low density diversity is proposed. By accurately estimating the noise shape from diversity, the detector is noise adapted and optimal detection will be achieved. The trade-off caused by this diversity is negligible.

1 Introduction

With the rapid development of computers and information network, storage of and access to information become easier and more efficient. However, digital media has the ease to be copied and changed, thus a major obstacle for digital media distribution and related business is media security and copyright protection. Digital watermarking offers a new way to solve these problems.

Many algorithms proposed in the past few years have good performances, especially those based on careful perceptual analysis[1],[2]. As pointed out, one of the key issue in watermarking is the detection problem. In those earlier works the original image is used as reference in watermark extraction, while the requirement of original image will bring inconvenience to many applications. The most commonly used method for blind detection is a simple or normalized correlator, which is most suitable when the noise distribution is unknown [3]. For those additive or nonadditive spread spectrum watermarking schemes, usually the noise comes from the host signal itself when no attack occurs, thus optimal detector structure could be derived with the known host signal distribution, such as General Gaussian Distribution(DCT, DWT)[3],[4], Weibull Distribution (DFT)[5], and will have much better detection result comparing with the correlation detector. However, under attacks as compression, the detector performance will become worse suffering from the inaccurate estimation of actual noise distribution. In this paper, we propose to use a hybrid watermark with low density diversity to overcome this problem. Experiments show its good performance.

F. Petitcolas and H.J. Kim (Eds.): IWDW 2002, LNCS 2613, pp. 105–112, 2003.
© Springer-Verlag Berlin Heidelberg 2003

2 Perceptual Based Watermarking Embedding and Detection

It is widely accepted that transform domain watermarking must make full use of the Human visiual character to achieve robustness. For example, in the method proposed by Zeng[1] ,DCT or wavelet domain Just Noticeable Difference(*JND*) is used as a strength masking. The watermark is embedded as:

$$y = x + sw \tag{1}$$

where x and y are coefficient vectors before and after watermarking. s is the perceptual strength, w is the watermark signal. In [1], the host signal x is modeled by GGD with a zero mean pdf:

$$p(x) = Ae^{-|\beta x|^c} \tag{2}$$

$\beta = \frac{1}{\sigma}(\frac{\Gamma(3/c)}{\Gamma(1/c)})^{\frac{1}{2}}$, $A = \frac{\beta c}{2\Gamma(1/c)}$, Γ is the gamma function, c is the shape parameter.

Usually for natural images, $0.3 \le c \le 1$. The well known Laplacian and Gaussian distribution are special cases of GGD with $c = 1$ and $c = 2$.

Under the following hypothesis:

H_0 : $y = x$

H_1 : $y = x + sw$

The optimal ML detector is

$$\rho = \sum_{i=1}^{N} \beta^c (|y_i|^c - |y_i - s_i w_i|^c) \tag{3}$$

While after attacks such as compression, the watermark strength changes and the mask could not be estimated correctly, thus the above hypothesis doesn't hold any more. In his paper [6], Chen proposed a new detector as:

$$\rho = \sum_{i=1}^{N} sign(y_i)(|y_i|^{c-1} w_i) \tag{4}$$

Whatever detector one uses, the key problem is the estimation of GGD parameter c, because a fixed c is not optimal for different images, and the GGD shape will also change with various kinds and degrees of attacks. In [4], a ML method is used to calculate the shape parameter: By setting a candidate set (c_1, c_2), increase c from c_1 to c_2 with step Δ, the value which maximizes the ML estimator is considered the optimal c and will be used in watermark detection. The estimation is based on the watermarked image itself assuming it has the same distribution as the unmarked one. Experiments stand for this assumption. However, under severe attacks as high ratio compression, many coefficients will be attenuated or even quantized to zero, thus the watermarked and attacked coefficients will not have the same distribution as the host signal any more, and the estimation is no more accurate. For example, when the watermarked image compressed by jpeg2000 with ratio 30, the estimated shape parameter is $c = 0.3$, while the value corresponds to the maxim detection statistics is $c = 1.3$. Suppose the attacked watermarked coefficients is $y^{'}$, one may suggest to use $\hat{x} = y^{'} - \hat{s}w$ for estimation, while the difficulty is: 1) the actual strength $\hat{s}$ remains after attack couldn't be estimated without diversity. If $\hat{s}$ is supposed unchanged and directly calculated as in the embedding procedure, then $\hat{x}$ will be far from GGD under severe attacks. 2) the estimated value is not accurate enough in most cases.

In this paper we assume that the noise after attack is still GGD, and optimal detection happens when the estimated shape parameter is closest to the actual one. Under this assumption we suggest to use a hybrid watermark with diversity of low density to achieve the optimal detection issue.

3   Hybrid Watermark with Diversity of Low Density

The hybrid watermark proposed here is composed of two sub sequences, one stands for the copyright information, we call it true watermark, the other serves as a reference, the role of which is to estimate the shape parameter of GGD from the attacked watermarked image. The reference watermark is embedded the same way as the true watermark to assure the same robustness. The placement of reference watermark should also obey the following ways in order to have the same distortions under possible attacks. For those systems which only need a yes or no answer, the reference watermark must be placed in a random way evenly distributed over those embedding positions. While for those TDMA systems which have different watermarks in different places, a local diversity placed in the neighborhood will be a better choice. In general, the hybrid watermark W can be described as:

$$W = W_{true} \bigcup W_{ref} \tag{5}$$

$w(i)_{i \in P} \in W_{true}$, $w(i)_{i \in \bar{P}} \in W_{ref}$. P and $\bar{P}$ are position sets for the true and reference watermark respectively.

The density D of the embedded watermark is defined as

$$D = \frac{l_{ref}}{l_{true} + l_{ref}} \tag{6}$$

l_{ref} and l_{true} are watermark length. $D = 0$ means no diversity exists. In the next section, we will show a diversity of low density is enough for the estimation purpose.

During watermark detection, the reference watermark will be examined first, with shape parameter c varying from c_1 to c_2. The step Δ controls the estimation accuracy. Then c_{max}, which corresponds to the maximal detection statistic will be used to detect the true watermark. Such a search procedure will be fast because of the low density used.

This hybrid approach could be widely used to improve the watermark detection for a group of additive algorithms in which the noise is modeled as GGD, such as those image and video algorithms in DCT or DWT domain[7]. In this paper, we just use a simple additive method to show the effectiveness of diversity. The hybrid watermark is embedded through an additive way in the mid frequency DCT coefficients of each 8*8 block. We use 512*512 grayscale Lena for example. To avoid perceptual artifacts, *JND* constraints are considered to limit the embedding strength. The embedding density is $D = 1/32$. Searching area is between $c_1 = 0.1$ and $c_2 = 2$, $\Delta = 0.1$. The detector we use is as equation (3).

The detection statistic is defined in [1]:

$$q = \frac{\rho}{\sqrt{N}\sigma} \tag{7}$$

$$z_i = sign(y_i)(|y_i|^{c-1} w_i) \tag{8}$$

$$\sigma^2 = \frac{1}{N-1} \sum_{i=1}^{N} (z_i - \frac{1}{N}\rho)^2 \tag{9}$$

A larger q means lower probability of detection error. Figure 1(a),(b),(c) show the detection statistics of the true and reference watermark under no attacks, JPEG compression with Quality 30 and JPEG2000 compression with ratio 30 respectively. The optimal c is named c_{true} and c_{ref}. In (a) $c_{true} = c_{ref} = 1$ and (b) $c_{true} = c_{ref} = 1.4$; in (c), $c_{true} = c_{ref} = 1.3$. We could see that 1) Without attacks, the host signal follows the Laplacian distribution, while after compression, c will become larger, it is expected that under severe attacks, c tends to be 2 as pointed in [6]. 2) In all cases, the reference watermark estimates the optimal shape parameter well.

One of the key issue is that, the detection statistic of the true watermark shouldn't be affected much by the introduction of diversity. Figure 2 is the comparison of detection statistics between two cases: $D = 0$ and $D = 1/32$ after JPEG compression of Quality 30. Experiment shows that embedding such a reference watermark causes only a loss of about 1%-2% q value. Comparing with the gain from correctly estimation of c, such a trade off is worth.

Reducing the diversity length to $D = 1/64$ or $D = 1/128$ is also tested. When $D = 1/64$, the estimation accuracy is the same with $D = 1/32$ in the above experiments, while q loss is down to less than 1%. When $D = 1/128$, the q loss due to inaccurate estimation is even higher than the gain by using diversity. Thus $D = 1/64$ will be a better choice.

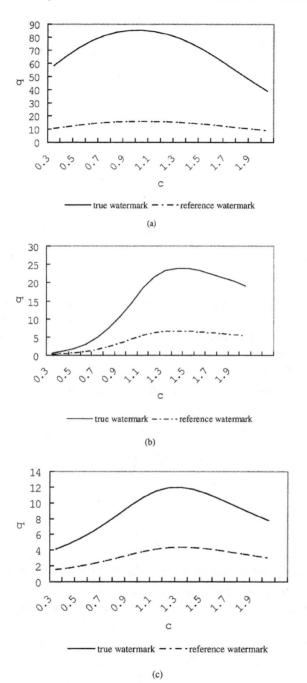

Fig. 1. Detection statistics compared between true and reference watermark. (a) No attacks, (b) JPEG compression with Quality 30, (c) JPEG2000 compression with ratio 30

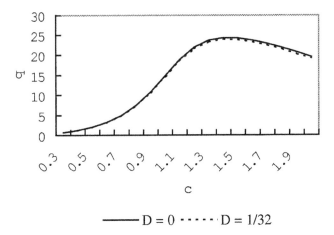

Fig. 2. Detection statistics compared between with diversity $D = 1/32$ and without diversity

It must be pointed out that the diversity here is not used as the evidence of the true watermark existence. In Hypothesis H_0, since the watermark doesn't exit, the estimated c by using the above approach is just a random value in the candidate set. Though this value will be used to detect the true watermark, it will not affect the final probability of false alarm P_{fp}.

The Neyman-Pearson principle is often used in watermarking detection to determine the threshold τ. Under C.L.T. , we have

$$P_{fp} = Q(\frac{\tau}{\sqrt{N}\sigma}) \tag{10}$$

Let

$$m = \frac{\tau}{\sqrt{N}\sigma} \tag{11}$$

The theoretic and experiment result of P_{fp} after JPEG 2000 compression of ratio 30 is shown in figure 3. (a) is under the optimal value $c = 1.4$. (b) is under a randomly selected c, here it is set to 0.8. We can see the theoretic and experimental value match well.

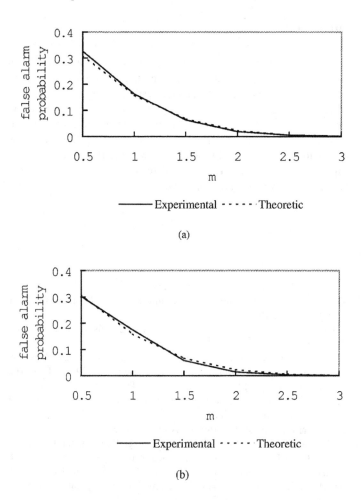

Fig. 3. Experimental and theoretic false alarm probability. (a) P_{fp} under $c = 1.4$, (b) P_{fp} under $c = 0.8$

This kind of diversity is also incorporate with our robust watermarking algorithm, which will be detailed in our paper elsewhere. The frequency domain titling template there also serves the function of diversity. It well estimates the channel state under various signal processing or geometric attacks. Under these circumstances, it raises the detection statistic by 20%-30%, compared with the correlation detector. Experiments show the algorithm could pass all the attacks in the Stirmark3.1 benchmark[7] and results in an average score of 1.

4   Conclusion

In this paper, a hybrid watermark is proposed to achieve optimal detection in perceptual based transform domain additive watermark. By using a low density diversity, the actual noise distribution could be accurately estimated, especially after severe attacks, thus the detector is noise adapted and the performance is improved with the estimated distribution parameter. The trade-off of introducing such a diversity is negligible, and the false probability will not be affected. We argue this method can be widely used in similar occasions for perceptual based image watermarking algorithms, either additive or multiplicative. Also it can be extended to transform domain video watermarking because of its effectiveness and simplicity.

References

1. Zeng, W., Liu, B.: A statistical watermark detection technique without using original images for resolving rightful ownerships of digital images. Vol.8. No.11. IEEE Trans. Image Processing, (1999) 1534–1548.
2. Podilchuk, C., Zeng, W.: Image-adaptive watermarking using visual models. Vol.16. No.4. IEEE J. Select Areas Commun. (1998) 525–539.
3. Hernandez, J. R., Perez-Gonzalez, F.: Statistical analysis of watermarking schemes for copyright protection of images. Vol87. No.7. Proc. of the IEEE. (1999) 1142–1166.
4. Hernandez, J.R., Amado, M., Perez-Gonzalez, F.: DCT-domain watermarking techniques for still images: detector performance analysis and a new structure. Vol.9. No.1. IEEE Trans. Image Processing. (2000) 55–68.
5. Barni, M., Bartolini, F.: A. D. Rosa etc, A new decoder for the optimum recovery of nonadditive watermarks. Vol.10. No.5. IEEE Trans. Image Processing. (2001) 755–766.
6. Chen, Q., Huang,T. S.: An additive approach to transform-domain information hiding and optimum detection structure. Vol.3. No.3. IEEE Trans. Multimedia. (2001) 273–284.
7. Kutter, M., F. Petitcolas, A. P., A fair benchmark for image watermarking systems, V3657. Proceedings of SPIE. San Jose, CA. Jan. (1999) 219–239.

Implications for Image Watermarking of Recent Work in Image Analysis and Representation

Ana Georgina Flesia and David L. Donoho

Department of Statistics, Stanford University
Sequoia Hall, 390 Serra Mall, Stanford, CA 94305-4065 USA
{flesia,donoho}@stanford.edu

Abstract. We consider the potential implications of recent developments in subfields of image analysis and image representation for watermarking and steganography. We consider three rapidly developing subfields: 1. Natural Scene Statistics; 2. Level Set Image Processing and Geometric Diffusion; and 3. Computational Harmonic Analysis. Each of these subfields has recently claimed progress either in characterizing or processing images. We interpret all such progress as implicitly or explicitly identifying invariants of real images. Such invariants are potential tools for studying the effects of watermarking or steganography in an image. We briefly survey these three subfields, give several examples of such invariants, and explore the effects of model watermarking schemes on such invariants.

Keywords. Image Watermarking, Image Steganography, Natural Scene Statistics, Geometric Diffusion by Level Set Methods, Total Variation, Inpainting, Interpolation, Computational Harmonic Analysis, Wavelets, Discrete Cosine Transform.

1 Introduction

The literature of digital watermarking of images has grown phenomenally over the last 5 years, due to the ubiquity of digital media. There are surveys [27,22, 32,31,44,38,37,21,26], books [10,23,25], workshops, conferences, and web sites, inventorying hundreds of active researchers. A striking fact about the literature is the wide range of potential scenarios for watermarking applications, and the attendant wide range of technical and social requirements for watermarking [4, 17,48,28].

These are accompanied by a wide range of conceptual levels displayed in the existing literature, from the relatively straightforward, tool-oriented, to more theoretically inclined [27,38].

In this more theoretical literature, one observes an emerging tradition of "importing sophistication" into the watermarking literature by adapting ideas from more established fields. Three such examples are particularly evident:

- Some works import ideas about the *human visual system* to design watermarking schemes which are more likely to be imperceptible to visual inspection while still providing strong marks [11,49,20,39].

F. Petitcolas and H.J. Kim (Eds.): IWDW 2002, LNCS 2613, pp. 113–129, 2003.
© Springer-Verlag Berlin Heidelberg 2003

- Other works import frameworks from digital communications, such as the concept of spread spectrum communications [12,2].
- In more recent work, for example marked in a special issue [24], the framework of information theory has been used.

This "importation algorithm" has generated many valuable developments and seems like a useful way to enhance the sophistication of watermarking literature.

In this paper, we propose that recent work in image analysis and representation can contribute new ideas to the watermarking literature. The work we shall discuss sheds light (explicitly or implicitly) on the *properties of real images*. We believe that *the watermarking literature lacks substantial discussion of the properties of real images, and that this discussion could inform the design of watermarking schemes and watermarking detectors.*

To make our point, we first think of the space of all possible N pixel images – for example the real vector space $(Z_b^3)^N$, consisting of arrays of 3 b-bit numbers at each pixel. Let's suppose for a moment that we could agree among ourselves to define a *space of real images* $\mathcal{R}$, a set containing all the images humans are ever likely to see. Without knowing very much about $\mathcal{R}$ this much would be clear: *real images occupy a tiny subset of the space of all possible images.* There are two approaches to this fact:

- Probability theory, allows us to precisely formulate the statement that almost every "possible image" looks simply like a realization of noise.
- Similarly we could say that the set of images with intelligible structure is of extremely low cardinality compared with the set of all possible N pixel images.

We prefer to think in geometric terms, and to say that for an N-pixel images, in some sense which remains to be made precise, the effective dimensionality of the set $\mathcal{R}$ of real images is $D << N$. The extra dimensions used in the N-pixel representation but not fully-employed by $\mathcal{R}$ represent redundancy in the image. A simple cartoon, in Figure 1, represents the situation: we caricature the collection $\mathcal{R}$ of real images as a linear subspace of a higher-dimensional space. This cartoon is obviously not correct, but will be useful for discussion purposes.

Watermarking perturbs a given real image in a way which is later detectable. With the cartoon model just presented, one could model this effect as displacement of original image data represented by a point R in $\mathcal{R}$ in such a way that it now lies outside the space $\mathcal{R}$. (The other possibility – moving an image around within $\mathcal{R}$ – does not currently seem like a realistic option, mostly because $\mathcal{R}$ is not a linear subspace, and we have no usable characterization of $\mathcal{R}$.)

Therefore, (conceptually, at least) completely "blind" watermark detection could be based on the principle of having a complete characterization of $\mathcal{R}$ and recognizing whether the image data being presented to us lie in $\mathcal{R}$ or not. Note that this point of view is quite distinct from much of the standard watermarking literature, which takes the point of view that the real image is a kind of noise and the watermark is a kind of signal, detected by matched filtering or similar

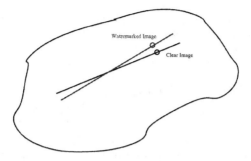

Fig. 1. Subspace of Natural Images

tools which are based on full knowledge of the watermarking schemes, and ignore the properties of real images [47].

Of course, the "space of real images" is not well characterized, and is certainly not the linear space depicted in our cartoon. It is very unlikely that there is any convenient mathematical characterization of this space, for there appears to be no precise list of quantitative properties which real images and only real images posses (but compare to Mumford and Gidas [34]). Therefore, the "blind" watermark detection principle just mentioned in the previous paragraph is not currently a practical option. However, it does serve as a useful organizing principle.

What we can expect is not to completely characterize the space of images, but instead to recognize certain *invariants*: properties which real images have, but manipulated images do not have. Identifying such invariants of images will have numerous implications for the field of image watermarking and, principally, put us in a better position to describe and understand the properties of watermarking schemes. If they are not strong enough to allow complete "blind" detection, they may perhaps allow advances in understanding how to design better watermarking schemes with more "natural" looking outputs.

In this paper we will consider recent developments in image analysis and image representation as sources for useful invariants. We describe several invariants and test them in an exploratory way with reference to watermarking, by asking: how do certain model watermarking schemes affect these invariants?

The invariants we consider will be drawn from three rapidly developing fields in which recent developments claim to be based on improved understanding of the structure of real images.

– *Natural Scene Statistics.* Over the last 15 years, an extensive literature has developed concerning the properties of naturally-occurring images. Driven by researchers from fields of vision, psychology, biology, and theoretical neuroscience, this literature aims to understand the statistical properties of naturally occurring images and to make predictions about how those statistical properties might have driven the evolution of the human visual system. Important discoveries in this field include scaling properties of natural images and tree-structured predictability of natural images [35,36,46,42].

– *Level Sets and Geometric Diffusion Techniques.* Over the last 10 years or so, ideas arising in applied mathematics (numerical solution of nonlinear partial differential equations) have been used in image processing for various purposes (noise removal and deconvolution), reporting surprisingly good results compared with traditional linear filtering ideas. A central idea in this literature is to view an image not as a collection of pixels, but instead as a collection of level sets (think of the level lines on a topographic map). This different point of view makes visible certain image properties which would be hard to express otherwise. A key, yet effectively hidden, assertion made by this literature is that the level sets of a real image exhibit substantial continuity and smoothness, and that exploiting this smoothness makes improved image processing possible [41,40].

– *Computational Harmonic Analysis and Data Compression.* Over the last 20 years, a series of new tools for signal and image representation have been developed in applied mathematics, beginning with the wavelet transform, and expanding through a host of "designer transforms", such as wavelet packets, cosine packets, ridgelets, curvelets, and other tools. A key assertion made by this literature is that such tools can give a more efficient representation of certain features of real data than existing tools on which classical compression tools are based [7,8,9,13,14].

Each of these three areas in some sense represents advances in understanding the structure of 'real' images. In the paper to follow, we will quickly review some of the work just mentioned, and the claims which have recently been made. We will then show that these claims imply the existence of certain image invariants, which we believe will be useful in watermarking.

In this exploratory work, we hope to illustrate the following central point: fields outside of watermarking frequently discover invariants of "real images" that may have relevance to watermark detection, understanding and processing. We expect that as it comes to be generally recognized that the structure of 'real images' is essential to high quality watermarking, interactions between the communities listed above will become common.

While this is a rather weak achievement in comparison to delivering an integrated watermarking system, we believe that injecting these ideas into the watermarking discourse will be valuable for the watermarking community as well as the image representation and analysis community.

2   Natural Scene Statistics

A number of interesting questions have motivated researchers to study the statistics of natural images and scenes. What are the relationships between gray values at distant pixels? Is it possible to define a probability law for natural images? Do natural images obey simple invariants? What is the relationship between the responses of the cortical cells of certain animals and the statistics of images of their habitat? What is the relationship (if one exist) between the morphology of the visual organs of certain animals and the statistics of images of their surrounding world?

A quick review of the findings of the field would state that most of the statistical studies of natural images are concerned with either first and second statistics (through the power spectrum, the covariances, the coocurrences) or additive decompositions of images, see [46,43]. Some of the findings in the second group that are relevant for our discussion are summarized as follows:

- Wavelets and related bases (having localized, multiscale, oriented basis elements) are in some sense "optimal" representation of images, (see [3,35, 46]).
- The distribution of wavelet coefficients of natural images has been empirically measured to be far from Gaussian, and closer to a heavy tailed distribution, (see [45]). Prediction rules for the absolute values of coefficients have been devised, based on neighboring coefficients across scales and orientations, (see [42]) .
- Wavelet transforms exhibit correlations between amplitudes at different scales and common locations, as pointed out by Simoncelli and collaborators on several papers; the nature of these statistics have been discussed by the authors in [15]. In that paper, the authors showed that the edges structure of an image accounts for most of the correlation present in the image.

Hence, Natural Images, if they are viewed as "noise" as is often the case in watermarking, is a very special kind of noise: non gausssian, non independent, with non linear higher-order relations.

Implications of Natural Scene Statistics for Watermarking. Watermarking is possible because the human perceptual process discards significant amounts of data when processing media. This redundancy is, of course, central to the field of lossy compression. Watermarking exploits the redundancy by hiding encoded watermarks in them. The key to our discussion is to show that even when watermarking does not *perceptually* change the image, it does change its statistics.

Watermarking's effect on parent-child properties. Buccigrossi and Simoncelli [6] have developed a probability model for natural images, based on empirical observation of their statistics in the wavelet domain. They have used this as a basis for successful image compression and noise removal programs and have studied a whole range of natural imagery to verify the model. Their findings have been widely replicated.

We will follow their notation, but use the simplest choice, Haar wavelets. In order to describe the relative position of wavelet coefficients in sub-bands, we call the coefficients in the same level and same position but different orientation cousins. We call the relationship of coarse-scale coefficients and fine-scale coefficients parent-child relationship.

In this section of the paper we intend to explore the dependency between parent and child wavelet coefficients at the same location on edge maps that have been watermarked in the spatial and DCT domains.

Consider two coefficients representing information at adjacent scales but the same orientation (e.g. horizontal) and spatial location. Bucigrossi and Simoncelli have plotted the conditional histogram of the energy (square) of the child coefficient conditioned to the energy of the corresponding coarse-scale parent coefficient, and found that typical localized image structures (edges), tend to have substantial power across many scales at the same spatial location. These structures are represented in the wavelet domain via superposition of basis functions at these scales. The signs and relative magnitudes of the coefficients associated with these basis functions will depend on the precise location, orientation and scale of the structure. Thus, measurement of a large coefficient at one scale means that large coefficients at adjacent scales are more likely. The correlation between squares of parent and child coefficients is widely accepted as an invariant of Natural Images.

Experiment. We now explore this invariant in the watermarking context. We construct a database of edges with different orientations, and calculate the correlation of parents and child energies. We will watermark this database and observe how much correlation has been disrupted.

- We consider first a crude watermarking scheme in the spacial domain. We construct a database of edges with different amplitudes, and we add a pseudo random noise W to our "edge image" E, multiplied by an strength factor δ

$$I = E + \delta W.$$

In Figure 2 below, we see that indeed for small δ there is high correlation between parent and child, and that as the watermark strength δ increases, the correlation between parent energy and child energy decreases. In fact, pure random noise should not induce parent-child correlation at all, since wavelet coefficients of noise are stochastically independent.

- This kind of disruption it is not only present on Edge Maps watermarked on the spatial domain. We may devise an analog experiment in the DCT domain, and we may consider adding the noise only to the medium frequencies, in order to make the watermark more robust to transformations (such as JPEG compression), see the Appendix for details. In Figure 2 below, we see that indeed for small δ there is high correlation between parent and child energies, and that as the watermarking strength δ increases, the correlation between parent energy and child energy decreases.

In short, a key invariant of Natural Imagery is diluted by watermarking.

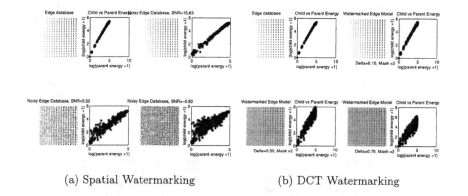

(a) Spatial Watermarking   (b) DCT Watermarking

Fig. 2. Wavelet parents and child: From left to right, top to bottom, watermark strength increases, and α and signal to noise ratio decreases.

3   Level Set Methods and Geometric Diffusion Techniques

Over the last decade it has been found that ideas originally arising in solution of nonlinear P.D.E's (e.g. for shock waves and other physical phenomena) could be used in image processing, for example, in problems of segmentation and image denosing. In general, the goal of most Level Sets denoising algorithms is to smooth the values of an image within homogeneous regions but not across the boundaries of those regions. They do this by smoothing "along" the level sets rather than "across" them. The idea is to preserve contrasts across level sets while performing substantial smoothing on the image [41,40].

More recently, the field has considered "inpainting", which attempts to fill in image information in a missing region based upon the image information available outside the region. The most recent approaches to (non-texture) inpainting aim to reconstruct missing regions by continuation of level sets (isophotes), using higher-order PDE's, Calculus of variations of a mixture of both [5,18].

In effect, the field is developing as if *a key invariant of images is the smoothness of their level sets.*

Implications of Level Sets Methods for Watermarking. Many watermarking schemes take advantage of the masking phenomenon. Masking refers to the fact that a component in a given audio or visual signal may become imperceptible in the presence of other signal called the masker. This masking effect has been used in the design of the image-dependent DCT watermark method described in the Appendix. There, to each sinusoid present in the signal (masking signal), another sinusoid (watermark) is added, having amplitude proportional to the masking signal [4]. Spatial masking refers instead to the fact that he human visual system is less sensitive to distortions around the edges and textured areas of the image than in smooth areas. This effect has also be exploited for watermarking by increasing the watermark energy locally in these masked areas [27]. The masking phenomenon helps improve the robustness of a watermark, since its energy could be increased (it is claimed), without degrading the visual image quality.

We claim that the techniques that take advantage of this phenomenon change the image in a *detectable way*, since the noisy structure of the watermark modifies the isophotes in a small region around the edges, making them wigglier, or breaking them in pieces.

Clear image

Watermarked image

Fig. 3. Contour lines computed by Matlab filled contour routine: Left, Clear Barbara, right, Wavelet watermarked Barbara.

Qualitative effects of Watermarking in Level Sets properties. A quick way to explore the level sets of the image is to plot them with a contour plot routine. The contouring algorithm of Matlab [30] treats the input intensity image as a regularly spaced grid, with each element connected to its nearest neighbors. The algorithm scans this image as a matrix, comparing the values of each block of four neighboring elements (i.e., a cell) in the matrix to the contour level values. If a contour level falls within a cell, the algorithm performs a linear interpolation to locate the point at which the contour crosses the edges of the cell. The algorithm connects these points to produce a segment of a contour line. A filled contour plot displays level lines calculated from the image and fills the areas between the level lines using constant colors, highlighting in this way the level sets.

A more indirect way of assessing changes in the topographic structure of a watermarked image would be evaluating the performance of algorithms that depend on the continuity and smoothness of the level sets of the input image. Unexpectedly reduced performance would suggest tampering with the invariant on which the algorithm definition is based.

Experiments

– We have watermarked the image called "Barbara" with two different schemes, one that introduces noise in the medium frequencies of the block

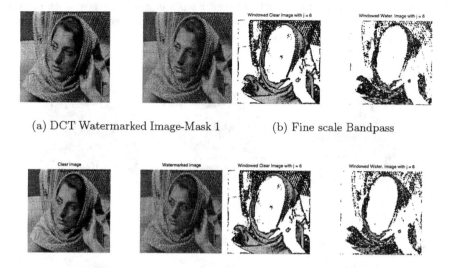

(a) DCT Watermarked Image-Mask 1   (b) Fine scale Bandpass

(c) Wavelet Watermarked Image   (d) Fine scale Bandpass

Fig. 4. First row: from left to right, Clear barbara, DCT Watermarked Barbara, Fine-scale Bandpass of Clear Barbara, Fine scale Bandpass of DCT Watermarked Barbara. Second row:from left to right, Clear barbara, Wavelet Watermarked Barbara, Fine-scale Bandpass of Clear Barbara, Fine scale Bandpass of Wavelet Watermarked Barbara.

DCT coefficients of the image and other that add noise to the biggest wavelet coefficients of the two finest scales. This approach has little effect on flat regions of the image. We can see in Figure 3 that the level sets of the face, hand and flat background are still reasonably smooth, but the scarf and the textured back of the chair show striking changes.

– We can explore this concept further, focusing on the structure of edges of the image by means of bandpass filter. We bandpassed the image to clean the flat regions and reveal only the fine details, see Figure 4. The contour plot routine of Matlab [30] finds points in the boundary of the level sets (called level lines) and interpolates to approximate the level lines. Watermarking completely disrupts this process, since each level line of the scarf of "Barbara' has been broken into pieces.

– We have seen that the connectivity and smoothness of the isophotes has been modified, so it is reasonable to expect image processing techniques as inpainting will be less successful. On Figure 5, first column we observe a clear image superposed with text. The size of the letters is quite small so the automatic text eraser procedure of Esedoglu [18] works its best. The next two columns show the same image watermarked with two different variations of the DCT scheme, and the output of the inpainting procedure, which was applied with the same parameters as it was with the original image. The text has been erased, but noise has taken its place. Several steps of anisotropic diffusion are necessary to remove the noise introduced by the watermark procedure, leading to excessive smoothing of the edges of the image.

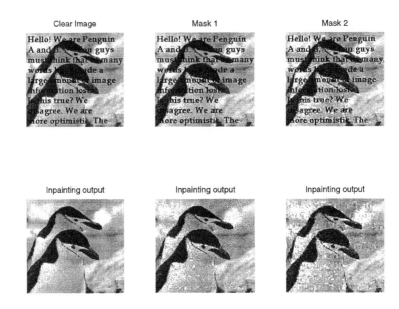

Fig. 5. Inpainting on Clear and Watermarked images with DCT scheme

We have introduced qualitative evidence of a disruption in the invariant of smoothness of level sets in images that have been watermarked. Quantitative evidence could be obtained by measuring the smoothness of the level lines. The most naive way would be to sum (integrate) a measure of the curvature of level sets along the level set, normalized by length.

4   Computational Harmonic Analysis

Wavelet analysis, and multiscale thinking in general, has grown in popularity in the last decade. The journal *Applied and Computational Harmonic analysis*, founded only in 1993, has become one of the most-cited journals in the mathematical sciences, and leading figures on wavelet research are among the most cited authors in the mathematical sciences. The imaginative appeal of multiscale and localized representation may account for the new popularity of wavelets.

A striking property of the "new wave" of multiscale transforms is the fast rate of decay of the sorted decomposition coefficients. Efficient non linear thresholding estimators may be devised thanks to this property, also called "sparsity' of the transform. The degree of sparsity of the decomposition of a given signal depends of the transform and the class or space where the signal belongs. Par example, ortho-normal wavelet basis are optimal, in the sense of maximizing sparsity, over the space of piecewise regular signals, i.e. smooth signals away of point singularities, and ridgelet basis/frames are optimal for representing smooth signals with singularities along straight lines [7,8,9].

CHA Implications for Watermarking. Transform domains are popular because many state of the art compression techniques such as JPEG and JPEG2000 employ this framework (block-based DCT, and Wavelet transform) and this allows for watermarking the compressed bit stream with only partial decoding. A simple way of applying some perceptual knowledge in the DCT domain is to watermark the mid-frequency components, since the low frequency components are very sensitive to distortion and the high frequency components can be removed without significantly affecting the original image quality [38].

In the wavelet case, it has been point out the importance of adding the watermark to the biggest coefficients of the selected subband since the current wavelet compression methods always keep these coefficients for reconstruction. Also, as the flat regions are represented by the biggest coefficients of the coarse scale subbands, the finer scale subbands should be selected to inject the watermark content [27,38].

Effects of watermarking on the sparsity of wavelet and ridgelet decompositions. The wavelet-based method described in the previous section introduces fewer artifacts in the image, which depends heavily on the selected noise variance, but also implies a simple way of detecting the presence of watermark content in a given copy of an image when comparing with the original image, since the sparsity of the wavelet decomposition is reduced.

There is not clear reason to expect a similar behavior on the wavelet decomposition of images that have been watermarked in the DCT domain, since the wavelets basis functions are not likely to react to noise added in a thin and elongated region of the frequency domain that does not match with their isotropic support.

In the other hand, digital ridgelets have better orientation and localization properties [13,14], so it could be the right domain to search for differences in the sparsity properties between clear and DCT watermarked images.

Our discussion in this section will focus in the effect that different watermaking schemes have over the sparsity invariant of the wavelet and ridgelet decomposition of selected images.

Experiments. We have performed some experiments to test the validity of our empirical analysis.

– We have applied the discrete wavelet transform to three images, "Barbara",' 'Wavelet watermarked Barbara" and "DCT watermarked Barbara", which have been obtained applying the methods described in the Appendix. In

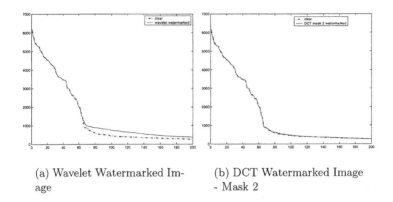

(a) Wavelet Watermarked Image

(b) DCT Watermarked Image - Mask 2

Fig. 6. Rearranged wavelet coefficients: left, wavelet watermarked image, right, DCT mask 2 watermarked image.

order to study the sparsity ofthe transform we have plotted the rearranged wavelet coefficients in Figure 6. We can observe that the wavelet watermarked image have a slower decay than the clear one, which is obvious result from the injection of noise on the second finer-subband of the transform. In the DCT domain, we do not observe any variation in the decay of the reordered coefficients.

– We have applied the digital ridgelet transform [16] in the same setting as the DCT transform, on 8x8 squares of the image. Higher ridgelet coefficients are observed on the DCT watermarked image, which is clear from visual inspection and from the plot of the reordered coefficients, see figure 7. No changes are observed in the decay of the ridgelet coefficients on the wavelet watermarked image.

We have introduced quantitative evidence that supports with our heuristic analysis, and suggests that an invariant of images, the sparsity of transform-domain representations, is disrupted by the watermarking procedure.

5   Conclusion

We have shown in this paper that watermarking disrupts the inter-scale correlations present in the wavelet coefficient pyramid on natural images. Previous work in steganalysis [19] has made a similar claim, so we are adding additional support to the hypothesis that watermarking changes the statistics of images in a way inconsistent with membership in the class of 'real' images.

Several currently popular methods of denoising and image enhancement depend heavily on the properties of the isophotes of 'real' images, such as smoothness and continuity. Evidence presented in this paper supports the claim that

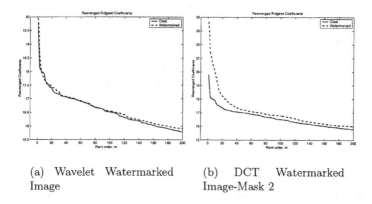

(a) Wavelet Watermarked Image

(b) DCT Watermarked Image-Mask 2

Fig. 7. Rearranged ridgelet coefficients: left, wavelet watermarked image, right, DCT mask 2 watermarked image.

watermarking systematically distorts the isophotes, making inpainting and other image processing tasks harder and less successful.

The DCT and wavelet domains have been widely used for watermarking purposes. Most DCT watermarking schemes produce modifications in the middle frequency band to coexist with JPEG lossy compression. Evidence presented in this paper shows that the discrete ridgelet transform is sensitive to the presence of chaff injected in that frequency band. Ridgelet coefficients are not particularly sensitive to the presence of chaff injected into the comparable wavelet subband.

What are the implications of these results for discourse in watermarking? We see several:

- *Talk about the structure of real images.* Watermarking is being applied on real imagery; whether it depicts natural or man-made scenes, it has attributes which distinguish it from arbitrary digital data. Many analyses of watermarking schemes treat the actual imagery as a noise and pay virtually no attention to its structure. Knowledge of that structure could contain valuable clues for blind detection, for tamper detection, and for artifact avoidance.
- *Do not restrict attention just to the usual suspects.* Wavelet and DCT domains are not the only domains which might be useful for designing watermarking schemes. Mathematicians are investigating completely new tiling schemes. Perhaps those are more appropriate for some purposes. As we have seen with ridgelets, they may also be more appropriate for blind detection, tamper detection and artifact control.

Future Work. We have follow the lead of Farid [19] and studied discriminant features based on first order statistics of wavelet coefficients, nd *predicted coefficients*. The rationale for this choice is that the high correlation between amplitudes of "parents", "children", "brothers" and "cousins" makes prediction possible [6], so it is likely that disrupted correlation will make prediction less accurate. Exploratory work has given 92% accuracy in discrimination between wavelet watermarked images and clear images, with 1% of false positives. The error rates with other imagery, like Digimarc marked images and mixtures of images marked in different domains, are less promising. We are currently working to improve performance in this area by constructing a more sophisticated discrimination rule for this set of features, based on modern machine learning tools like MART [29]. We are also studying different measures of smoothness, and basic statistics of ridgelet coefficients, as new features for discrimination.

References

1. Ambrosio, L. and Tortorelli, V.: Approximation of functionals depending on jumps by elliptic functional via Γ-convergence, Commun. Pure. Appl. Math., **43** (no. 8) (1990).
2. Barni, M., Bertollini, F., Cox, I. Hernandez, J. and Perez-Gonzalez, F.: Digital Watermarking for copyright protection: a communications perspective. IEEE Comunications Magazine August 2001 90–116.
3. Bell, A.J. and Sejnowski, T.J.: An information-maximization approach to blind separation and blind deconvolution. Neural Computation. **7** (1995) 1129–1159
4. Bender, W., Gruhl, D., Morimoto, N., Lu, A.: Techniques for data hiding. IBM Systems Journal. **35** (no 3,4) (1996) 313–336.
5. Bertalmio, M.,Sapiro, G., Ballester, C. and Caselles, C.: Image inpainting. Computer Graphics, SIGGRAPH 2000, July 2000.
6. Buccigrossi, R.W. and Simoncelli, E.P.: Image compression via joint statistical characterization in the wavelet domain. IEEE Transactions on Image Processing, **8**, (no.12) Dec. 1999 1688–701.
7. Candès, E.: Ridgelets: Theory and Applications. Ph.D. Thesis, Department of Statistics, Stanford University, 1998.
8. Candès, E and Donoho, D.: Ridgelets: The key to High-Dimensional Intermittency?. Phil. Trans. R. Soc. Lond. A. **357** (1999), 2495–2509.
9. Candès, E and Donoho, D.: Curvelets: a surprisingly effective nonadaptive representationof objects with edges. In: Albert Cohen, Christophe Rabut, and Larry L. Schumaker (eds.). Curve and Surface Fitting: Saint-Malo. Vanderbilt University Press, Nashville, TN. ISBN 0-8265-1357-3, 1999.
10. Cox, I., Bloom, J., Miller, M.: Digital Watermarking, Morgan Kaufmann Publishers (2001).
11. Cox, I., Lilian, J., Leighton, T.: Secure spread spectrum watermarking for multimedia. IEEE Transactions on image processing. **6** (no.1) (1997) 1673–1687.
12. Cox, I., Miller, M. and Mckeillips, A.: Watermarking as communications with side information. Proceeding of the IEEE **87** No.7 July 1999 1127–1141.
13. Donoho, D.: Orthonormal Ridgelets and Linear Singularities. SIAM J. Math Anal. **31** (no 5) (2000) 1062–1099.
14. Donoho, D. Ridge Functions and Orthonormal Ridgelets. Journ. Approx. Thry. **111** (2001) 143–179.
15. Donoho, D.L., Flesia, A.G.: Can recent innovations in harmonic analysis "explain" key findings in natural image statistics?. Network: Computation in Neural Systems **12** (no.3) (Natural Stimulus Statistics Workshop 2000, Long Island, USA, Oct. 2000.) IOP Publishing Aug. 2001 371–93.

16. Donoho, D.L., Flesia, A.G.: Digital ridgelet transform based on true ridge functions. To appear in Beyond Wavelets. J. Stoeckler and G. Welland (Eds). Academic Press, December 2002.

17. Dugelay, J.L. and Roche, S. A survey of current watermarking techniques. In: Katzenbeisser, S. and Petitcolas, F. (eds). Information Hiding, Techniques for Steganography and Digital Watermarking, Computer Security Series, Artech House (2000) 121–148.

18. Esedoglu, S. and Shen, J.: Digital Inpainting based on the Mumford-Shah-Euler image model. European J. Applied Mathematics, in press, 2002

19. Farid, H: Detecting steganographic messages in digital images. Technical Report 2001-412, Dartmouth College, Computer Science.
    http://www.cs.dartmouth.edu/ farid/publications/tr01.html.

20. Hannigan, B., Reed, A. and Bradley, B.: Digital watermarking using improved human visual system model.

21. Hartung, F. and Kutter, M.: Multimedia watermarking techniques. Proceeding of the IEEE. **87** (no.7) July 1999 1079–1107.

22. Herrigel, A., O Ruanaidh, J., Petersen, H. Pereira, S. and Pun, T.: Secure copyright protection techniques for digital images. In: Aucsmith, D. (ed.): Information Hiding. Lecture Notes in Computer Science, Vol. 1525, Springer-Verlag, Berlin Heidelberg New York (1998) 169–190.

23. Information Hiding, techniques for steganography and digital watermarking. In: Computer Security Series. Katzenbeisser, S. and Petitcolas, F. (eds), Artech House (2000).

24. Information theoretic aspects of digital watermarking. Special Issue of Signal Processing. Elsevier for EURASIP, **81** (no.6) June 2001 1117–1119.

25. Johnson, N., Jajodia, S. , Duric, Z.: Information Hiding: Steganography and Watermarking-Attacks and Countermeasures. Kluer Academic Publishers (2000).

26. Kutter, M. and Hartung, F.: Introduction to watermarking techniques. In: Katzenbeisser, S. and Petitcolas, F. (eds). Information Hiding, Techniques for Steganography and Digital Watermarking, Computer Security Series, Artech House (2000).

27. Langelaar, G., Setyaman, I. and Lagendijk, R.: Watermarking digital image and video data. A state of the art overview. IEEE Signal Processing Magazine. **17** (no.5) September 2000 20–46.

28. Maes, M., Kalker, T., Linnartz, J.P., Talstra, J., Depovere, G., Haitsma, J.: Digital watermarking for DVD Video Copy protection. IEEE Signal Processing Magazine. Sept. 2000 47–57.

29. MART- Multiple Additive Regression Trees. *http://www-stat.stanford.edu/ jhf/R-MART.html*

30. Matlab -The MathWorks. *http://www.mathworks.com/*

31. Memon, N. and Wah Wong, P.: Protecting Digital Media Content. Comunications of the ACM. **41** (no.7) July 1998 35–43.

32. Miller, M., Cox, I., Linnartz, J.P. and Kalker, T.: A review of watermarking principles and practices. In: Parhi, K. and Nishitani, T. (eds.) Digital Signal Processing in Multimedia Systems, Marcel Dekker Inc. (1999) 461–485.

33. Mumford, D. and Shah, J.: Optimal approximation by piecewise smooth functions and associated variational problems. Comm. Pure. Appl. Math., vol. 42, no. 4, 1989.

34. Mumford, D. and Gidas, B.: Stochastic models for generic images. Technical report, Division of Applied Mathematics, Brown University, 1998.
    http://citeseer.nj.nec.com/mumford99stochastic.html

35. Olshausen, B. and Field, D.: Emergence of simple-cell receptive field properties by learning a sparse code for natural images. Nature **381** (1996) 607–609.

36. Olshausen, B and Field, D.: Natural Image statistics and efficient image coding. Network: Computation on neural systems. **7** (1996) 3333–3339.

37. Petiticolas, F., Anderson, R. and Kuhn, M.: Information Hiding: a survey. Proceeding of the IEEE **87** (no.7) July 1999 1062–1078.

38. Podilchuk, C. and Delp, E.: Digital watermarking algorithms and applications. IEEE Signal Processing Magazine. July 2001 33–46.

39. C. Podilchuk, W. Zeng.: Image-adaptive watermarking using visual models. (1998).

40. Sapiro, G.: Geometric Partial Differential Equations and Image Processing. Cambridge University Press, January 2001.

41. Sethian, J.A.: Level Set Methods and Fast Marching Methods: Evolving Interfaces in Computational Geometry, Fluid Mechanics, Computer Vision, and Materials Science. Cambridge University Press, 1999 Cambridge Monograph on Applied and Computational Mathematics.

42. Portilla, J., Simoncelli, E.P.: A parametric texture model based on joint statistics of complex wavelet coefficients. International Journal of Computer Vision, **40** (no.1) (2000) p. 49–71.

43. Ruderman, D.: The statistics of natural images. Network. **5** (no 4) (1993) 517–548.

44. Swanson, M., Kobayashi, M. and Tewfik, A.: Multimedia data-embedding and watermarking technologies. Proceedings of the IEEE. **86** (no.6) June 1998 1064–1087.

45. Simoncelli, E. and Adelson, E.: Subband Transforms In: John Woods (ed.) Subband Image Coding. Kluwer Academic Publishers Norwell MA, 1991 143–192.

46. Simoncelli, E.P., Olshausen, B.A.: Natural Image Statistics and Neural Representation. Annual Review of Neuroscience, **24** (2001) 1193–1215.

47. Su, J., Hartung, F., Girod, B.:Channel Model for a Watermark Attack. Proc. Security and Watermarking of Multimedia Contents, San Jose, CA, SPIE, **3657** January 1999 159–170.

48. Voyatzis, G. and Pitas, I.: The use of watermarks in the protection of digital multimedia products. Proceeding of the IEEE **87** (no.7) July 1999 1197–1207.

49. Wolfgang, R. and Podilchuk, C.:Perceptual watermarks for digital images and video. Proceeding of the IEEE. **87** (no.7) July 1999 1108–1126.

Appendix:Watermarking Experiments

The most straightforward way to watermark an image in the spatial domain is to add a pseudorandom noise pattern to the luminance value of its pixels. We may make the watermark image content dependant before adding it to the cover image by multiplying the random noise pattern by a binary image in order to increase the watermarking load in specific regions of the cover image. The binary image could be the produced by an edge detector, so flat regions will have lower watermark context that heavy textured regions or edges. The same principle could be applied to other domains. For example, a crude DCT Watermarking Scheme may be defined by the next algorithm:

- Compute the 8*8 block DCT.
- Grab coefficients in each block that lie in the range $5 <= k+l <= 8$, (Mask 1), or $3 <= k+l <= 5$, (Mask 2), where (k, l) is the index of DCT coefficients within a block.
- Multiply this band of coefficients by a mask $(1 + \delta w)$ where w is pseudo random uniform $[-1, 1]$ and $\delta < 1$.
- Invert the transform.

We should notice that the modification of the $3 <= k + l <= 5$ coefficients (Mask 2) introduces more noise in the textured areas of the image.

Another example, a crude Wavelet Watermarking Scheme may be defined by the next algorithm:

1. Let wt be the wavelet transform of the image I.
2. Look at the wavelet coefficients one scale removed from the finest scale. Select the M1 largest coefficients at this scale, and multiply this group of coefficients by w1, a pseudo random uniform[-1,1].
3. Look at the wavelet coefficients of the finest scale and select the M2 largest coefficients at this scale. Multiply this group of coefficients by w2, a pseudo random uniform[-1,1].
4. Let W=[0 w1 w2] be the rearranged wavelet coefficients array, where zero sets for the untouched scales. Invert the transform of (wt + k W).

On Watermarking Numeric Sets*

Radu Sion, Mikhail Atallah, and Sunil Prabhakar

Computer Sciences Department and
The Center for Education and Research in Information Assurance,
Purdue University, West Lafayette, IN, 47907, USA,
[sion, mja, sunil]@cs.purdue.edu,
http://www.cs.purdue.edu/homes/sion

Abstract. *Digital Watermarking*, [3] [4] [5] [6] [7] [8] [9] [11] [12] [16] [17] [18] can be summarized the technique of embedding un-detectable (un-perceivable) hidden information into data objects (i.e. images, audio, video, text) mainly to protect the data from unauthorized duplication and distribution by enabling provable rights over the content.
In the present paper we address the issue of rights protection in the framework of numeric data, through resilient information hiding. We're looking into the fundamental problem of watermarking numeric collections and propose resilient algorithms. To the best of our knowledge there is no work specifically addressing the problem of watermarking this type of data. The wide area of applicability of the problem ranging from numeric database content to stock market analysis data, makes it especially intriguing when considering a generic solution and particularities of its various applications. Given a range of associated numeric constraints and assumptions we provide a solution and analyze associated attacks. Our solution is resilient to a multitude of attacks, including data re-sorting, subset selection (up to 40% data loss tolerance), linear data changes etc. Finally we present and discuss a proof-of-concept implementation of our algorithm.

1 Introduction

Extensive research has been conducted on the problem of watermarking multimedia data (images, video and audio), however there is relatively little work on watermarking other types of data. More recently, the focus of watermarking for digital rights protection is shifting toward data types such as text, software, and algorithms. Since these data types are designed for machine ingestion and have well defined semantics (as compared to those of images, video, or music), the identification of the available "bandwidth" for watermarking is as important a challenge as the algorithms for inserting the watermarks themselves. Existing

---

* Portions of this work were supported by Grants EIA-9903545, IIS-9985019 and IIS-9972883 from the National Science Foundation, Contract N00014-02-1-0364 from the Office of Naval Research, and by sponsors of the Center for Education and Research in Information Assurance and Security.

F. Petitcolas and H.J. Kim (Eds.): IWDW 2002, LNCS 2613, pp. 130–146, 2003.
© Springer-Verlag Berlin Heidelberg 2003

research has addressed the problems of software watermarking [2] [10] [15] and natural language watermarking [1]. Here we study the issue of watermarking numeric collections and propose algorithms for resilient watermarking.

Thus, in this paper we explore how Alice makes sure she can safely distribute a valuable numeric collection to Tim Mallory and others. Of course she also wants to be able to prove later on to Jared that the data in Tim's possession (possibly maliciously modified) is her creation and/or assert some other rights over it.

The algorithm introduced proves to be resilient to various important classes of attacks, including data re-shuffling/sorting, massive subset selection, linear data changes, random item(s) alterations attacks.

The paper is structured as follows. Section 2 presents the considered framework issues and main associated challenges. Section 3 presents our solution. Section 4 introduces a practical example illustrating our algorithm. Section 5 discusses conclusions and defines our current ongoing efforts as part of a broader frame of future envisioned research.

2   The Problem

Let $\mathbb{S}$ be a set of n real numbers $\mathbb{S} = \{s_1, ..., s_n\} \subset \mathbb{R}$, Let $\mathbb{V}$ be the result of watermarking $\mathbb{S}$ by minor alterations to it's content. For now we assume $\mathbb{V} = \{v_1, ..., v_n\} \subset \mathbb{R}$ is also of size n. Let a string of bits, w of size $m << n$ be the desired watermark to be embedded into the data ($|w| = m$). We will use the notation w_i to denote the i-th bit of w.

2.1   Data Usability

In the following we define a certain value (allowable "usability") metric of a data collection that will enable us to determine the watermarking result as being valuable and valid, within permitted/guaranteed error bounds. Thus, our algorithm relies on the knowledge of the guaranteed (e.g. at watermarking/outsourcing time) restrictions/properties required of the actual data.

For each relevant subset $S_i \subset \mathbb{S}$ let $G_i = \{G_1{}^i, ..., G_p{}^i | G_j{}^i : subsets(\mathbb{S}) \to \mathbb{R}\}$ be a (possible empty) set of "usability metric functions", that S_i has to satisfy within a certain set of allowable (i.e. guaranteed result error bounds) usability intervals $G_i{}^\delta = \{((g_1{}^i)_{min}, (g_1{}^i)_{max}), ..., ((g_p{}^i)_{min}, (g_p{}^i)_{max})\}$, such that the following "usability condition" holds: $G_j{}^i(S_i) \in ((g_j{}^i)_{min}, (g_j{}^i)_{max}) \forall j \in (1, p)$.

In other words we define the allowable distortion bounds for the given input data ($\mathbb{S}$) in terms of "usability" metrics (see "usability" in [14]) which are given at watermarking time and are defined by the actual purpose (see "usability domain" in [14]) of the data.

Example

One simple but extremely relevant example is the *maximum allowable mean squared error* case, in which the usability metrics are defined in terms of mean squared error tolerances as follows:

$$(s_i - v_i)^2 < t_i \quad \forall i = 1, ..., n \quad (1)$$
$$\sum (s_i - v_i)^2 < t_{max} \quad (2)$$

where $\mathbb{T} = \{t_1, ..., t_n\} \subset \mathbb{R}$ and $t_{max} \in \mathbb{R}$ are defining the guaranteed error bounds at data distribution time. In other words $\mathbb{T}$ defines the individual elements allowable distortions in terms of mean squared error (MSE) and t_{max} the overall permissible MSE.

Many other semantic and numeric constraints can be imagined with respect to a given application and data set. This paper does not focus on any particular complex constraint case but rather on the overall concept. Analysis of different types of constraints is to make the object of a distinct, future research effort.

We define the *general problem* of watermarking the set $\mathbb{S}$ as the problem of finding a transformation from $\mathbb{S}$ to another item set $\mathbb{V}$, such that, given all possible imposed usability metrics sets $\mathbb{G} = \cup G_i$ for any and all subsets $S_i \subset \mathbb{S}$, that hold for $\mathbb{S}$, then, after the transformation yields $\mathbb{V}$, the metrics should hold also for $\mathbb{V}$ [1]. We call $\mathbb{V}$ the "watermarked" version of $\mathbb{S}$.

One interesting issue here is identifying the original set items *after* watermarking. That is, how do we "recognize" an item after it has been changed slightly. This is the subject of Section 3.2 where we devise a scheme for item labeling that works well enough to be suitable for our watermarking purposes.

2.2   Attacks

Having formulated the problem as above, before attempting any solution, let's first outline classes of envisioned attacks.

A1. Subset Selection. The attacker can randomly select and use a subset of the original data set, subset that might still provide value for it's intended purpose (subtractive attack).

A2. Subset Addition. The attacker adds a set of numbers to the original set. This addition is not to significantly alter the "valuable" (from the attacker's perspective) properties of the initial set versus the resulting set.

A3. Subset Alteration. Altering a subset of the items in the original data set such that there is still value associated with the resulting set. A special case needs to be outlined here, namely (A3.a) a linear transformation performed uniformly to all of the items. This is of particular interest as such a transformation preserves many data-mining related properties of the data, while actually altering it considerably, making it necessary to provide resilience against it.

A4. Subset Re-sorting. If a certain order can be imposed on the data then watermark retrieval/detection should be resilient to re-sorting attacks and should not depend on this predefined ordering.

---

[1] In other words, if $\mathbb{G}$ is given and holds for the initial input data, $\mathbb{S}$ then $\mathbb{G}$ should also hold for the resulting data $\mathbb{V}$.

Given the attacks above, several properties of a successful solution surface. For immunity to **A1**, the watermark has to be embedded in overall collection properties that survive subset selection (e.g. numeric confidence intervals, see later).

If the assumption is made that the attack alterations are within problem distortion bounds, defined by the usability metric functions (otherwise the data might loose it's associated value), then **A3** should be defeat-able by embedding the primitive mark in resilient global item set properties.

As a special case, **A3.a** can be defeated by a preliminary normalization step in which a common divider to all the items is first identified and divided by. For a given item X, for notation purposes we are going to denote this "normalized" version of it by $NORM(X)$.

Because it adds new data to the set, defeating **A2** seems to be the most difficult task, because it implies the discovery of the possible data usability domains [14] for the attacker. That is, we have to be able to pre-determine what the main uses (for the attacker) for the given data set/type are.

3   A Solution

Our solution for the *simplified problem* consists of several steps. First, we deploy a resilient method for item labeling, enabling the required ability to "recognize" initial items at watermarking detection time (i.e. after watermarking and/or attacks). In the next step we ensure attack survivability by "amplifying" the power of a given primitive watermarking method. The amplification effect is achieved by the deployment of secrets in selecting collection subsets which will become input for the final stage, where a primitive watermarking method is deployed on selected secret subsets.

3.1   Overview

As an overview, the solution for the simplified problem reads as follows.

Encoding

Step E.1. Select a maximal number of unique, non-intersecting (see below) subsets of the original set, as described in Section 3.3.

Step E.2. For each considered subset, (E.2.1) embed a watermark bit into it using the encoding convention in Section 3.4 and (E.2.2) check for data usability bounds. If usability bounds exceeded, (E.2.3) retry different encoding parameter variations or, if still no success, (E.2.3a) try to mark the subset as invalid (i.e. see encoding convention in Section 3.4), or if still no success (E.2.4) ignore the current set [2]

---

[2] This leaves an invalid watermark bit encoded in the data that will be corrected by majority voting at extraction time.

We repeat step E.2 until no more subsets are available for encoding. This results in multiple watermarking patterns embedded in the entire data collection.

Many other implementations of this solutions are possible. For example checking for data usability could be done at an even more atomic level, such as inside the bit-encoding procedure, selection of intersecting subsets could be allowed, etc.

Decoding

Step D.1. Using the keys and secrets from step E.1, recover a majority of the subsets in E.1, all of them if no attacks were performed on the data.

Step D.2. For each considered subset, using the encoding convention in Section 3.4, recover the embedded bit value and re-construct watermarks.

Step D.3. The result of D.2 is a set of copies of the same watermark with various potential errors. This last step uses a majority voting scheme to recover the highest likelihood initial mark.

In the following we introduce more details on the actual building blocks of the overview above.

3.2   Item Labeling for Set Elements

Watermarking a data collection requires the ability to "recognize" *most* of the collection items before and after watermarking and/or a security attack. This is especially important as a response to attacks of type **A4**. In other words if an item was accessed/modified before watermarking, e.g. being identified with a certain label L, then hopefully at watermark detection time the same item is still identify-able with the same label L or a known mapping to the new label.

Bringing this a little bit further, making some less restrictive assumptions, we would like to be able to identify *a majority of the initial elements of a subset* after watermarking and/or attacks. As we will see, "missing" a small number of items is not making it much worse as the marking method is resilient to that.

While research efforts of the authors include work in this area (see "tolerant canonical labeling" in [13]) we are going to present a simplified solution here, tailored to the particularities of the current problem.

Our solution is based on lexicographically sorting the items in the collection, sorting occurring based on a one-way, secretly keyed, cryptographic hash of the set of most significant bits (MSB) of the normalized (see Section 2.2) version of the items. The secret one-way hashing ensures that an attacker cannot possibly determine what the actual item ordering is. Then, in the next step (see Section 3.3), subset "chunks" of the items are selected based on this secret ordering. This defeats **A4** as well as any attempts to actually deploy statistical analysis to determine the secret subsets.

More formally, given a collection of items as above, $\mathbb{S} = \{s_1, ..., s_n\} \subset \mathbb{R}$, and a secret "sorting key" k_s, we induce a secret ordering on it by sorting according to a cryptographic keyed hash of the most significant bits of the normalized items. Thus we have $index(s_i) = H(k_s, MSB(NORM(s_i)), k_s)$.

The MSB space here is assumed to be a domain where minor changes on the collection items (changes that still satisfy the given required usability metrics) have a minimal impact on the MSB labels. This is true in most cases (as usually the given usability metrics are related to preserving the "important" parts of the original data). If not suitable, a different labeling space can be envisioned, one where, as above, minor changes on the collection items have a minimal impact.

3.3   Algorithm

Current watermarking algorithms draw most of their court-persuasion power [14] from a secret that controlled watermark embedding (i.e. watermarking key). Much of the attack immunity associated with an watermarking algorithm is based on this key and it's level of secrecy.

Given a weak partial marking technique (e.g. (re)setting a bit), a strong marking method can be derived by repeatedly applying the weak technique in a keyed fashion on different (secretly selected) parts of the object to be watermarked.

In this section we present the two main steps of our watermarking scheme that come in after labeling the data collection items (that is, we assume the ability to identify most of the items here).

Let $\mathbb{K} = \{k_1, ..., k_m\}$ be a set of m keys of n bits each.

Step One: Power Amplification

This step performs exactly the *power amplification* role, as outlined above, namely selecting (based on set of selection secrets/keys) subsets of the initial data on which to apply a simple watermarking method later on, achieving overall a high degree of resilience and power.

Generic Solution: We define $S_i = \{s_j \in \mathbb{S} | (k_i)_{bitj} = 1\}, i = 1, ..., m$. In other words each $S_i \subset \mathbb{S}$ is defined by selecting a subset of $\mathbb{S}$ fully determined by it's corresponding key $k_i \in \mathbb{K}$ (see Figure 1(a)).

The main purpose of this step is to amplify the power [14] of the general watermark. The next step will simply consider each S_i to be marked separately by building on a simple watermarking method. The result will be at least a m-bit (i.e. $i = 1, ..., m$) overall watermark bandwidth (unless multiple embeddings and majority voting are considered, see Section 3.5) in which each bit is embedded/hidden in each of the marked S_i.

Note: In building the subsets S_i we do not consider elements s_j which are subject to very restrictive usability metrics (e.g. with corresponding $t_j = 0$, i.e. no available encoding bandwidth). If any of the considered keys are selecting one of those unalterable elements, we simply generate another key instead.

We presented the generic solution above for illustrative purposes. It works well for cases when exact item labeling is available and there are no concerns of

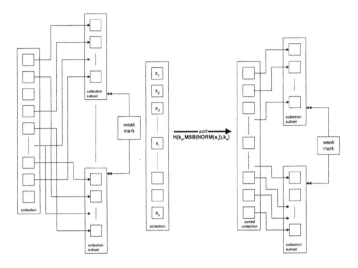

Fig. 1. Primitive Mark Power Amplification. (a) Keyed selection of subsets. This assumes the ability to uniquely and consistently identify items before and after watermarking and/or attacks. (b) Subset selection after sorting on keyed hash of the most significant bits (MSB) of the normalized data items. This enables recovery after various attacks, including re-shuffling/sorting and linear changes.

attacks of the types **A2** and **A1** (i.e. subset addition, selection). The following idea takes also into account these concerns.

Actual Solution: Considering the ability to induce a secret ordering on the collection items as presented in Section 3.2, we define an alternate method to select subsets as required by power amplification. Let k_s the sorting key as above. After inducing the secret ordering by sorting the collection $\mathbb{S} = \{s_1, ..., s_n\} \subset \mathbb{R}$ on $index(s_i) = H(k_s, MSB(NORM(s_i)), k_s)$, we build the subsets S_i as "chunks" of items from the collection, a "chunk" being a set of adjacent items in the sorted version of the collection (see Figure 1(b)).

This increases the ability to defeat different types of attacks including "cut" and/or "add" attacks (e.g. **A1** , **A2**), by "dispersing" their effect throughout the data, as a result of the secret ordering. Thus, if an attack removes 5% of the items this will result in each subset S_i being 5% smaller. If S_i is small enough and/or if the primitive watermarking method used to encode parts of the watermark (e.g. 1 bit) in S_i is made resilient to these kind of (minor) transformations (See Figure 4) then the probability of survival of most of the embedded watermarks is higher.

Additionally, in order to provide resilience to massive "cut" attacks, we will select the subset "chunks" to be of sizes equal to a given percent of the overall data set (i.e. not of fixed absolute sizes). This guarantees a certain adaptability of our subset selection scheme, assuring later on the retrieval of the watermark even from, say, half of the original data.

For another discussion on the size of the subsets S_i see Section 3.5. For now it just suffices to say that all the subsets are equally sized and this size is to be considered a part of the overall watermark encoding secret.

Depending on the particularities of the desired result, as well as the data's usability domain, different keyed subset selection methods may be devised, more appropriate to the envisioned types of attacks.

Step Two: Watermarking

Once each of the to-be-watermarked secret (keyed) sets S_i is determined, the problem reduces itself to finding a reasonable, not-very-weak (i.e. better than "coin-flip", random occurrence) algorithm for watermarking a medium-small sized set of numbers. The problem here is to find a direct watermarking method that allows reliable encoding of a single bit value in this set of numbers.

3.4   Encoding and Primitive Watermarks

The previous "amplification" provides most of the hiding power of our application (as happens in many current watermarking techniques where secrets are an important avenue for hiding as well as protecting the watermark). The next step actually encodes the watermark bits into the provided sub-collections.

One desired property of an encoding method is the ability to retrieve the encoded information without having the original data. This can be important especially in the case of very large dynamic databases (e.g. 4-5 TBytes of data) where data-mining portions were outsourced at various points in time. It is unreasonable to assume the requirement to store each outsourced copy of the original data. Our method satisfies this desiderata.

Confidence Violators

We are given S_i (i.e. one of the subsets secretly selected in the previous step) as well as the value of a watermark bit b that is to be encoded into S_i. The bit encoding procedure follows.

Let v_{false}, v_{true}, $c \in (0,1)$, $v_{false} < v_{true}$ be real numbers (e.g. $c = 90\%$, $v_{true} = 10\%$, $v_{false} = 7\%$). We call c a *confidence factor* and the interval (v_{false}, v_{true}) *confidence violators hysteresis*. These are values to be remembered also for watermark detection time. We can consider them as part of the encoding key.

Definition: Let $avg(S_i) = \frac{\sum x_j}{|S_i|}$, $\delta(S_i) = \sqrt{\frac{\sum (avg(S_i) - x_j)^2}{|S_i|}} \forall x_j \in S_i$. Given S_i and the real number $c \in (0,1)$ as above, we define $v_c(S_i)$ to be the *number of items of S_i that are greater than* $avg(S_i) + c \times \delta(S_i)$. We call $v_c(S_i)$ the number of positive "violators" of the c confidence over S_i, see Figure 2.

Mark encoding convention: Given S_i, c, v_{false} and v_{true} as above, we define $mark(S_i) \in \{true, false, invalid\}$ to be *true* if $v_c(S_i) > (v_{true} \times |S_i|)$, *false* if $v_c(S_i) < v_{false} \times |S_i|$ and *invalid* if $v_c(S_i) \in (v_{false} \times |S_i|, v_{true} \times |S_i|)$.

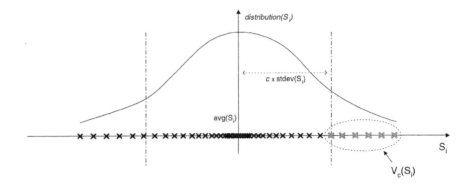

Fig. 2. Distribution of sample (normal) item set S_i. Encoding of the watermark bit relies on altering the size of the "positive violators" set, $v_c(S_i)$.

In other words, the watermark is modeled by the percentage of positive "confidence violators" present in S_i for a given confidence factor c and confidence violators hysteresis (v_{false}, v_{true}).

Actually watermarking the data (i.e. to the desired mark values) in this case resumes to modifying the component elements of S_i such as to yield the necessary value for $v_c(S_i)$, while satisfying all the given data "usability" constraints $\mathbb{G}$.

It is to be noted that many minor technical issues remain to be solved with the actual encoding method itself. For example, in order to maintain the actual mark reference (i.e. the mean of all values of S_i, $avg(S_i)$), items in S_i are to be altered in pairs. Other simple technical tweaks had to be taken into account.

Getting back to the encoding procedure, the question arises on how to perform the required item alterations so as to also satisfy the given "usability" metrics (i.e. $\mathbb{G}$) for the data in case. There are two possible approaches.

The first approach simply performs the primitive watermarking step (e.g. for S_i) and then checks for data usability with respect to $\mathbb{G}$. If watermarking altered main usability restrictions, simply ignore S_i and consider the next secretly selected subset to encode the rest of the watermark. This will result in errors in the encoded marks but by using majority voting (see Section 3.5) over a large number of encoded mark copies in the data, the errors will (hopefully) be eliminated in the result.

This approach is very attractive for dynamically generated/shaped data where the selected subsets S_i will have small sizes and the mark redundancy will be high even in small amounts of the original data.

The previous approach does not make optimal use of the existing bandwidth in the provided subset S_i. Another idea would be to check for data usability after *each* item alteration and adjust the encoding behavior accordingly. This can happen for example by choosing another item (if available) if the current considered one does not preserve data usability after alteration. While more optimal, this approach presents higher computing overhead at watermarking time.

The ideal approach is probably a combination of the previously presented ideas. Our implementation is based on the first approach although minor tweaks could bring it closer to a combination among the two.

3.5   Discussion on Resilience

A decision needs to be made determining the size of the subsets selected in the amplification step (i.e. $|S_i|$). Given that our method embeds 1 bit per subset we have a total mark bandwidth of $\frac{|S|}{|S_i|}$ bits. Thus the size of the selected subsets determines directly the total mark encoding bandwidth.

This can and should be considered as a fine-tuning step for the particular data usability metrics provided. If those metrics are too restrictive, more items will be needed inside S_i to be able to encode one bit while still preserving required usability. On the other hand if the usability metrics are more on the relaxed side, S_i can be very small, sometimes even 10-15 items. This enables for more encoding bandwidth overall.

S usually is large enough to provide for multiple embeddings of the original mark which is a requirement in order to survive subset "cut" attacks (i.e. to preserve the mark even inside a "cut" subset of data).

We can embed the main watermark no more than $\frac{|S|}{|S_i| \times m}$ times. At watermark detection time, after recovering all the watermark copies from the given data *majority voting* over all the recovered watermark bits is deployed (or any other error correcting method for that matter) in order to determine the most likely initial watermark bits, see Figure 3.

bits	5	4	3	2	1	0
w_0	1	0	1	1	1	0
w_1	1	0	1	0	1	0
w_2	1	0	0	0	1	1
w_{result}	1	0	1	0	1	0

Fig. 3. Majority voting over three recovered watermark copies for a 6 bit sized original watermark.

Another interesting point to be made here is considering the inherent attack-vulnerability of the watermarking scheme. As shown also in previous research

[14], bringing the watermarked data as close as possible to the allowable distortion bounds ("usability vicinity" limits) is of definite benefit in making the result's data usability as fragile as possible to any attack.

An attacker will be faced with the problem of removing/altering the watermark and now any changes he performs with this intent have an increased likelihood of making the data invalid with respect to the guaranteed usability metrics[3], thus removing or at least diminishing its value.

In effect we integrated this idea also in our primitive encoding implementation. Not only do we embed as many watermark copies as possible, but also, as watermark embedding progresses, a certain embedding aggressiveness factor increases, determining actual changes to the data to be performed more and more up to the permitted limit and not only as required.

Note: The *incremental* increase of the aggressiveness factor is needed so as to make sure that at least several copies of the mark were embedded successfully, before changing the data too aggressively might not allow for entire mark copies to be embedded (i.e. while maintaining data usability).

We performed some initial attack-related experiments on various data sets and determined promising features of our embedding method. More experiments are to follow and results should become available online.

The "confidence-violators" primitive set encoding proves to be resilient to a considerable amount of randomly occurring uniformly distributed surgeries (i.e. attacker with no extra knowledge, in this case item removals) before watermark alterations occur. Even then, there exists the ability to "trace" or approximate the original watermark to a certain degree (i.e. by trying to infer the original mark value from an invalid set). Most of the considered data tolerated up to 20-25% data loss before mark alterations occurred, as illustrated also in Figure 4.

Thus, our watermarking scheme provides resilience for a set of attack types, including re-sorting (**A4**), subset selection (e.g. up to 25-30% data removal), massive subset selection (e.g. watermark preserved even in half of the data if data halved randomly), linear changes (e.g. adding/multiplication), random item(s) alterations attacks that preserve data usability.

3.6 Analysis

In the following we are analyzing the above presented algorithm from a more theoretical perspective, with the final goal of determining bounds associated to the embedding resilience and its attackability.

Note: Given current space constraints, for the scope of this analysis we are going to consider "cut and remove" and data alteration attacks. It can be shown that data addition and/or alteration attacks can be reduced to this case.

---

[3] Because the watermarking process already altered the data up to its usability metrics limits.

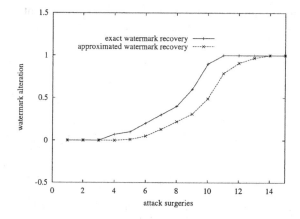

Fig. 4. Experiments on resilience to surgeries (data loss, "cut" attacks). The item set size considered was 35, experiments were performed on 10 different sets of close to normally distributed data. Various other parameters: $v_{false} = 5\%, v_{true} = 9\%, c = 88\%$. The average behavior is plotted here. Up to 25% data loss was tolerated gracefully by most the tested data.

Let us assume a primitive 1-bit encoding method for subsets (of subset size denoted by s) that is resilient to a minimum $s \times l$ random "surgeries" (data item removals and/or alterations), $l \in \mathbb{R}$. This resilience can be guaranteed by varying the encoding parameters presented in Section 3.4.

For now we are going to assume a most general scenario by not assigning values for l. Also let us consider a error correcting mechanism (e.g. majority voting) able to correct $e \times \frac{n}{s} \times \frac{1}{m}$ bit errors where, as above, n is the number of total items in the input set, m is the bit-size of the watermark to be embedded and $e \in \mathbb{R}$, $e \geq 2$. In other words e naturally models the error correcting power proportional to the ratio of total available bandwidth to watermark size. Again, in order to keep a maximum degree of generality, we are not assigning values for e at this point.

Let $P(s, a'')$ be the average success probability (i.e. actual bit-flip) of a random, a'' sized (i.e. a'' surgeries) attack on a 1-bit encoding subset of size s. The assumption of resilience to l surgeries of the subset encoding can be thus also expressed as $P(s, x) = 0, \forall x \leq l$.

Given the above, the question we ask now is: *What is the probability of success of an attacker aiming at destroying at least one watermark bit, as a function of the amount of damage (i.e. number of surgeries) ?*

An answer to the above immediately enables the computation of resilience and attackability bounds of the watermarking algorithm by relating the required damage for a successful attack to the maximum permissible damage levels etc.

First let us compute the local (i.e. at subset level) amount of surgeries that are taking place in the case of an a-sized (i.e. a surgeries) global attack on the entire marking scheme.

Because of the additional sorting and one-way hashing step (see Section 3.3), for illustrative purposes we are going to introduce a simplifying assumption, namely that of an uniform distribution of all the surgeries among the individual subsets. That is, in the following $a'' = a \times \frac{s}{n}$.

Now let us compute the probability of an a-sized attack affecting (e.g. flipping) exactly t bits in the underlying data bandwidth, before error correction, $P_t(s, a)$:

$$P_t(s, a) = C_{\frac{n}{s}}^t \times P(s, a'')^t \times (1 - P(s, a''))^{n-t} \tag{1}$$

Now given our e-bit error correction ability, the probability that one watermark bit is altered by an a-sized attack becomes:

$$P_1(a) = 1 - \sum_{i=1}^{e} (P_i(s, a)) \tag{2}$$

Getting back to $P(s, a'')$ let us recollect the fact that it actually represents the average success probability (i.e. actual bit-flip) of a random, a'' sized (i.e. a'' surgeries) attack on a 1-bit encoding subset of size s. There also exists the assumption of resilience to l surgeries of the subset encoding.

As the bit-encoding method depends highly on input data and its distribution as well as on the actual values of the involved encoding parameters (e.g. c, v_{false}, v_{true}) it becomes impossible to provide an exact, in-depth analysis of the actual value of $P(s, a'')$ for arbitrary input data sets.

Given a certain fixed data set, it might be possible to actually exactly determine the value of $P(s, a'')$ but to no useful effect as much of the power of the encoding lies in its ability to watermark arbitrary input.

Another method of analyzing $P(s, a'')$ could take the form of an experiment, sampling its value over a large number of potential different data inputs. We are proposing to pursue this avenue in future research. For the scope of the current analysis, given also associated space constraints, we are going to reasonably approximate $P(s, a'')$.

Remember that we introduced the assumed average l tolerated surgeries per 1-bit encoding. We know that, on average, $P(s, x) = 0, \forall x \leq l$. Let us assume that $a'' > l$. Then we approximate

$$P(s, a'') = q \times \frac{a'' - l}{s}, \forall a'' \in (l, s) \tag{3}$$

where $q \in \mathbb{R}, q \geq 1$ is a input data characteristic normalization constant. Now we can rewrite equation 1 as

$$P_t(s, a) = C_{\frac{n}{s}}^t \times (q \times \frac{a'' - l}{s})^t \times (1 - (q \times \frac{a'' - l}{s}))^{n-t} \tag{4}$$

For illustration purposes, by substituting $t = 1, n = 10000, s = 50, a = 1000, l = 4, q = 1$, and continuing the computation we obtain a very promising sample result

$$P_1(50, 1000) = \frac{1}{200} \times \frac{1}{50} \times (\frac{49}{50})^{9999} \simeq 0 \tag{5}$$

namely that there is a surprisingly low probability of destroying one bit in the underlying data by a 1000-sized attack on an input set of 10000 where the subsets are of size 50 and subset encoding is tolerant to at least 4 item-surgeries.

Note: The approximation introduced for $P(s, a'')$ is not accurate. An exponential behavior, indeed proportional to $\frac{a''-l}{s}$ can be observed experimentally for large enough values of a''. Subject for future research is to determine (e.g. experimentally) the exact shape of $P(s, a'')$ for normally distributed input data, for example, and then re-assess the above numbers.

4   Implementation and Experiments

This section presents aspects of our proof-of-concept implementation and some of the results obtained on various data input.

4.1   The nrx.* Package

nrx.* is our test-bed implementation of the algorithms presented in this paper. It is written using the Java language. The package receives as input a watermark to be embedded, a secret key to be used for embedding, the input data (in a special file format) as well as a set of external *usability plug-in modules*. The role of the plug-in modules is to allow user defined usability metrics to be used at run-time without recompilation and/or software restart (We implemented the case of the maximum allowable mean squared error usability metric). The software then uses those metrics to re-evaluate data usability after each atomic watermarking step as explained in Sections 3.3 and 3.1.

Once usability metrics are defined and all other parameters are in place, the watermarking module (see Figure 5) starts the process of watermarking. A rollback log is kept for each atomic step performed (i.e. 1-bit encoding) until data usability is assessed and confirmed. This allows for "rollbacks" in case usability is not preserved by the current atomic operation.

Watermark embedding continues until a maximal number of watermark copies have been embedded into the data, while preserving the guaranteed usability metrics.

Watermark recovery takes as input the key used in embedding, the input data known to contain the watermark and recovers the set of watermark copies initially embedded. A final step of majority voting over the recovered copies completes the recovery process.

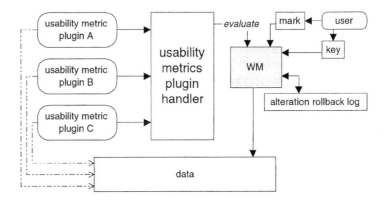

Fig. 5. The nrx.* package. Overview.

4.2 Experiments

For exemplification purposes we generated synthetic input data for nrwm.*. The size of the generated set was 10000, the set item values being uniformly distributed in the interval $(1, 1000)$. We considered the MSE usability metric case and conditioned our generated data to a maximum of 2% overall and 1% individual allowable MSE change (See Section 2.1). The experimental setup hardware consisted of a 1GHz CPU linux box with Sun JDK 1.3.1 and 384MB RAM. Algorithm parameters were adjusted repeatedly in an attempt to maximize the number of embedded copies, establishing them around $c = 88\%, v_{false} = 5\%, v_{true} = 9\%$. Using the confidence violators encoding method with the above specified parameters we were able to repeatedly (for different generated input data) embed a total of over watermark 120-130 bits in the set of size 10000. The considered watermark consisted of 24 bits. We were able to resiliently embed at least 5 copies of the watermark each time, allowing for a final enforcing step of majority voting, as discussed in Sections 3.1 and 3.5. We then performed attack experiments on parts of the data in order to experimentally assess encoding resilience and obtained encouraging results, some presented in Figure 4. Pre-processed parts of the original data as well as their watermarked version are soon to be found at http://www.cs.purdue.edu/homes/sion/wm/nrwm.

5   Conclusions and Future Research

In the present paper we introduced a solution to the problem of watermarking a numeric collection by (i) defining a new suitable mark encoding method for numeric sets and (ii) designing an algorithmic securing mapping (i.e. mark amplification) from a simple encoding method to a more complex watermarking algorithm. We also developed a proof of concept implementation of our algorithms under the form of a Java software package, **nrx.***.

Further research should investigate a model of attacks in this new domain. A more detailed attack-ability analysis needs to be performed. A full-fledged commercial watermarking application could be derived from our proof-of-concept software. Finally, different applications for our numeric collection marking method could be envisioned and pursued, such as watermarking relational data.

Note: Recently the algorithms and implementation presented in this article became part of a larger, industry-size watermarking application for relational data (WMDB). Most of the future research in this are will be performed on this new implementation platform. An online link to WMDB is http://www.cs.purdue.edu/homes/sion/wm/wmdb.

References

1. M.J. Atallah, V. Raskin (with M. Crogan, C. Hempelmann, F. Kerschbaum, D. Mohamed, and S. Naik). Natural language watermarking: Design, analysis, and a proof-of-concept implementation. In *Lecture Notes in Computer Science, Proc. 4th International Information Hiding Workshop, Pittsburgh, Pennsylvania.* Springer-Verlag, 2001.

2. Christian Collberg and Clark Thomborson. On the limits of software watermarking, August 1998.

3. Ingemar Cox, Jeffrey Bloom, and Matthew Miller. Digital watermarking. In *Digital Watermarking.* Morgan Kaufmann, 2001.

4. Ingemar J. Cox and Jean-Paul M. G. Linnartz. Public watermarks and resistance to tampering. In *International Conference on Image Processing (ICIP'97)*, Santa Barbara, California, U.S.A., 26–29 October 1997. IEEE.

5. Ingemar J. Cox, Matt L. Miller, and A. L. McKellips. Watermarking as communications with side information. *Proceedings of the IEEE (USA)*, 87(7):1127–1141, July 1999.

6. Edward J. Delp. Watermarking: Who cares? does it work? In Jana Dittmann, Petra Wohlmacher, Patrick Horster, and Ralf Steinmetz, editors, *Multimedia and Security – Workshop at ACM Multimedia'98*, volume 41 of *GMD Report*, pages 123–137, Bristol, United Kingdom, September 1998. ACM, GMD – Forschungszentrum Informationstechnik GmbH, Darmstadt, Germany.

7. Stefan Katzenbeisser (editor) and Fabien Petitcolas (editor). Information hiding techniques for steganography and digital watermarking. In *Information Hiding Techniques for Steganography and Digital Watermarking.* Artech House, 2001.

8. Bob Ellis. Public policy: New on-line surveys: Digital watermarking. *Computer Graphics*, 33(1):39–39, February 1999.

9. M. Kobayashi. Digital watermarking: Historical roots. IBM Research Report RT0199, IBM Japan, Tokyo, Japan, April 1997.

10. J. Palsberg, S. Krishnaswamy, M. Kwon, D. Ma, Q. Shao, and Y. Zhang. Experience with software watermarking. In *Proceedings of ACSAC, 16th Annual Computer Security Applications Conference*, pages 308–316, 2000.

11. Fabien A. P. Petitcolas, Ross J. Anderson, and Markus G. Kuhn. Attacks on copyright marking systems. In David Aucsmith, editor, *Information Hiding: Second International Workshop*, volume 1525 of *Lecture Notes in Computer Science*, pages 218–238, Portland, Oregon, U.S.A., 1998. Springer-Verlag.

12. Fabien A. P. Petitcolas, Ross J. Anderson, and Markus G. Kuhn. Information hiding – a survey. *Proceedings of the IEEE*, 87(7):1062–1078, July 1999. Special issue on protection of multimedia content.
13. Radu Sion, Mikhail Atallah, and Sunil Prabhakar. On watermarking semistructures. In *(submission for review), CERIAS TR 2001-54*, 2002.
14. Radu Sion, Mikhail Atallah, and Sunil Prabhakar. Power: Metrics for evaluating watermarking algorithms. In *Proceedings of IEEE ITCC02, CERIAS TR 2001-55*. IEEE Computer Society Press, 2002.
15. R. Venkatesan, V. Vazirani, and S. Sinha. A graph theoretic approach to software watermarking. In *Proceedings of the Fourth International Hiding Workshop, IH01*, 2001.
16. G. Voyatzis, N. Nikolaidis, and I. Pitas. Digital watermarking: an overview. In S. Theodoridis et al., editors, *Signal processing IX, theories and applications: proceedings of Eusipco-98, Ninth European Signal Processing Conference, Rhodes, Greece, 8–11 September 1998*, pages 9–12, Patras, Greece, 1998. Typorama Editions.
17. Jian Zhao and Eckhard Koch. A generic digital watermarking model. *Computers and Graphics*, 22(4):397–403, August 1998.
18. Jian Zhao, Eckhard Koch, Joe O'Ruanaidh, and Minerva M. Yeung. Digital watermarking: what will it do for me? and what it won't! In ACM, editor, *SIGGRAPH 99. Proceedings of the 1999 SIGGRAPH annual conference: Conference abstracts and applications*, Computer Graphics, pages 153–155, New York, NY 10036, USA, 1999. ACM Press.

Watermarking Techniques for Electronic Circuit Design

Edoardo Charbon[1] and Ilhami Torunoglu[2]

[1] Swiss Federal Institute of Technology, Lausanne, Switzerland
edoardo.charbon@epfl.ch
[2] Canesta Inc., San Jose, California U.S.A.
ilhami@canesta.com

Abstract. Enforcing copyright laws related to circuit design is usually hard, since discovery and proof of infringements are required beyond reasonable doubt. Proving that a given circuitry is trivially derived from a patented technique or method is in general a painstakingly slow task, often requiring reverse-engineering and forensic analysis of fabricated chips. These techniques are so complex that their application to large collections of commercial products is almost always prohibitive. Watermarking is one of several techniques available today to deter copyright infringement in electronic systems. The technique consists of implanting indelible stamps in the circuit's inner structure, while not disrupting its functionality or significantly degrading its performance. In this paper a series of methods is proposed for the creation of watermarks at several stages of the design cycle, from high-level design to layout. Algorithms are described for implanting robust watermarks to minimize the overhead and, ultimately, to reduce the impact on performance. Detection methods are discussed in the presence of infringement. The resilience of the methods in several tampering regimes is estimated.

1 Introduction

The share of electronic designs based on complex, fully integrated systems on silicon is growing at exponential rate. A great increase in operating speeds and design productivity is expected, provided that typical chip design cycle is significantly shortened. System components are available to designers in electronic form rather than in a fully packaged format. Such components, known as virtual components, must be delivered for a particular application according to a specific contract. Due to the new medium of storage and exchange, virtual components are prone to infringements and abuses, i.e. uses beyond the original contracts and/or by unauthorized integrators.

The protection of Intellectual Property (IP) rights of authors and integrators is an emerging multi-disciplinary field encompassing several aspects of today's IC design process. Common legal devices, such as patents, trade secrets, copyrights, and non-disclosure agreements are aimed at deterring potential infringement. However, the real Achille's heal of the system is currently the enforcement of such

F. Petitcolas and H.J. Kim (Eds.): IWDW 2002, LNCS 2613, pp. 147–169, 2003.
© Springer-Verlag Berlin Heidelberg 2003

rights. The goal of IP protection as a whole is to provide necessary technologies to make enforcement a more manageable task while deterring infringement at all levels of a design.

A potentially effective scheme requires the capability of effectively detecting and subsequently tracking IP infringement cases. This task can be accomplished by a process known as *watermarking*. The method consists of embedding a unique code, or watermark, which exploits the IP's unique features. Fundamental requirements for a watermark are that it be (1) *transparent*, i.e. not interfering with the design functionality, (2) *robust*, i.e. hard to remove or forge, (3) *detectable*, i.e. easy to extract from the design. The process used for managing watermarks must not necessarily be proprietary, while the code used in the encryption process should be secret for any released IP.

Watermarking has been proposed to protect digital audio-visual IPs. The literature is very extensive on the subject (see [1] for a comprehensive description of digital watermarking focused on these applications). Here we mention only two works [2,3] because they allow us to introduce some of the techniques used in this paper. The main method described in [2,3], though with small variations, essentially consist of superimposing a pseudo-random noise to the signal of interest. Such noise, though completely inaudible (or invisible in the case of an image), can be easily detected via digital signal processing methods.

Schemes based on watermarking have been recently proposed for electronic IPs as well. In [4,5] the watermark assumes the form of a extraneous bit stream, hidden inside large Field Programmable Gate Arrays (FPGAs). The mark is stored in some of the unused configurable control logic blocks of the FPGA. Each unused lookup table is responsible for storing a single bit in the code. All the configurable control elements used in the watermark are then routed in the design for mimetic purposes. This is done in such a manner to avoid any impact on the original functionality. The method has later been refined in [6] where the signature is modified before being embedded so as to mimic the statistical properties of the existing design, hence reducing detectability. One issue in our opinion still remaining in this approach is the fact that to date watermarked lookup tables do not reflect any functionality, thus they are prone to elimination if optimization algorithms are used.

In [7,8] it was proposed to incorporate several watermarks, distributed over all the abstraction levels of a given design. The techniques differ depending on the abstraction level they are applicable to. At the physical design level, the watermark assumes the form of a set of topological constraints governing the relative position, orientation, and, possibly, scaling of the devices or gates of the circuit. At structural and RTL level, constraints on the structure of a selected set of nets are used to represent the watermark. Watermarks are created at multiple levels of hierarchy simultaneously. This is provably a very robust and flexible techniques since it requires the elimination of watermarks placed at every level of abstraction. Erasing one level, by resynthesizing a logic circuitry for example, may erase the watermarks created at that abstraction level and, possibly, at lower levels, while leaving higher abstraction levels (and their watermarks) intact. As expected, this is the a particularly costly and complex scheme. Another advantage of this scheme is the fact that forgery can be traced and a history of tampering actions can be derived.

Several authors have proposed to use other design constraints to implant watermarks. In [9] fixed placement and delay constraints implemented the watermark. In [10] a sequence of nodes in a multi-level logic function was permuted according to a seeded pseudo-random selection scheme. In [11,12] schemes have been proposed to implant watermarks in regular sequential functions by modifying the original function in a structured fashion. In [9], the authors proposed two methods for embedding signatures in a design. The first method, general in nature, can be applied to several abstraction levels. It consists of adding clauses to a satisfiability problem. For convenience, the authors restricted themselves to a subset of the problem known as 3SAT, where each clause added to the original problem codes a sequence of symbols or a section of the signature to be embedded. IF a design can be represented in terms of a 3SAT formulation, then it will be possible to embed an arbitrary signature in it. The second method is not applicable to IPs at the highest abstraction level, as it consists of formulating the signature in terms of a set of delay sub-constraints which are found in delay constrained signal paths. Constraints on floorplanning block relative locations are also used to embed a signature.

In the case more than one party is involved in creation of an IP, any of the above techniques does not guarantee that the infringements can be tracked. Watermarking should be performed simultaneously at various levels of abstraction [7]. The goal is to improve the robustness of the approach and to allow quick and accurate tracking of the last licensee, who ultimately caused the infringement. In this paper we will describe a consistent strategy for incorporating watermarks in an electronic circuit at all abstraction levels, i.e. in all phases of a design flow.

At least two types of watermarking schemes exist. The first scheme, known as *active watermarking*, consists of integrating the watermark as a part of the design process, thus allowing the creation of an arbitrarily high number of uniquely watermarked designs. In the second scheme, known as *passive watermarking* or *fingerprinting*, one creates a unique and compact representation of a design at any abstraction level. This representation, known as *digital signature*, can be used to track infringement after it occurred by simply extracting the signature from an existing design and comparing it with the original one. Note that this scheme does not require any modification or redesign of the IP, thus making it attractive for use in existing, already released designs. To avoid false claims, a third party organization should maintain a database of all registered signatures for which protection is sought [13]. Both approaches are robust, since the deletion of the watermark results, with high probability, in the removal of wanted functionality.

IP protection based on watermarking consists of two phases: *synthesis* and *detection*. The synthesis phase is fully characterized by (a) a set of algorithms translating design features onto a unique watermark, and (b) P_u, the odds that an unintended watermark is detected in a design. The detection phase is fully characterized by (c) P_m, the probability of a miss and (d) $P_f = P_u$, the probability of a false alarm. The set of algorithms proposed in this paper are all classifiable based on the above criteria.

In order for any protection scheme to be effective it is necessary to define how design flows must be modified, if at all. Moreover, to allow effective infringement detection, a well-defined detection protocol must be set up. A well-known example of such protocol is the one used by law enforcement organizations to identify criminals based on natural fingerprints and, more recently, DNA samples found on the scene. In the case of IP infringements, all existing prevention and detection methods are generally used simultaneously to ensure maximal impact.

The paper is structured as follows. Section 2 describes methods to implant a watermark at the highest level of abstraction, i.e. at the Hardware Description Language (HDL) levels. Section 3 outlines the creation of a watermark at an intermediate level, i.e. at a structural level. Section 4 describes watermarking techniques at the lowest levels of abstraction, i.e. at the physical implementation of the circuit. A number of examples are presented in Section 5.

2   HDL Level Watermarking

At high abstraction levels it is necessary to focus on a structure that is simple enough for a general watermarking method and frequent enough to cover a large number of designs. We selected a generic sequential function, since it is a simple and well-understood entity and it is ubiquitous.

In its most general form, a sequential function is a function that transforms input sequences into output sequences. Regular sequential functions are functions such that at any stage the output symbol depends only on the sequence of input symbols which have been already received. Any regular sequential function operating on finite input/output sets can be specified by means of a Finite State Machine (FSM).

A FSM is a discrete dynamical system translating sequences of input vectors into sequences of output vectors and it is generally represented by State Transition Graphs (STGs) and State Transition Tables (STTs). A STG is a graph whose nodes represent the states of the FSM and whose edges determine the input/output conditions for a state to state transition. By convention, an edge is labeled by the input/output pair causing the transition.

In real-world sequential designs, although not explicitly specified using STGs and STTs, FSMs appear in different forms. For example, case statements in VHDL and Verilog HDL are represented as FSMs using a STG or STT by HDL compilers. FSMs also appear in embedded software, especially to define the device drivers and interface protocols. In large sequential designs, usually several such small FSMs exist which can be used to watermark the entire design. By watermarking all or a selected subset of these FSMs, tampering resilience can be reached while ensuring the method's feasibility.

The essence of this technique is to hide the watermark in an unused input/output symbol sequence. This task can be performed using the STG or STT representation of the regular sequential function. By visiting every state and finding the unused input/output symbol pairs, one can determine the candidate subset of such symbol pairs at each state in the FSM. This procedure however requires exponential time with respect to the number of reachable states. Heuristics can therefore be employed, as we will see later, in order to make the scheme feasible.

The complete procedure consists of the following phases. First, the required input/output symbol sequence length, which satisfies given uniqueness constraints, i.e. constraints on P_u, is computed. Second, a path of visited states must be selected and the corresponding input/output symbol pairs required to exercise such path is computed. In case the degrees of freedom of the FSM are insufficient to generate a long enough path, then one can augment the input and/or output spaces by increasing the input and/or output alphabets. The estimation of P_u and the derivation of the length of the input/output symbol sequence can be found in [14]. Finally, by connecting the states, one can generate a trace in the FSM. Some selections of input/output symbol sequences and the states may generate large FSMs.

To capture the principle of the proposed techniques, consider the example of Figure 1. The original FSM is depicted in Figure 1(a) in terms of its STG. The FSM has two input bits and one output bit. Assume one has decided that a watermark of length 2 is satisfactory and suppose the proposed watermark is represented by input/output sequence $((00,1)(11,0))$. Figure 1(b) illustrates the new FSM obtained after augmentation and state selection.

Assume that the input/output pairs available are not sufficient to generate a sequence of desired length. In this case, the number of inputs is first incremented by one (for illustrative purposes). Two extra transition relations can hence be added. The resulting FSM is depicted in Figure 1(c).

In the remainder of the paper we will restrict ourselves to deterministic FSMs, using the same notation of [15] and [16].

Definition 1 *Let a FSM be a tuple* $M = (\Sigma, \triangle, Q, q_0, \delta, \lambda)$, *where* Σ *and* $\triangle$ *are respectively the input and output alphabets,* Q *is a finite set of states,* $q_0 \in Q$ *is the initial state,* $\delta(q,a) : Q \times \Sigma \to Q \bigcup \{\phi\}$ *is the transition relation, and* $\lambda(q,a) : Q \times \Sigma \to Q \bigcup \{\epsilon\}$ *is the output relation.*

$q \in Q$, $a \in \Sigma$, $b \in \triangle$ refer to a state, an input and an output, respectively. ϕ denotes an unspecified next state while ϵ is an unspecified output. A FSM can be identified by the mapping of all its input and output sequences, or *IO mapping*.

Definition 2 *An IO mapping is defined to be the sequence of input/output pairs* $((a_1, b_1), (a_2, b_2), \ldots, (a_k, b_k)) \in (\Sigma \times (\triangle \bigcup \{\epsilon\}))^k$ *specifying the output sequence of the FSM for a given input sequence.*

Let us define Σ^* and $\triangle^*$ as the sets of all strings in Σ and in $\triangle$, respectively. Let $s = (a_1, \ldots, a_k) \in \Sigma^*$ be an arbitrary input sequence and let $d = (b_1, \ldots, b_k) \in \triangle^*$ be an output sequence. Moreover, define $\lambda(q, s)$ to be the output symbol of the FSM and $\delta(q, s)$ its state when s has been applied in state q. String s is said to be contained in M iff a state reached by applying s to state q_0 is still in M, i.e. iff $\delta(q_0, s) \in Q$.

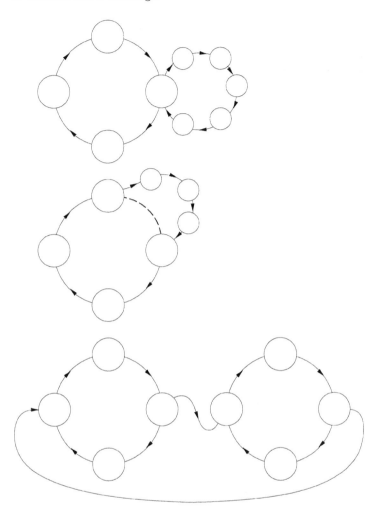

Fig. 1. An example of two possible ways of watermarking a FSM: a) original FSM; b) adding transitions; c) augmenting input and adding transitions

Completely specified FSMs (CSFSMs) contain every element of set Σ^*, i.e. every input sequence in Σ^* results in a unique output sequence in $\triangle^*$. An incompletely specified FSM (ISFSM) is one in which there exist some transition relations with unspecified destination and/or output, i.e. there exist a set of input sequences for which no output is specified. Call $I_u \subset \Sigma^*$ such set. Conversely, there exist a set of output sequences which can be produced only by unspecified input sequences. Call $O_u \subset \triangle^*$ such set. The problem of minimizing the number of states in CSFSMs can be solved in polynomial time [17]. For ISFSMs the problem is known to be NP-complete [18]. Algorithms for reducing such machines are proposed in [15,16,17].

Let $M' = (\Sigma', \triangle', Q', q'_0, \delta', \lambda')$ be an ISFSM and $\mathcal{P}_{M'}$ be the set of all possible completely specified implementations of M'. Thus, for each $p \in \mathcal{P}_{M'}$, every element of I_u and O_u is eventually associated to an element of $\triangle^*$ and Σ^*, respectively. Let us select an arbitrary sequence $s_\sigma \subset I_u$ and the corresponding output sequence $d_\sigma \in \triangle^*$. Let tuple $\sigma = \{s_\sigma, d_\sigma\}$, call it *IO signature*.

Consider first an active watermarking regime. The problem of synthesizing a watermark for an ISFSM M' is equivalent to that of finding a minimum sized machine M'', whose specified IO mapping has been augmented by an IO signature σ on specification of M'. It is also required that robustness constraint specified as $\overline{P_m}$ and $\overline{P_u}$. be satisfied. The problem is formulated as following

Problem 1. Minimize size of M'', s.t.

$$P_m \leq \overline{P_m} \ , \quad P_u \leq \overline{P_u} \ , \tag{1}$$

where $\overline{P_m}$ and $\overline{P_u}$ are constraints on the watermark robustness. Note that the size is measured in terms of added states and logic.

Problem 1 can be partitioned into two subtasks. The first subtask consists of computing the size of IO signature σ so as to satisfy the constraints on the confidence. The second subtask is that of finding the actual IO signature so as to minimize the overhead of M''. The IO signature must be generated with some degree of randomness to ensure that, using the same algorithm one cannot generate an identical code. The randomized algorithm is controlled by key k. The key k is provided by the user to control the generation of the IO signature and of the sequence of states activated by the it. k is used to select from n best state sequences and IO signatures. In this case, the minimality of the overhead might not be guaranteed.

In case keeping the IO signature secret were not possible, then one of the following approaches could be used. The authentication of the generated IO signature can be achieved by registering the key of a specific design in a third party database, similarly as in copyright and trademark registration.

An alternative solution is that of explicitly creating an IO signature based on the method proposed in [12]. The user specifies a string which is converted into a number by standard one-way hash function like MD5. In this manner, one can guarantee that there will be no two identical IO signatures generated by two different strings and it is computationally intractable to obtain the string from the IO signature. Using this signature, one can find a state sequence that minimizes the overhead, even though an absolute minimum can not be guaranteed.

Synthesizing watermarks in CSFSMs requires first that the machine be translated onto a ISFSM. This can be accomplished by extending the input and/or output alphabets Σ and $\triangle$. The resulting machine is then handled by solving Problem 1. Hence, the procedure can be seen as a preprocessing step to a general watermark synthesis step.

A passive watermarking scheme consists of generating signature σ from a given ISFSM without modifying the machine itself. The process consists of first minimizing the FSM using, for example, the techniques proposed in [15], thus synthesizing a CSFSM. Then, a subset of all the sections of the non-specified IO mapping are designated as a IO signature. Randomization of the signature, controlled by key k, used to select unspecified IO sequences. Hence, the probability of accidentally synthesizing the same watermark are bounded by the degrees of freedom of the algorithm and/or by its level of randomization.

Let us now formally analyze the problem of finding a IO signature which optimizes the overhead of a FSM. Let $q' \in Q'$ denote a state in an ISFSM M' and let q'_0 be its reset state. Let $I_u^{(q')}$ be the set of all the input configurations in q' for which no next state is specified, call such configurations *free*. Define U' to be the set of all the states with incompletely specified transition relations, i.e. $U' = \{q' \in Q' \mid |I_u^{(q')}| > 0\}$. The total number of free input configurations n is bounded as follows

$$n \leq n_{max} = \sum_{q' \in Q'} |I_u^{(q')}|. \qquad (2)$$

Every state $q' \in U'$ must necessarily be reachable $|I_u^{(q')}|$ times, using each time one of the remaining free input configurations in $I_u^{(q')}$. Suppose that a sequence x exists of all the visited states, call s the input sequence which forces x. The resulting output sequence d, of length n, will be one of $[2^{|\triangle|}]^n$ possible implementations. Hence, the odds that an identical sequence be produced by M is

$$P_u = \frac{1}{[2^{|\triangle|}]^n - 1}. \qquad (3)$$

The second term of the denominator is given by the fact that one of such sequence will result from the given input sequence in the CSFSM in $\mathcal{P}_{M'}$. By setting $P_u \leq \overline{P_u}$ and solving (3) with respect to n one obtains

$$n \geq n_{min} = \frac{1}{|\triangle|} log_2 \left| 1 + \frac{1}{\overline{P_u}} \right|. \qquad (4)$$

In some cases it is not possible to satisfy both (2) and (4) to meet specification (1), i.e. $n_{min} > n_{max}$. Hence, either (1) must be relaxed and/or n_{max} must be increased.

Suppose constraints (2) and (4) are satisfied, then an output sequence $d_\sigma \in \triangle^*$ and the states which can produce it must be selected. The required output is generated by an n-long sequence of states in U'. The sequence can be seen as a path $p_\sigma = (q'_0, u'_1, \ldots, u'_{n-1})$ covering a subset of the states in U', with or without repetition. It is assumed, but it is not necessary, that $q'_0 \in U'$. If this were not the case, a different first state, say $q''_0 \in U'$, could be selected for p_σ and input sequence s_σ would need to be augmented by an input sequence s such that $\delta'(q_0, s) = q''_0$. The generation of p_σ does not contribute to the probability of coincidence P_u, but it does determine the impact state minimization will have on the final machine. The second factor impacting the effectiveness of the optimization is the selection of input sequence s_σ. The third factor is a constraint on the overhead necessary to implement a given IO signature.

For a given output sequence d_σ, input sequence s_σ is generated in two steps: selection of p_σ and derivation of s_σ. Sequence p_σ represents a path through n

of the states in U' from the original STG. Every time a state u' is touched by the path, it looses one of its $|I_u^{(u')}|$ free input configurations. We propose to use an algorithm based on the Euler path search which can be targeted to minimize the number of visited states and/or to maximize the number of remaining free configurations per state.

As an illustration, consider the ISFSM example given earlier. For each state assume there exist three out of four free input configurations. Assume that $n = 2$, then two possible paths p_σ are shown in Figure 2 (a) and (b). In the example of Figure 2 (a) the number of inputs was unchanged, while in 2 (b) it was incremented by one. Consider the example of Figure 2 (a). Path p_σ, represented

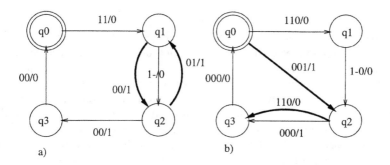

a)   b)

Fig. 2. Two possible paths p_σ for a given U': a) path based on minimum visited states criterion; b) path based on maximum remaining free configurations

in bold, is selected by maximizing the number of remaining free configurations per state. Note that the path may begin in a state other than the reset state q_0. In this case, one must additionally find the input sequence leading to p_σ's initial state.

Once p_σ for Figure 2 (a) has been selected, input sequence s_σ is derived from a path on a decision tree rooted in q_0 and whose leaves correspond to state u'_{n-1}. The solid bold line in Figure 3 represents p_σ, while the dotted line shows the path needed to reach p_σ's initial state. At each level i exactly $|I_u^{(u'_i)}| < |\Sigma|$ branches exist. Each branch represents the decision of using a certain free input configuration at a given state. There exists $\Pi_{i=1}^n |I_u^{(u'_i)}|$ possible paths connecting the root state q_0 to u'_{n-1}. One or more of these paths is associated with the smallest CSFSM $M \equiv M'$. The problem of finding such path is NP-complete since in best case the machine associated with one path must be synthesized, which in itself is an NP-complete problem. As an illustration, if the path represented in bold in Figure 3 is used for ISFSM M', the resulting IO signature is $\{s_\sigma, d_\sigma\} = \{(1,1,0,0,1,0); (0,0,1)\}$.

Several alternatives are proposed for the generation of the input sequence s_σ to minimize overhead. The first method consists of performing an exhaus-

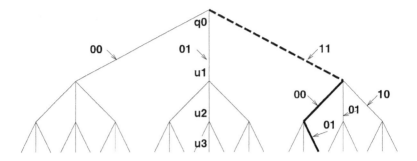

Fig. 3. Decision tree to compute s_σ

tive search of the decision tree. For each path a CSFSM is synthesized and the smallest machine is selected. The second method is a Monte Carlo approach, in which a set of input sequences are selected at random from all the feasible ones. The CSFSMs corresponding to such sequences are generated and the smallest one is selected. The third method is based on a branch-and-bound search. At each level of the tree an estimate is computed for the machine associated with each sub-tree underlying any decision. Such estimate is computed using a Monte Carlo approach. All the sub-trees with higher estimates are pruned, while the surviving trees are explored into the next level, i.e. the next state of p_σ. The search stops at the leaves. The complete algorithm for active watermarking in FSMs is described as follows:

1. if the FSM is CSFSM then augment Σ
2. compute the minimum size of s_σ, n_{min}, from $\overline{P_u}$
3. if $n_{min} > n_{max}$ then augment Σ or $\triangle$
4. using k, randomly generate new output sequence $d_\sigma \in \triangle^*$
5. compute path p_σ
6. compute input sequence s_σ

As a byproduct of Step 6 the FSM is synthesized. A passive watermarking scheme is applied to ISFSMs only. The method assumes that randomization can be introduced by the FSM synthesis. It consists of converting the original ISFSM onto a CSFSM using a given optimization criterion. Then, an IO signature is selected at random from all the possible ones available. The only way to synthesize a CSFSM from the original ISFSM which contains an identical IO signature is to use the same synthesis engine with an identical set of parameters and optimization criteria. Hence, P_u can be derived in this case as the inverse of all possible machines which can be generated from an ISFSM of a certain size and structure with the given engine.

Detecting a signature $\sigma = \{d_\sigma, d_\sigma\}$ entails applying input sequence s_σ to the machine and observing the output sequence d_σ, as shown in Figure 4. In absence of tampering, necessarily $d = d_\sigma$ and $P_m = 0$, i.e. no misses are possible. To properly analyze the effects of tampering, let us consider the following scenarios:

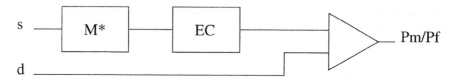

Fig. 4. Detection of signature under some tampering

1. specifications on the IO mapping of the original machine are known,
2. IO mapping of the original machine is not known but the STG of the modified machine is known,
3. no STG is known.

In case (1), infringement cannot be prevented, since the aggressor can resynthesize the FSM from specifications using techniques proposed, e.g. in [16].

In case (2) the aggressor may either: (a) modify state transition relations, i.e. changing the output or next state associated with a transition relation, or (b) apply the techniques proposed in this paper to watermark CSFSMs. In both cases, part or the totality of the watermark will be unchanged, but it may be corrupted locally. Tampering (a) may in fact result in a change in the functionality of the machine, it is therefore counterproductive. Tampering (b) will only result in literal swaps and deletions within pairs of reset states, similar to gene deletion within DNA sequences.

To combat tampering (2)b, we propose an approach based on the concept of *genome search*. Such approach was successfully used in topological watermarking [7,8]. The method is essentially a selective pattern matching. It is assumed for simplicity that the output d_σ is a chain of sequences all rooted in a single reset state q_0. This restriction is however not necessary as multiple reset states can be used. Suppose the IO signature is

$$p_\sigma = (q_0, q_2, q_1, q_0, q_3, q_4, q_0, q_1, q_2, q_0)$$
$$\{s_\sigma, d_\sigma\} = \{ (01, 01, 00, 10, 01, 00, 11, 10, 01); (0, 1, 1, 0, 1, 0, 1, 1, 1) \}.$$

Suppose that tampering has removed or corrupted the median section of d_σ, i.e. $(0, 1, 0)$, then the sections of the IO signature which are still intact can be matched to σ using the `genome_search` algorithm described in detail in [7]. The algorithm returns an estimate of the probability that the design contains in fact watermark σ. Note that by construction, it is known when the reset state is reached. Hence, the boundary symbols or *operons* of each "gene" are known. Also note that if this or any other error correction algorithm is used, then our estimation of P_u is un upperbound on the true value, i.e. it is an optimistic estimate. It this case changes to the way P_u is estimated should be applied based on the details of the algorithm. An alternative method is that of using correction schemes such as CRC to detect and correct corrupted subsequences.

Finally, consider case (3), let us analyze the possible attempts to remove the watermark using netlist manipulations. Obviously, it is not possible to foresee all possible tampering techniques. Instead, we will analyze those that are more likely to be performed under following assumptions.

Assumption 1 *A netlist or a structural HDL description is available for tampering.*

Assumption 2 *All input and output pins are well documented and extra I/O pins (if any) used for watermarking are introduced as extra test pins and/or signal pins.*

In [12] it has been proven that generating a STG from a given netlist is an NP-Complete problem. For medium and large scale FSMs, it is unlikely that the STG can be obtained from its netlist. Therefore, if the netlist is obtained by reverse engineering, the aggressor has no other options but to perform one of the following modifications to remove or hide the watermark: (a) embed the FSM into a bigger one, (b) delete some of the circuitry related to the test inputs, (c) Add dummy I/O bits and/or shuffle the bit order using unknown mapping functions.

In scenario (a), the aggressor tries to hide the watermark under a wrap to mask the original IP from input/output probing. The watermark is still intact but it may not be easily observable, if at all possible. In this case, the detection technique proposed earlier cannot be exploited. However, simulation or on-chip measurements can be used to logically insulate the original IP from the wrap.

In scenario (b), by knowing that the watermark should be related to the extra test pins, the aggressor might try ro remove the registers and circuitry related to those inputs. In this case. the attempt would damage the original behavior because the IO signature is an integral part of the FSM. Therefore, this attempt shall not be successful.

In scenario (c), the aggressor adds new dummy input and/or output bits and dummy circuitry to the FSM. In this case IP forensic can use the following exhaustive method. Let us assume that there were n input bits and m output bits in the original watermarked FSM. Moreover assume that d_n and d_m extra bits have been added. Then, one needs to apply the input sequence to each possible subset of n bits of the $n + d_n$ inputs. The output is observed to reconstruct the correct sequence. Although it is time consuming, it is guaranteed that the IO mapping can be found exactly, since the watermark is intact.

3   Structural or Netlist Watermarks

Let us now introduce a mathematical formalism which helps describing the watermarking algorithms described in the following two sections. Let Σ^* be the set of all strings in a finite alphabet Σ, e.g. $\Sigma = \{0, 1\}$. Assuming there exists a compact representation or signature for a given design at some abstraction level, let $s \in \mathcal{S}$ be one of all possible physical implementations of the design and let σ_s be its signature. Define *signature mapping* $\mathcal{S} \rightarrow \Sigma^* : \mathcal{M}$ as the mapping of a subset of all the layout features onto a signature $\sigma_s = \mathcal{M}(s)$. Let us define $\mathcal{S} \to \mathcal{S} : \mathcal{F}$ as a mapping which transforms implementation s onto a new implementation $s' = \mathcal{F}(s)$.

The structural level of abstraction is an intermediate representation of a circuit. Generally, after a compilation phase behavioral representations can be converted into a physical implementation by constructing the symbolic connectivity map of all the necessary electrical devices. Such map is usually represented in terms of a schematic or a netlist.

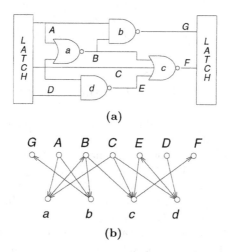

(a)

(b)

Fig. 5. *(a)* Gate-level circuit; *(b)* Connectivity graph

As an illustration consider graph $G(N, E)$ as a compact representation of a schematic or netlist. The nodes of the graph correspond to general blocks, or single devices, as well as nets. The (directed) edges define connectivity. Let us define $\mathcal{H}$ as the set of all blocks in Ω. Let $\mathcal{N}$ be the set of all nets, with $E = \mathcal{H} \cup \mathcal{N}$. Let $\mathcal{O}_n$ be the set of edges in net $n \in \mathcal{N}$ which are connected to an output. The set of edges leading to an input is called $\mathcal{I}_n$, while the set of edges connected to a high-impedance pin or pass transistor gate is called $\mathcal{P}_n$. For simplicity, we assume that exactly one edge can be connected to an output, i.e. $|\mathcal{O}_n| = 1$, this condition is however not necessary. The pin number $|n|$ and the type and port of the gates connected by n are necessary but not sufficient properties to uniquely identify the net. A set of constraints on sets $\mathcal{O}_n$, $\mathcal{I}_n$ and $\mathcal{P}_n$ for each net, can be imposed so as to make these properties define the net uniquely, to all practical purposes.

Let us now consider the gate-level circuit in Figure 5(a) and the corresponding connectivity graph of Figure 5(b).

Let $\mathcal{N}' \subseteq \mathcal{N} = \{n \in \mathcal{N} : |n| \text{ is prime}\}$. Next, impose the following constraints on each net $n' \in \mathcal{N}'$:

$$\mathcal{O}(n') = \{\text{gates of type } \omega_{\mathcal{O}}(|n'|)\};$$
$$\mathcal{I}(n') = \{\text{gates of type } \omega_{\mathcal{I}}(|n'|)\}; \; |\mathcal{I}(n')| = \ell_{\mathcal{I}}(|n'|); \quad (5)$$
$$\mathcal{P}(n') = \{\text{gates of type } \omega_{\mathcal{P}}(|n'|)\}; \; |\mathcal{P}(n')| = \ell_{\mathcal{P}}(|n'|),$$

where $\omega_{\mathcal{O}}(), \omega_{\mathcal{I}}(), \omega_{\mathcal{P}}(), \ell_{\mathcal{I}}()$ and $\ell_{\mathcal{P}}()$ are net size-dependent parameters, generated using, for example, a parametrized pseudorandom sequence determined by key k.

One can trivially infer that an arbitrary signature can be implanted in the structure of the netlist. Such signature can be at the hart of the watermark, which, in this case, is known as a *structural watermark*. In the case of Figure 5, Equations (5), written compactly, form the signature for net $\mathcal{C}$ as: $\sigma_C(\mathcal{C}) = (latch; a, d, c, 3; -, 0)$.

4   Watermarking Physical Implementations

A particular mapping often used to generate design signatures from given physical implementation of a circuit. The same technique can be used to implant an arbitrary signature in terms of an extraneous active or inactive circuit. Let us assume that the granularity of the original circuit is given. As a result, the set of fundamental components, such as transistors or standard cells, is determined. Call such components *atomic blocks* and Ω their set. In s, every component $\omega \in \Omega$ may have multiple instantiations.

A layout implementation defines a set of all relative positions and orientations of every component instantiation in the circuit. Interconnect can be represented in a similar fashion where components are replaced by pins, Steiner points, and bends. A composition, containing the details of all relative positions and orientations, is called *topology*. Let us now use the layout's atomic blocks, pins, Steiner points, and interconnect bends, which are in turn represented by a set of primitives called *bubbles*, as proposed in [19]. A bubble is a point associated with a given layer. Let B be the set of all bubbles in the design. Every atomic block is mapped onto m distinct bubbles according to a specific mapping $\Omega \to B : \mathcal{B}$, where m is a finite natural number. For simplicity, but without loss of generality, suppose that m is constant over Ω. Note that $|B|$ grows linearly with the number of atomic blocks and pins.

Paths can be represented by a continuous curve of finite length which begins and ends in a bubble. Such curve is known as *rough routing* [20]. The design rules of a given technology can be seen as minimum spacing constraints between the perimeters of bubbles and paths. Alternatively, after proper scaling of the design rules, one can consider bubbles as points, and paths as curves of zero-thickness. For simplicity we have adopted this convention. Let *topological routing* be an equivalence class of rough routings connecting its pins. Two rough routings of a wire are equivalent when one can be obtained from the other by continuous deformation with no violations of any of the scaled design rules. Assume that every pair of bubbles is connected by an edge, then if a topological routing crosses such an edge, it is said to *intersect topologically* the edge.

If every region in the layout is partitioned in simply connected regions, each containing no bubbles, then such regions are called *simple regions*. Figure 6(a) shows an interconnect and some obstacles, while Figure 6(b) depicts the corresponding partition into simple regions. The rough routing connecting bubble 4 to 0 can be represented in terms of the sequence of all topological intersections. In this case such a sequence is: $\sigma = (\overline{23}, \overline{13}, \overline{37}, \overline{36}, \overline{38}, \overline{58}, \overline{59}, \overline{50})$. Note that symbol $\overline{X_i\,X_j}$ represents the topological intersection of the rough routing with the edge spanned by bubbles X_i and X_j. Define E_ℓ as the set of all simple regions in a

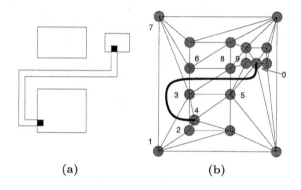

(a)   (b)

Fig. 6. Bubbles and rough routings

given layer ℓ and a *planar subset* $T_\ell \subset E_\ell$ as one in which distinct edges do not intersect or they intersect at only one of the vertices. In addition, if T_ℓ has a convex boundary or *convex hull*, it is said to be maximally planar. Under these conditions, T_ℓ is called *triangulation* [21]. Let us now assume that an arbitrary triangulation T_ℓ is in place for each layer. Let B_ℓ be the set of all the bubbles associated with T_ℓ. For convenience, although not needed, let us set four bubbles at the extremities of the union of all the layers, so as to encompass every layer.

Sequence σ is a non-unique representation of all the rough routings associated with the class of this topological routing. Hence, to make such representation resilient to minor modifications, it is necessary to convert it onto a canonical form. This is done simply removing adjacent identical edges, which form so-called *loops*. The unique canonical form of an arbitrary topological routing τ is called *topological signature* σ_τ. The complexity of loop removal is higher when it involves a large number of rough routings. The process in this case must be recursively performed.

Triangulations are not unique. However if the method used to obtain a certain triangulation is an invariant, then the signature is also invariant for a certain design. Figure 7(a) for example shows a simple layout based on standard cells

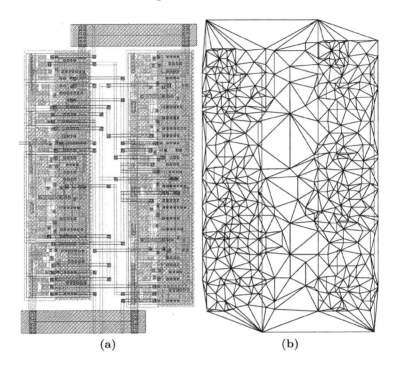

(a)   (b)

Fig. 7. *(a)* Layout; *(b)* Associated triangulation

organized in two rows with the corresponding interconnect. Figure 7(b) shows a possible triangulation of the associated topology. The computational scheme and circuit topology determine the final result [21].

Let us recall that the uniqueness of a signature is defined by probability P_u, its robustness by P_m. Topological intersections are unique for a given design and triangulation, while a triangulation is determined by the utilized algorithm and by set B. For each layer the number of possible triangulations grows factorially as $(|B_\ell| - 1)!/3!$, hence it is reasonable to choose a layer ℓ^* which maximizes $|B_\ell|$ over all layers. By a conservative estimate, N_T, the total number of possible triangulations over all layers, is then $N_T \geq (|B_{\ell^*}| - 1)!/3!$. Suppose now that all N_{ℓ^*} topological routings in ℓ^* consist of N_i i-terminal nets, $i = 2, \ldots, N_{max}$. Then, all N_{ℓ^*} topological routings can be represented in terms of N' two-terminal sub-routings, with $N' = \sum_{i=2}^{N_{max}} N_i (i - 1)$. As a consequence, the number of possible topological signatures can be computed as $N_\sigma \geq N_T \binom{N'}{2}$, hence the estimate of P_u becomes $\overline{P_u} \leq \frac{1}{N_\sigma}$. For example, suppose that for a given design $|B_{\ell^*}| = 20$, $N_{\ell^*} = 10$, $N_2 = 3, N_3 = 5, N_4 = 2$. Then, $N_\sigma \geq (20 - 1)!171/3! = 3.5 \times 10^{18}$, hence $\overline{P_u} \leq 2.9 \times 10^{-19}$.

In the absence of tampering $P_m = 0$, i.e. the signature extracted from a topology matches 100% with the one which is registered in the signature bank.

If tampering has occurred, it needs to be modeled in order to properly estimate its effects on P_m. Let us consider the following tampering attempts: (1) routing modification, (2) atomic block modification, and (3) atomic block move and/or addition/deletion. Attempt (1) does not change triangulation, however it may cause changes in the signature. Such changes are of three basic types: symbol addition, deletion and swap. More than one symbol may be involved in the change at any time, however, when this occurs, the change can be modeled in terms of a composition of simple symbol modifications. Attempts (2) and (3) may change the triangulation. However, their effects can be modeled in terms of simple symbol operations.

Define P_r as the probability that a symbol change occurs. Then, the probability that a signature of size t mutates is $P_t = \sum_{j=1}^{t} \binom{|B|}{j} [P_r]^j \times [(1 - P_r)]^{|B|-j}$.

Hence, for example, if $t = 1$ and $P_r = 10^{-5}$, then $P_m \leq 9 \times 10^{-6}$.

Signature detection consists of the following phases

1. bubble extraction
2. transformation inference
3. bubble matching
4. triangulation
5. signature computation

The initial layout is flattened and all its layers are extracted and deconstructed into polygons or basic standard cells. Using standard slicing techniques [22], the layout is partitioned in rectilinear areas encompassing exactly one atomic block. The complexity of this operation is $O(|\Omega| \, log|\Omega|)$ where $|\Omega|$ is the number of objects in the layout. Using mapping $\mathcal{B}$, the design is entirely converted into a bubble-based representation in $O(|\Omega|)$ time (phase 1).

In order to detect the presence of blocks with known signatures embedded in the design, one has to infer the most likely orientation of every candidate block. This operation is performed by matching complex interconnect patterns present in both the host and the embedded design. Consider the designs of Figure 8. Suppose the interconnects shown in shaded lines are to be used to determine the orientation of the embedded circuit within the host. Let us first catalog all the interconnects present in both layouts in order of size (equal to the number of interconnect segments) in $O(n \log n)$ time. Then, for each pair of interconnects of identical size, a transformation $(\triangle x, \triangle y, \theta, s_x, s_y)$ is derived which maximizes the number of points that can be transformed from the embedded to the host design. Note that s_x, s_y represent a possible scaling operation. Deriving $(\triangle x, \triangle y, \theta, s_x, s_y)$ requires the solution of a system of eight linear equations for each pair of candidate interconnects in the worst case. Then, the most frequently occurring transformation is selected. The solution time of each system of equations is constant, the worst case time complexity is therefore quadratic in the number of interconnects of identical size. (phase 2).

Next, the bubble representation of the host needs to be matched with that of the transformed embedded design. This procedure is accomplished by superimposing the designs and by assigning every bubble in the host to exactly one

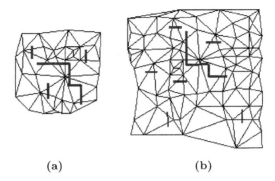

(a)   (b)

Fig. 8. Transformation inference: *(a)* embedded, *(b)* host design

in the embedded design which minimizes the Euclidean distance. The search is initially performed within a zero range, which is augmented multiple times by a unit length until a neighbor is found. Figure 9 shows the range search process (phase 3).

Finally, using optimal algorithms, a Delauney triangulation is computed in $O(|B| \, log|B|)$ time for both designs [21, p. 241] (phase 4).

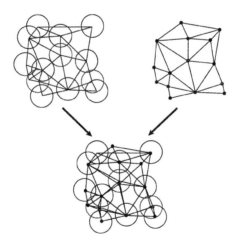

Fig. 9. Principle of range search

The line segment intersection algorithm is used for the computation of the edges being intersected by each topological routing. The complexity of this operation is again $O(|B| \, log|B|)$ [21, p. 285]. The signature is derived from this information in a straightforward way (phase 5). In summary, the complexity of entire signature detection process is $O(n \, log \, n)$, where n is the number of atomic blocks, pins and Steiner points in the topology.

5 Examples

5.1 HDL Level

In our experiments we have used FSMs from the IWLS93 benchmark set. The tools were implemented in C/C++ and run under UNIX and Linux operating systems. Watermarking was performed on ISFSMs as well as CSFSMs. Constraint $\overline{P_u}$ was selected so as to require, in some cases, expansion of Σ and/or Δ. The increase in the number of states $|Q|$ and input/output bits $|\Sigma|$ is expressed by the area estimates. The estimates are based on technology mapping obtained with SIS[23] using the MSU script. Table 1 lists all relevant experimental data and specifications on the robustness of the watermark. For the FSM minimization stage in the algorithm the tools STAMINA and NOVA[15] were used. The area results are based on the actual circuit implementation after technology mapping obtained via SISand relate to the number of gates.

Table 1. IWLS 93 FSM benchmarks. The number of States and the number of I/O pins refer to the original FSM, while I/O chg. refers to the modified FSM. Overhead is the extra area of the modified FSM

circuit	# states	# I/O	# I/O chg.	n_{min}	orig. FSM area	CPU	Monte Carlo area	CPU	$\overline{P_u}$	Overhead
s27	6	4/1	1/3	9	632	0s	1.53k	0.1s	1.4×10^{-11}	143%
bbara	10	4/2	1/1	10	1.16k	0.1s	2.01k	0.1s	9.3×10^{-10}	73%
dk14	7	3/5	1/0	7	1.48k	0.1s	1.84k	0.1s	2.9×10^{-11}	24%
styr	30	9/10	1/0	4	8.6k	0.1s	10.69k	0.1s	9.1×10^{-13}	22%
bbsse	16	7/7	1/0	10	2.28k	0s	2.62k	0.1s	2.9×10^{-11}	6.3%
cse	16	7/7	1/0	5	3.84k	0.1s	4.08k	0.1s	2.9×10^{-11}	6%
sse	16	7/7	0/0	3	2.29k	0s	2.43k	0.1s	4.7×10^{-7}	5.9%
ex1	20	9/19	0/0	4	5.37k	0.1s	5.55k	0.1s	1.3×10^{-23}	3.2%
ex1	20	9/19	0/0	2	5.37k	0.1s	5.40k	0.1s	3.6×10^{-12}	0.6%
viterbi	68	15/59	1/0	2	13.49k	1.5s	13.61k	15s	3.0×10^{-36}	0.8%
dec	56	16/23	1/0	2	14.75k	0.5s	14.78k	5s	1.4×10^{-14}	0.2%
scf	121	27/56	0/0	2	20.97k	3.4s	21.02k	34s	1.9×10^{-34}	0.2%

As expected, larger FSMs require less overhead for comparable robustness. Note, as shown in benchmark ex1, that overhead can be traded for smaller values of $\overline{P_u}$. These overhead results are comparable to the ones obtained in [12]. The overhead of benchmark s27 was excessively high due to the increase of the output alphabet. Such expansion was however necessary to boost the watermark's confidence.

Exhaustive search could be performed only in sse due to the extreme computational complexity of the method. The CPU time in this case was 1.0 second for an area of 2.33k gates. For the other circuits an estimate of a lowerbound of the time required by the search can be computed. Such time estimates are derived multiplying the time required by one minimization with the minimum number of free configurations, i.e. $2^{|I_u^{(min)}|} n_{min}$, where $|I_u^{(min)}| = \min_{q' \in U'} |I_u^{(q')}|$.

In the Monte Carlo approach a maximum of ten input sequences s_σ was explored. Alternatively one could select such upperbound based on some estimate or measurement of the standard deviation of the minimized machine's size.

5.2 Structural and Physical Implementation Levels

A complete pass in a typical design flow was simulated in order to verify the suitability of the approach. The tools utilized in the flow were implemented in C/C++ running under UNIX/LINUX operating systems. All CPU times are referred to a Sun UltraSparc 2 with 256MB of memory. The experiments were based on a set of MCNC 86 and ISCAS 85/89 benchmarks. Each circuit was synthesized and mapped to a SCMOS technology using SIS[24]. Place&route was performed by TIMBERWOLFSC-4.1[25].

To simulate the registration phase, a signature was generated for each benchmark. Then, small modifications were introduced in every benchmark to check whether the signature was resilient to "official" Engineering Change Orders (ECOs) and scaling. Later, a variable number of random non signature-invariant mappings $\mathcal{F}$ were performed on the benchmark's layout so as to maximize the potential damage to the circuit. $\mathcal{F}$ introduced changes on atomic blocks, pins, Steiner points, and nets, uniformly distributed over the entire circuit. Three types of modifications were implemented: (1) translation/rotation, (2) swap, and (3) stretch, aimed at simulating illegal tampering. The signatures associated to the modified designs were compared with the original ones. Finally, the benchmarks were entirely redesigned and the signatures were again compared to the original ones, thus estimating the event that a design could be mistakenly detected even when a "legal" redesign had taken place.

Table 2 reports circuit data, such as device, IO pin, and net count. The signature matching rates are given for several modification densities, simulating an ECO applied to the circuit. The signature was constructed with a minimum net size n_n of 2, 3, 4 or 10 terminals, while no net size upperbound N_n was used. As expected, small ECOs generally resulted in perfect matching, while

Table 2. Signature matching with ECOs and re-design

circ.	n_n/N_n	dev./ IO/nets	ECO density 5 %	ECO density 10 %	re-des.	CPU [s]
s27	$2/\infty$	69/5/96	99.05	96.68	8.24	76.9
s27	$3/\infty$		100	100	7.80	53.0
s27	$10/\infty$		100	100	4.28	43.0
s444	$2/\infty$	709/9/932	100	93.0	10^{-6}	1598
s444	$10/\infty$		100	93.5	10^{-6}	1087
s832	$4/\infty$	1686/37/2127	100	-	10^{-6}	1950
s832	$10/\infty$		100	-	10^{-6}	1620
s1196	$10/\infty$	2105/28/2682	100	96.0	10^{-6}	2383

re-designs resulted in very low matching rates. Moreover, small circuits were less robust to tampering than large ones, due to the lower number of degrees of freedom available to their design.

For the detection phase a large benchmark was selected as the host design. Small benchmarks were embedded, at random locations, in the host. The detection algorithm was run on this example to extract the original signature of the host as well as that of the embedded designs. In various experiments the embedded circuits made up 1% to 10% of the entire host. Finally, tampered circuits were embedded in the host to verify the robustness of the approach in the presence of multiple levels of tampering. Table 3 summarizes the results of the detection experiment. Despite the presence of embedded circuits, the host still maintained high signature matching (rows 3-6 in Table 3). The recognition algorithm performed well in identifying both untampered embedded circuits and heavily tampered ones.

Table 3. Signature matching with embedded circuits

embedded circ.	host circ.	n_n/N_n	ECO density 0 %	ECO density 10 %	CPU [s]
s27	s1196	$1/\infty$	73.8	73.8	218
s27	s1196	$2/\infty$	72.7	72.7	218
s27	s1196	$5/\infty$	72.7	72.7	218
s1196	-	$1/\infty$	100.0	99.2	1241
s1196	-	$2/\infty$	100.0	99.0	1241
s1196	-	$5/\infty$	100.0	98.6	1241

6   Conclusions

Protecting copyrights of intellectual property providers and integrators has become a serious problem. It arises from the fact that electronic circuits are readily available in a form of virtual blocks at any abstraction levels, thus allowing for abuses and theft. Several methods have been described to generate watermarks at various levels of hierarchy during the electronic design flow. Modifications to the flow have been outlined to integrate watermarks at all abstraction levels. Ways of effectively detecting the presence of a watermark have been suggested so as to minimize the disruption of product cycles while allowing forensic analysis of large numbers of suspected circuits. If supported by an enforcement infrastructure at the place of fabrication, the described methods are effective in detecting and tracing intellectual property infringement before fabrication, thus minimizing potential litigation.

References

1. I. J. Cox, M. L. Miller, J. A. Bloom. Digital Watermarking. Morgan Kaufmann, 2001.
2. M. D. Swanson, B. Zhu, and A. H. Tewfik. Transparent robust image watermarking. In *Proc. IEEE International Conference on Image Processing*, volume 3, pages 211–214, September 1996.
3. L. Boney, A. H. Tewfik, and K. N. Hamdy. Digital watermarks for audio signals. In *Proc. IEEE International Conference on Multimedia Computing and Systems*, pages 473–480, June 1996.
4. J. Lach, W. H. Mangione-Smith, and M. Potkonjak. Fpga fingerprinting techniques for protecting intellectual property. In *Proc. IEEE Custom Integrated Circuit Conference*, pages 299–302, May 1998.
5. J. Lach, W. H. Mangione-Smith, and M. Potkonjak. Robust fpga intellectual property protection through multiple small watermarks. In *Proc. IEEE/ACM Design Automation Conference*, pages 831–836, June 1999.
6. J. Lach, W. H. Mangione-Smith, and M. Potkonjak. Signature hiding techniques for fpga intellectual property protection. In *Proc. IEEE International Conference on Computer Aided Design*, pages 194–198, November 1998.
7. E. Charbon. Hierarchical watermarking in IC design. In *Proc. IEEE Custom Integrated Circuit Conference*, pages 295–298, May 1998.
8. E. Charbon and I. Torunoglu. Watermarking layout topologies. In *Proc. IEEE Asia South-Pacific Design Automation Conference*, pages 213–216, January 1999.
9. A. Kahng, J. Lach, W. H. Mangione-Smith, S. Mantik, I. L. Markov, M. Potkonjak, P. Tucker, H. Wang, and G. Wolfe. Watermarking techniques for intellectual property protection. In *Proc. IEEE/ACM Design Automation Conference*, pages 776–781, June 1998.
10. D. Kirovski, Y. Y. Hwang, M. Potkonjak, and J. Cong. Intellectual property protection by watermarking combinational logic synthesis solutions. In *Proc. IEEE International Conference on Computer Aided Design*, pages 194–198, November 1998.
11. I. Torunoglu and E. Charbon. Watermarking-based copyright protection of sequential functions. In *Proc. IEEE Custom Integrated Circuit Conference*, pages 35–38, May 1999.
12. A. L. Oliveira. Robust techniques for watermarking sequential circuit designs. In *Proc. IEEE/ACM Design Automation Conference*, pages 837–842, June 1999.
13. E. Charbon and I. Torunoglu. Copyright protection of designs based on multi source IPs. In *Proc. IEEE International Conference on Computer Aided Design*, pages 591–595, November 1999.
14. I. Torunoglu and E. Charbon. Watermarking-based copyright protection of sequential functions. *IEEE Journal of Solid State Circuits*, SC-35(3), pages 434–440, 2000.
15. T.Villa, T.Kam, R.Brayton, and A.Sangiovanni-Vincentelli. *Synthesis of Finite State Machines: Logic Optimization*. Kluwer Academic Publ., Boston, MA, 1997.
16. J. M. Pena and A. L. Oliveira. A new algorithm for the reduction of incompletely specified finite state machines. In *Proc. IEEE International Conference on Computer Aided Design*, pages 482–489, November 1998.
17. G. De Micheli. *Synthesis and Optimization of Digital Circuits*. McGraw-Hill, 1994.
18. C. F. Pfleeger. State reduction in completely specified finite state machines. *IEEE Trans. on Computers*, C-22, pages 1099–1102, 1973.

19. T. Whitney. *Hierarchical Composition of VLSI Circuits*. PhD thesis, California Institute of Technology, 1985.

20. J. Valainis, S. Kaptanoglu, E. Liu, and R. Suaya. Two-dimensional ic layout compaction based on topological design rule checking. *IEEE Trans. on Computer Aided Design*, CAD-9(3), pages 260–275, March 1990.

21. F. P. Preparata and M. I. Shamos. *Computational Geometry. An Introduction*. Springer, second edition, 1988.

22. R. H. J. M. Otten. Automatic floorplan design. In *Proc. IEEE/ACM Design Automation Conference*, pages 261–267, June 1982.

23. E. M. Sentovich, K. J. Singh, C. Moon, H. Savoj, R. K. Brayton, and A. L. Sangiovanni-Vincentelli. Sequential circuit design using synthesis and optimization. In *Proc. IEEE International Conference on Computer Design*, pages 328–333, October 1992.

24. E. M. Sentovich, K. J. Singh, L. Lavagno, C. Moon, R. Murgai, A. Saldanha, H. Savoj, P. R. Stephan, R. K. Brayton, and A. L. Sangiovanni-Vincentelli. Sis: A system for sequential circuit synthesis. Memorandum UCB/ERL M92/41, UCB, Univ. of California, Berkeley, CA 94720, May 1992.

25. C. Sechen and A. L. Sangiovanni-Vincentelli. Timberwolf3.2: A new standard cell placement and global routing package. In *Proc. IEEE/ACM Design Automation Conference*, pages 432–439, 1986.

A SVD-Based Fragile Watermarking Scheme for Image Authentication

Sung-Cheal Byun[1], Sang-Kwang Lee[1], Ahmed H. Tewfik[2], and Byung-Ha Ahn[1]

[1] Kwangju Institute of Science and Technology,
1 Oryong-dong, Puk-gu, Kwangju 500-712, Korea
{Scbyun, Sklee, Bayhay}@Kjist.ac.kr,
[2] 4-174 EE/CSCI Building, 200 Union St. SE Minneapolis, MN 55455, USA
{Tewfik}@Ece.umn.edu

Abstract. A fragile watermarking scheme is proposed for authentication of images. We exploit singular values of singular value decomposition(SVD) of images to check the integrity of images. In order to make authentication data, the singular values are changed to the binary bits using modular arithmetic. The binary bits, authentication data, are inserted into the least significant bits(LSBs) of the original image. The pixels to be changed are randomly selected in the original image. The advantages of this scheme are that i) we can detect any modification of watermarked images, ii) the quality of watermarked images is very high because only a few bits of authentication data are embedded. We also propose an extension algorithm to provide localization. Experimental results show that the proposed fragile watermarking scheme can be applied to the authentication applications.

1 Introduction

Watermarking techniques for the protection of intellectual property rights have been developed for various areas such as broadcast monitoring, proof of ownership, transaction tracking, content authentication, copy control, and device control [1]. The requirements that watermarking systems have to comply with are always based on application. A number of watermarking algorithms have been proposed for twenty years [2][3].

In this paper we focus on the authentication of images. Cryptography is probably the most common method used to authenticate the integrity of digital data. It is accomplished by digital signature, which assures confidentiality, authentication, integrity, and non-repudiation. The signature is attached to the encrypted content. On the other hand, fragile watermarking offers some advantages over simple digital signatures, including: i) signature stays with image, ii) it can be made insensitive to some changes, such as when the image undergoes D/A-A/D or JPEG, and iii) it can be used to localize changed area.

Friedman proposed a trusted digital camera, which embeds a digital signature for each captured image. With the digital signature he can verify that the image is not changed with as well as can identify a specific camera that pictured

F. Petitcolas and H.J. Kim (Eds.): IWDW 2002, LNCS 2613, pp. 170–178, 2003.
© Springer-Verlag Berlin Heidelberg 2003

the image [4]. Yeung and Mintzer proposed an authentication watermark that uses a pseudo random sequence and a modified error diffusion method to protect the integrity of images [5]. Lin and Chang proposed a scheme to insert authentication data in JPEG coefficients so that the authentication watermark has some resilience against JPEG compression [6]. Wong and Memon proposed a secret and public key image watermarking schemes for grayscale image authentication [7]. All of these embed too many information to identify the image's integrity. It results in the degradation of original images. In some applications like medical photographs, the original image should not be changed in some degree. Fridrich et al. proposed invertible fragile watermarking schemes, in which the distortion due to authentication can be removed to obtain the original image data [8]. But, the algorithm should be added to JPEG compressors and decompressors.

In the proposed scheme, although we embed only a few bits of authentication data we can detect any modification of the watermarked image. The singular values of SVD are used for authentication data. There was only one SVD based watermarking work [9]. In the paper they propose a robust watermarking method, embedding a watermark in SVD domain. In our scheme, the quality of the watermarked image is very high. We also provide an extension algorithm to provide localization. Localization is useful because knowledge of where an image has been altered can be used to infer: i) the motive for tampering; ii) possible candidate adversaries; and iii) whether the alteration is legitimate [2]. The specific locations where changes have been made are reflected in the extracted watermark, which indicates the attacked area. The remainder of this paper is organized as follows. Proposed watermarking scheme is described in Section 2. Simulations of our method with respect to attacks are conducted in Section 3. Finally, conclusions are given in Section 4.

2   Proposed Watermarking Algorithm

The basic idea of this scheme is to embed authentication data extracted from the original image to the images. For authentication we check if the embedded information is changed or not in the receiver side. We consider these points below.

2.1   Watermark Insertion

Let's consider a still image O of size M-by-N pixels as an original image. The watermark insertion procedure for the original image is shown in Fig. 1. N pixels are randomly selected with a key in the original image O. The same key is used in the watermark extraction procedure. The number of N should be the same as the dimension of singular values of SVD. LSBs of the selected pixels are set to zero. And then, in order to make authentication data we compute singular values of the image O'.

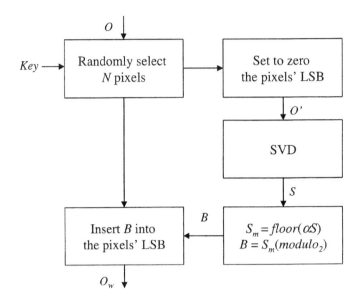

Fig. 1. Watermark insertion scheme

Let A be a general real M-by-N matrix. The SVD of A is the factorization

$$A = USV^T \tag{1}$$

where U and V are orthogonal, and

$$S = diag(\sigma_1, \ldots, \sigma_k), k = \min(M, N) \tag{2}$$

where $diag$ means diagonal matrix with $\sigma_1 \geq \ldots \geq \sigma_k \geq 0$. The σ_i are called the singular values, the first k columns of V the right singular vectors and the first k columns of U the left singular vectors. The singular values S are multiplied by multiplying factor α so that any modification can be detected. In the experiments, we show that the bigger the multiplying factor, the more sensitive to changes to the image, but which is not in every case. And then, the multiplied values are set to the floor integer values:

$$S_m = floor(\alpha S) \tag{3}$$

In order to generate binary bits from S_m, we use modular arithmetic

$$B = S_m(modulo_2) \tag{4}$$

where B is a binary string of size k. Modular arithmetic is simply division with remainder, where we keep the remainder and throw everything else away. In general, the expression $a(modulo_m)$ means to divide a by m and keep the remainder. The result of modular arithmetic consists of binary bits. The binary bits are inserted into the LSBs of randomly selected pixels. Embedding binary bits B forms a watermarked image O_w.

2.2 Watermark Extraction and Verification

The extraction and verification procedure for the embedded watermark from received images is shown in Fig. 2. We choose N pixels to find the location of the embedded bits. The key used in the embedding process is used for selection of the pixels. And then, extract LSBs from the pixels. The computation of feature information is the same as in the insertion procedure. We compare the LSB strings with the computed authentication data.

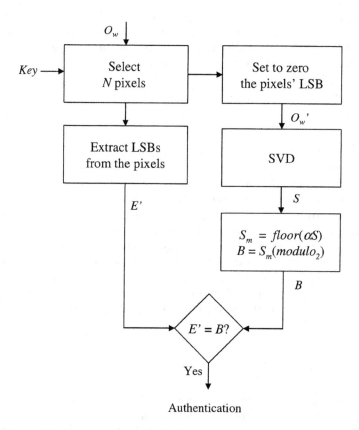

Fig. 2. Watermark extraction and verification scheme

If the watermarked image is not changed and correct key is used, the extracted watermark from the received image is equal to the feature information. When the watermarked image was changed by any processing, or improper key is used to extract the watermark, the extracted watermark is not same as authentication data.

2.3   Extension Algorithm for Localization

Attackers try to change an image without any noticeable artifacts. We should design our watermark to detect any modifications and to indicate the locations where changes have been made. With this proposed algorithm, we can accomplish the two objectives. At first, LSBs of an original image are set to zero. A binary logo image W of size J-by-K is used for a watermark. The generation of authentication data is the same as described in section 2.1. Because the size of watermark W and authentication data B are small in comparison to the size of original image O, it is tiled to make B' and W' respectively, which is the same size as O. The proposed scheme exploits the characteristics of a exclusive OR(XOR) function, in which if we know two inputs among three element in XOR function, then the rest can be derived.

The authentication data B' are combined with the binary watermark W' using a bit by bit XOR operation. That is, the result L is

$$L = B' \oplus W' \tag{5}$$

where $\oplus$ is the XOR operation. Finally, the result L is embedded into the LSB of randomly selected pixels by a key. The same key is used for the watermark extraction procedure. It forms a watermarked work O_w. Fig. 3 presents watermark embedding procedure to find the positions of changed data.

In order to extract the embedded watermark, we perform a bit-wise XOR operation between tiled authentication data B' and extracted bits E' to form the binary watermark. If the watermarked image was not changed and correct keys are used, the derived watermark from the equation of $W'' = B' \oplus E'$ provides the embedded watermark W. That is, if some pixel's values are changed by attackers, the extraction procedure indicates that the received image is not authentic. If LSBs of watermarked images are changed, we can detect locations where images have been changed.

3   Experimental Results

A series of experiments show that our watermark is equal to authentication data if there is no change of the watermarked image. The change of watermarked image results in difference between extracted strings and authentication data extracted from received image. For the experiments, we use gray "rocks" image of size 256×256 as an original image.

Fig. 4 shows the original and watermarked images. The watermarked image shows the same image quality to the original image as shown in Fig. 4 (b). The difference between two images is only 256 bits of LSB among the 65536 pixels (i.e. 256×256 pixels). If we use a correct user key and follow the watermark extraction procedure given in Fig. 2, the extracted strings are equal to extracted authentication data. When the watermark is extracted from the unwatermarked image, or by using incorrect key, or by changing the watermarked image with

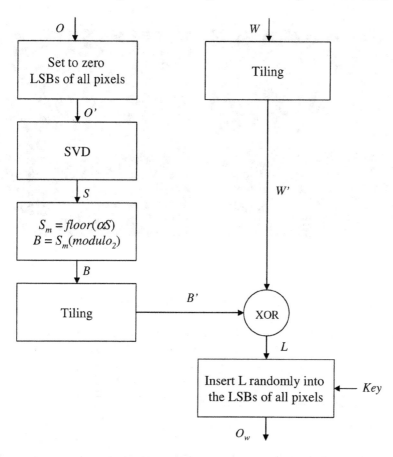

Fig. 3. Watermark insertion for localization

any processing technique, the extracted watermark is not equal to feature information.

Table 1 shows the number of different bits extracted from watermarked image and 1 bit changed watermarked image, respectively, according to the multiplying factor α. We can adjust the sensitivity by changing multiplying factor to the σ_i. In the experiment, we use 1000 as a multiplying factor α. In general, the bigger the multiplying factor, the more sensitive to changes to the images. According to the applications, the multiplying factor can be adjusted. For example, if we need high security the multiplying factor should be increased.

The comparison of a few binary bits between watermarked image and 1 bit changed watermarked image is given in Table 2. The sequences of bits are completely different even if only one bit is changed. Note that although we embed 256 bits of authentication data, only 10 bits of the data are enough to verify the image's integrity. According to applications we can adjust the number

(a)   (b)

Fig. 4. (a) Original image and (b) watermarked image

Table 1. The number of different bits extracted from watermarked image and 1 bit changed watermarked image, respectively, according to multiplying factor α

α	10	10^2	10^3	10^4	10^5	10^6	10^7
Diff*	7	54	112	130	119	126	134

*: the number of different bits

of binary bits of authentication data extracted from images. Because the singular values are very sensitive to any modification, it is enough to embed only few bits instead of whole N bits of information. Table 3 shows the authentication results against various attacks. Only when the images are unchanged the images are considered as the authentic images. Recall that this watermark is designed for authentication of the original image. That is, if someone changes some bits of the image by any image processing techniques, the watermark extraction procedure indicates that the received image is not authentic.

Table 2. Comparison of first ten binary bits extracted from watermarked image and 1 bit changed watermarked image, respectively

k	1	2	3	4	5	6	7	8	9	10
E'*	1	0	0	1	1	0	0	0	0	1
B**	1	0	1	1	1	1	1	0	1	1

k: the order of binary bits
*: extracted binary bits, **: authentication data

Table 3. Authentication results against various attacks

Integrity	Yes	No
Unchanged	○	
Unwatermarked		○
Compressed		○
Filtered		○
Scaled(down or up)		○
Pixel changed (by positions)		○
Pixel changed (by values)		○
Cropped		○
Wrong key used		○

In the experiments for extension algorithm, if the key is incorrect, or the image is not watermarked, or change is given to the watermarked image, then we can't extract our watermark as given in Fig. 5 (b). Especially, when someone changes LSBs in the watermarked image, the specific locations of the change are reflected at the output of the watermark extraction procedure. Fig. 5 shows the original watermark (a), extracted watermark (b) from images corrupted by any signal processing techniques, and extracted watermark (c) that indicates the specific area where changes have been made.

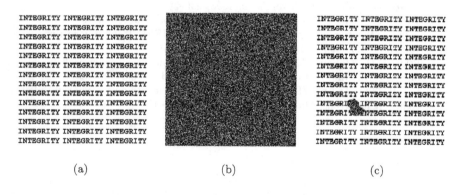

(a)   (b)   (c)

Fig. 5. (a) Original watermark, (b) extracted watermark from images corrupted by any signal processing techniques, and (c) extracted watermark from the image where pixel values are changed

4   Conclusions

In this paper, we present a fragile watermarking scheme for still images. In order to check integrity of the received images, we exploit singular values of SVD of images. Images can be represented with unique singular values. The singular values, authentication data, are very sensitive to any modification. The advantages of this scheme are; i) we can detect any modification such as compressing, filtering, scaling, changing of pixel values and positions, cropping, and using wrong key, ii) the image's quality is very high because only a few bits of authentication data are embedded. In the proposed extension algorithm, the extracted watermark localizes the changes of pixel's values in the original image. Results show that the proposed fragile watermark scheme can be applied for the image authentication.

References

1. Cox, I., Miller, M., Bloom, J.: Digital watermarking. Morgan Kaufmann Publishers (2001)
2. Podilchuk, C., Delp, E.: Digital watermarking: algorithms and applications. IEEE Signal Processing Magazine, vol. 18 (2001) 33–46
3. Lee, S., Jung, S.: A survey of watermarking techniques applied to multimedia. Proc. IEEE International Symposium on Industrial Electronics, vol. 1 (2001) 272–277
4. Friedman, G.: The trustworthy digital camera: Restoring credibility to the photographic image. IEEE Trans. Consumer Electron., vol. 39 (1993) 905–910
5. Yeung, M., Mintzer, F.: Invisible watermarking technique for image verification. Proc. ICIP vol. 2 (1997) 680–683
6. Lin, C., Chang S.: A robust image authentication method surviving JPEG lossy compression. Proc. SPIE, vol. 3312 (1998) 296–307
7. Wong, P., Memon, N.: Secret and public key image watermarking schemes for image authentication and ownership verification. IEEE Trans. Image Processing, vol. 10 (2001) 1593–1601
8. Fridrich, J., Goljan, M., Du, R: Invertible authentication watermark for JPEG images. Proc. Information Technology: Coding and Computing (2001), 223–227
9. Liu, R., Tan, T: An SVD-based watermarking scheme for protecting rightful ownership. IEEE Trans. Multimedia, vol. 4 (2002) 121–128

A DWT-Based Fragile Watermarking Tolerant of JPEG Compression

Junquan Hu[1], Jiwu Huang[1], Daren Huang[1], and Yun Q. Shi[2]

[1] School of Information Science and Technology, Zhongshan University, Guangzhou,
510275,PRC
isshjw@zsu.edu.cn
[2] Dept. of ECE, New Jersey Institute of Technology, Newark, NJ 07102, USA.
shi@adm.njit.edu

Abstract. In this paper, we propose a novel DWT-based fragile watermarking scheme by exploiting the characteristics of the human visual system (HVS). Multi-resolution tamper detection and image fusion are applied to watermark detection and accurate tamper region location. To distinguish between incidental and malicious modifications, some effective rules are presented. Mathematical morphology operations are used to improve the detection performance. Experiment results demonstrate that the watermark is fragile to malicious tamper and robust against high quality lossy image compression.

1 Introduction

Fragile watermarking plays an important role in image authentication. An effective fragile watermarking scheme should be [1,2]: 1) Perceptual invisibility; 2) Ability to detect and locate any tampered region made in an image; 3) Ability to tolerate alteration resulted from JPEG lossy compression.

Several fragile watermark techniques have been reported recently. Yeung *et al.* [3] proposed an elegant scheme that authenticates individual pixels, but it has a serious security flaw if the same logo and key are reused for multiple images. Some schemes [4,5,6] overcame it partially by enlarging the space of keys. Nowadays, fragile watermark has been advanced to semi-fragile in order to tolerate some special operations (image compression, image enhancement, and so on). For example, after a special modulation, Lin *et al.* [7] proposed a semi-fragile scheme that can tolerate JPEG lossy compression. Its weakness is the capacity is limited by the parameters adopted by the author. Kundur *et al.* [8] utilized the space-frequency localization of wavelet transform. The mark is embedded by special modulation. Tamper detection at multi-resolution was achieved. However, the values they used for modulation are monotonously increased from high resolution to low resolution. It thus results in perceptible distortion of watermarking images.

In this paper, a new DWT-based fragile watermark scheme is proposed. Motivated by quantization used in image compression, we embed the mark based on the features of HVS. Multi-resolution tamper detection is achieved. Hence, the detection becomes more flexible. Any malicious tamper can be detected and the tampered regions can be

F. Petitcolas and H.J. Kim (Eds.): IWDW 2002, LNCS 2613, pp. 179–188, 2003.
© Springer-Verlag Berlin Heidelberg 2003

located accurately with the proposed algorithm. The watermark thus generated also can tolerate high quality lossy image compression.

This paper is organized as follows. Section 2 and Section 3 describe the watermark pyramid and the algorithm. Section 4 and Section 5 analysis the fragility of the scheme and tamper detection. In Section 6, mathematical morphology and image fusion is introduced. Experimental results are showed in Section 7. Finally, we draw the conclusion and discuss the future work in Section 8.

2 Watermark Pyramid

In our work, the watermark is a binary logo. For multi-resolution tamper detection and convenience to embed, we construct an image pyramid of the logo by resolution reduction. The resolution reduction (RR) scheme suggested by JBIG is adopted in this paper. By RR, the current pixel value is calculate according to the following formula:

$$h = 4h_{22} + 2(h_{12} + h_{21} + h_{23} + h_{32}) + (h_{11} + h_{13} + h_{31} + h_{33}) - 3(l_{01} + l_{10}) - l_{00} . \tag{1}$$

If $h > 4.5$ then the pixel value is 1 otherwise 0. All parameters are illustrated in Fig.1.

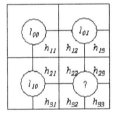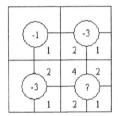

Fig. 1. Pixel weight for resolution reduction, where low-resolution pixels are shown as circles and the high ones are shown as squares. The pixel "?" is decided according to h

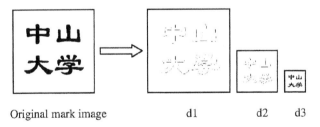

Original mark image   d1   d2   d3

Fig. 2. The pyramid structure of the watermark after resolution reduction

In this way, we generate the pyramid structure of our logo image as shown in Fig.2.

3   Watermark Embedding and Extraction

The mark is embedded into some specific sub-bands after the DWT applied to an image. According to the requirements of invisibility and tolerance towards lossy compression, the marks are embedded into the lower frequency sun-band and middle frequency sub-band. To embed, the L-level DWT is firstly applied, where L is a positive integer. Then, to a specific channel, we calculate

$$Q_{i,j} = \begin{cases} 0 & \lfloor f(i,j)/JND(i,j) \rfloor \text{ is even} \\ 1 & \lfloor f(i,j)/JND(i,j) \rfloor \text{ is odd} \end{cases} \tag{2}$$

Where $f(i,j)$ denotes a DWT coefficient's magnitude, $JND(\cdot)$ is the element in the corresponding Watson's quantization matrix [9], $\lfloor . \rfloor$ is the floor function. We adopt Watson's quantization matrix because it has taken into consideration the features of HVS. Define $s = \lfloor f(i,j)/JND(i,j) \rfloor$. To a pre-specified positive integer m, we divide the interval $[sJND(i,j),(s+1)JND(i,j))$ into 2^{m-1} equal parts, and denote the length of each part as $length$. The ordinal number of the part in which a coefficient is located is denoted as $t \in [1,2,3,\cdots,2^{m-1}]$. We embed m bits of the mark data at once, and denote the first bit by $w(i,j)$, the remaining m-1 bits by r in decimal scale with $r \in [0,1,2,3,\cdots,2^{m-1}-1]$. The specific rule for coefficient alteration is as follow:

$$\tilde{f}(i,j) = \begin{cases} JND(i,j) \cdot s + (r+0.5) \cdot length & \text{if } Q_{i,j} = w(i,j) \\ f_1 & \text{otherwise} \end{cases} \tag{3}$$

$$f_1 = \begin{cases} JND(i,j) \cdot (s+1) + (r+0.5) \cdot length \\ \quad \text{if } (t = r+1 \text{ and } length/2 < (f(i,j) - JND(i,j) \cdot s - r \cdot length)) \text{ or } t > (r+1) \\ JND(i,j) \cdot (s-1) + (r+0.5) \cdot length \\ \quad \text{if } (t = r+1 \text{ and } length/2 > (f(i,j) - JND(i,j) \cdot s - r \cdot length)) \text{ or } t < (r+1) \end{cases} \tag{4}$$

If we want to extract the watermark, L-level DWT is operated on possible marked image firstly. Denoting the DWT coefficients as $f'(i,j)$. Similar to the Q_{ij}, s and ordinal number t used in the embedding procedure, Q'_{ij}, s' and t' are calculated according to the same rule with $f(i,j)$ replaced by $f'(i,j)$. Hence, the extracted watermark is:

$$w = Q'_{i,j} \cdot 2^{m-1} + t' . \tag{5}$$

Then we extract m bits mark just by transforming w to binary scale.

4   Fragility of the Watermark

Theoretically, the capacity of the data to embed will become larger with the increasing of m in our scheme, but it will make the system more fragile. On the other hand, the system should tolerate some especial image processing like JPEG lossy compression and filtering to some extent. The reason is obvious because of the wide distribution of JPEG images in Internet. Thus, if the system tolerates compression, we can make the authentication more effective. Therefore, we should design a scheme that can tolerate some special attacks but still make precise result of tamper detection. The case of filtering is similar. Hence, the problem we should to resolve is the tamper classification. According to [8], there are two types of degradations on a given image region, incidental distortion and severe distortion. The authors of [8] modeled the magnitude changes caused by incidental distortion and malicious tampering as Gaussian distributions with small and large variances, respectively. Furthermore, the distributions of malicious tamper and incidental distortion are denoted as $N(0,\sigma_M{}^2)$ and $N(0,\sigma_I{}^2)$, respectively. Then from [10], we know that there is a relation between σ_M and σ_I, i.e. $\sigma_M = c \cdot \sigma_I$ with $c > 1$. Based on this, we can estimate the fragility of our watermark. Firstly, let the distribution of the distortion is $N(0,\sigma_v{}^2)$. Thus, the probability of correctly extracted mark is:

$$p = \frac{2}{length}\int_0^{length}[erf(\frac{\xi}{2\sigma_v})]d\xi \quad . \tag{6}$$

where $erf(\cdot)$ is standard error function, $length$ and m are the same as in section 3.

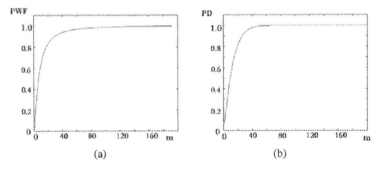

Fig. 3. (a) The relation between m and the probability of watermark false extracted (PWF); (b) The relation between m and the probability of dense of the error detection pixel (PD)

Then, the probability of false extracted mark is $p_e = 1 - p$, as shown in Fig.3 (a). The figure shows that the larger the m, the higher the probability of watermark false extracted, hence the higher fragility of the system. Please note that the fields we choose to embed watermark is important to the fragility. Fragility after embedding to each channel can be calculated by using of the formula of p_e. According to the formula, the watermark is more fragile if we embed it into the coefficients at the lower resolution. This is because of that the higher the resolution, the larger the threshold and hence the large the value allowed altering. Additionally, in order to survive from lossy compression, the mark should not be embedded into the higher frequency components since high frequency usually removed after JPEG compression. Thus, we embed mark into the coefficients of middle resolution and lower resolution, e.g. *HL* and *LL*.

5   Tamper Detection

Let $W'(i,j)$ denote the extracted watermark. We denote the difference mark as (11):

$$D(i, j) = |W(i, j) - W'(i, j)| . \qquad (7)$$

This means that if $W'(i,j)$ equal to $W(i,j)$ then the pixel in difference image has value 0, and 1 otherwise. Thus the difference image is binary with black pixel represents mark extraction error. Hence, we can locate the tamper pixel just according to difference image. We have discussed the basic features that an effective fragile watermark should have, and moreover, we hope our system should bring us the following features: (1) the system should confirm the type of certain attack; (2) the system should extract the correct mark if the image suffered from incidental modification; (3) the system should locate and characterize malicious tamper in any case. Thus, we should use an effective detector that can distinguish malicious tamper from incidental modification. For this, we carefully examine difference image extracted after both malicious tamper and incidental modification. In the case of incidental modification, we have known that the magnitude changes on the coefficients can be modeled as a Gaussian distribution with smaller variance. Moreover, we find that most of watermark error pixels are isolated on the difference image. Contrarily, most of the mark errors pixels are assembled. According to this observation, we can distinguish them just by examine if mark error pixels are sparse or dense. The definition of dense and sparse is defined as follows. For a mark error pixel, it is a dense pixel if at least one of its eight neighbor pixels is a mark error pixel, and a sparse pixel otherwise. Now, let us analyze this issue in statistical way. Let $x(i,j)$ and $p(x)$ denote the current pixel in difference image and its mark error probability that we have defined in Section 4, respectively. Thus, to this pixel, the probability of dense is $p_d=1-(1-p(x))^8$. We show this in Fig.3 (b). From the figure, we find that the probability becomes more and more close to 1 with the increasing of m. As a result, serious distortion will be introduced to image even if it was suffered from subtle alteration. Therefore, m should be selected carefully to achieve lower probability of dense. On the other hand, even if m has been selected appropriately, we also need some united rules to classify the type of tamper. For this, some preliminary parameters should be defined. For a fixed resolution level $l \in [1,2,3,....,L]$, we define these parameters as follows:

$$area_{l,dense} = \{\text{The total of dense pixel}\} . \qquad (8)$$

$$area_{l,sparse} = \{\text{The total of sparse pixel}\} . \qquad (9)$$

$$area_{l,\,total} = area_{l,dense} + area_{l,sparse} . \qquad (10)$$

$$area_l = \{\text{The total pixel of channel } l\} \; . \tag{11}$$

$$\lambda_l = \frac{area_{l,total}}{area_l} \; , \delta_l = \frac{area_{l,dense}}{area_{l,total}} \; . \tag{12}$$

Now, we define the following rules to judge whether a modification is malicious or incidental:

1. If $\lambda_l = 0$ for every resolution level $l \in [1,2,3,....,L]$, then the tested image is neither maliciously tampered nor incidental distorted.
2. If there exists some $l \in [1,2,3,....,L]$, such that $\lambda_l > 0$ and $\delta_l \leq \alpha$, where the threshold is selected carefully. Generally, we fix it between 0.5 and 1.then the tested image encountered only incidental distortions.
3. If $\delta_l > \alpha$ for every $l \in [1,2,3,....,L]$, then the tested image is maliciously tampered.

6   Mathematical Morphology and Image Fusion

We have mentioned that most of the mark extraction errors caused by incidental modification are isolated. Moreover, since we used eight neighbors to determine if one pixel is dense or not, hence, many mark error pixels not caused by malicious modification are looked as caused by malicious modification. Therefore, the result should not be precisely. Hence, we should propose a technique to wipe off those noise-liked sparse mark error pixels, while make dense region caused by malicious modification more compactly. To do so, MM (mathematical morphology) operations [11] can be adopted. Using properly operations with certain structuring elements, we hope the noise-liked pixel should be removed and the compact tamper regions can be created. Let us take into account the difference image $D(i,j)$, which is a binary image. The dilation of $D(i,j)$ with structuring element s is defined as $D \oplus s$, and the erosion is $D \ominus s$. The size of structure element used in these operations determines the size of the objects that will be removed from the image or the size of the gaps that will be filled. We employ a sequence of morphological operations on $D(i,j)$, that is:

$$D' = D \oplus s_1 \ominus s_2 \oplus s_3 \; . \tag{13}$$

The first dilation uses s_1 to create compact regions .The erosion with s_2 is to remove the noise-liked mark error pixel due to lossy compression and the final dilation with s_3 restores the original size of the compact regions. Obviously, the selection of structure element is important. From Bartolini's previous work, the size of structure element can be calculated using order statistics. After above operations, we should increase the threshold α because of the increasing of δ_k for all level k. Because sparse pixels decrease and dense pixel increase, the percentage of dense pixel in error pixel increased accordingly. Here we set $\alpha = 0.9$. Therefore, we use those rules defined in last section to get more precise tamper detection result.

Because the resolution reduction version marks are embedded into corresponding resolution level, thus, the difference images we got just reflect the impression of tamper in each fixed resolution level. We have no knowledge about integrated information of tamper. However, it is useful to build more detailed information about

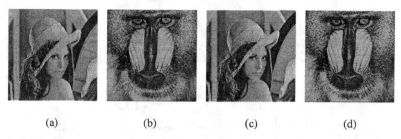

(a)   (b)   (c)   (d)

Fig. 4. Original image and watermark image (a), (b) Original image; (c) Watermark image (PSNR=38.43 dB); (d) Watermark image (PSNR=31.86 dB)

the tamper. To do so, image fusion is adopted. Image fusion [12] refers to the processing and synergistic combination of image information from various knowledge sources to provide a better understanding image. Especially to the different resolution images with the same scene, image fusion seems to obtain a better knowledge of the scene than the knowledge obtained using only one image. M. Costantini *et al.* [12] proposed a general method to fuse image with different resolution. In his scheme, the fused image is obtained by solving a constrained quadratic highly parallelizable minimization problem. As to our scheme, the difference images with gradual increasing resolution version are obtained by mark extraction procedure. Even though the information about tamper from some fixed resolution level is obtained, we also want to get more from the point of view from integrated difference image. Hence, the image fusion scheme described above is adopted. After such an operation, an integrated difference image is obtained. We use it to get more integrated and exact tamper detection result.

7   Experimental Results

We have tested our algorithm on the "Lena" and "baboon" images, both of 256×256×8 bits, while having quite different texture complexities. L=3,and m is fixed as 4 in our experiments because lower p_d (p_d=0.09) can be obtained. The PSNR of the watermarked images (as shown in Fig. 4) are 38.43 dB and 31.86 dB, respectively. Many experiments have been done to demonstrate the effectiveness of tamper detection with the proposed scheme. Fig. 6 shows that the extracted watermarks from the marked image corrupted by JPEG compression at the different compression rates by using our scheme. Obviously, when the quality factor is higher than 50%, we can discern the content of the mark easily. The case with quality less than 50% should be judged as serious distortion. In order to prove the effectivity of the proposed scheme, we compare its performance with that reported in [8]. The PSNR of the marked image with Kundur and Hatzinakos' scheme is 34.26 dB under the conditions of Δ=4 and 3-level DWT on the "Lena" image, lower than 38.43 dB obtained with our scheme. Moreover, perceptible distortion has been introduced to the marked image as the

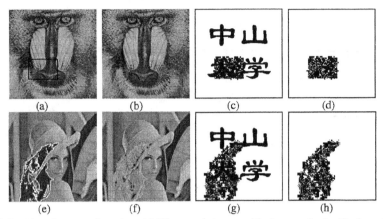

Fig. 5. Results of tamper detection. (a) Watermark image with the area in the black rectangle will be replace with original image; (b) The image after replacing;(c), (d) The mark extracted and difference image;(e) Watermark image with the hair will be brighten;(f) The image after brighten;(g), (h) The mark extracted and difference image

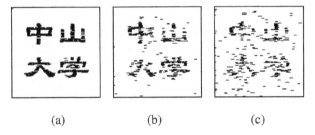

Fig. 6. The mark extracted from the watermark image compressed by JPEG with quality factor (a) 90, (b) 70, and (c) 50, respectively

increasing of Δ and the decomposition level. The authors of [8] just list the detection images for the various resolution levels, and the ground they used to judge on whether an image is tamper with or not is a parameter named tamper assessment function, which is similar to the parameter λ adopted in our scheme. Numerical results of the parameters on "Lena" image are listed in Table 1, where MM means mathematical morphology operations. According to the parameters calculated with different schemes, the types of tamper are determined based on our rules, and we find that the proposed scheme can tolerate JPEG lossy compression with quality factor high than 70%. Compare to [8]'s scheme, the value of tamper assessment function in our scheme is lower in each resolution level. It declares that our scheme is more robust to JPEG compression since more details are preserved after encode and much less watermark false is arisen. We also tested the fragility to malicious tamper and the capacity to locate the tamper areas under malicious tamper. To do so, the contents in the rectangle region (as showed in Fig. 5(a)) are replaced by those of the original image. The detection results show us clearly that tamper occurs in this region, as in

Fig. 5(d). Another experimentation is showed in Fig. 5(e), where Lena's hair is brightened. The detection result is showed in Fig. (f).

Table 1. The type of tamper. "$\sqrt{}$" : Incidental tamper. "$\times$" : Malicious tamper. " / ": is not computed (since the area of replacement is variable, is also variable and hence is not helpful to decision masking)

Attack Para.	Method	JPEG lossy compression					Tamper
		90%	80%	70%	60%	50%	Replacing
λ_1	Scheme in [8]	0.053	0.112	0.146	0.157	0.200	/
	Without MM	0.021	0.121	0.298	0.396	0.443	/
	After MM	0.006	0.035	0.089	0.171	0.149	/
λ_2	Scheme in [8]	0.163	0.276	0.340	0.359	0.400	/
	Without MM	0.322	0.441	0.463	0.495	0.492	/
	After MM	0.075	0.218	0.276	0.292	0.296	/
λ_3	Scheme in [8]	0.419	0.508	0.539	0.542	0.560	/
	Without MM	0.234	0.476	0.502	0.519	0.573	/
	After MM	0.233	0.338	0.319	0.315	0.313	/
δ_1	Without MM	0.108	0.253	0.421	0.923	0.932	1
	After MM	0.667	0.806	0.852	0.977	0.961	1
δ_2	Without MM	0.873	0.927	0.954	0.953	0.959	1
	After MM	0.961	0.989	0.993	0.993	0.992	1
δ_3	Without MM	0.803	0.981	0.992	0.987	0.985	1
	After MM	0.988	0.992	0.992	0.994	0.994	1
Type	Without MM	$\sqrt{}$	$\sqrt{}$	$\times$	$\times$	$\times$	$\times$
	After MM	$\sqrt{}$	$\sqrt{}$	$\sqrt{}$	$\times$	$\times$	$\times$

8   Conclusions

In this paper, we embed the watermark based on HVS and DWT. The features of proposed algorithm are as follows:
1. The algorithm constructs a pyramid structure of the watermark for multi-resolution tamper detection;
1. According to the visual model, the algorithm modifies the coefficients to reduce the perceptible distortion;
2. The algorithm presents a new scheme for tamper detection by using image fusion. It makes the result of tamper detection more precise;
3. The algorithm can tolerate high quality JPEG lossy compression. Hence, the scheme is semi-fragile;

4. The algorithm provides a set of rules to distinguish malicious tamper from incidental tamper. According to our experiments, we distinguish the JPEG lossy compression with high quality factor from malicious tamper, hence the watermark system is robust to incidental tamper, and in the case of malicious tamper, tamper detection is also precise and localized.

Our future research will focus on how to enhance the capacity to tolerate the incidental tamper.

Acknowledgments. The work is supported by NSF of China (69975011, 60172067, 60133020), NSF of Guangdong (013164), China; New Jersey commission of Science and Technology via NJWINS, New Jersey commission of High Education via NJ-ITOWER, and NSF via IUCRC.

References

1. Fridrich, J.: Methods for Tamper Detection in Digital Images. Proc. of the ACM Workshop on Multimedia and Security, Orlando (1999) 19–23
2. Lin, E.T., Delp, E.J.: A Review of Fragile Image Watermarks. Proc. of the Multimedia and Security Workshop, Orlando (1999) 25–29
3. Yeung, M., Mintzer, F.: An Invisible Watermarking Technique for Image Verification. Proc. of the IEEE Int. Conf. on Image Processing, vol.2. Santa Barbaa (1997) 680–683
4. Memon, N., Shende, S. and Wong, P.: On the Security of the Yeung-Mintzer Authentication Watermark. Proc. of the IS&T PICS Symposium, Savannah (1999) 301–306
5. Fridrich, J., Memon, N. and Yeung, M.: Further Attacks on Yeung–Mintzer Fragile Watermarking Scheme. Proc. of the SPIE Electronic Imaging, San Jose (2000) 428–437
6. Fridrich, J., Goljan, M. *et al.*: New Fragile Authentication Watermark for Images. Proc. of the IEEE Int. Conf. on Image Processing (ICIP), Vol.1. Vancouver (2000) 446–449
7. Lin C-Y, Chang S-F: Semi-Fragile Watermarking for Authentication Jpeg Visual Content. SPIE Security and Watermarking of Multimedia Content II, San Jose (2000) 140–151
8. Kundur, D., Hatzinakos, D.: Towards a Telltale Watermark Techniques for Tamper-Proofing. Proc. of the IEEE Int. Conf. on Image Processing (ICIP), Vol.2. Chicago (1998) 409–413
9. Watson, B., Yang, G.Y., *et al.*: Visibility of Wavelet Quantization Noise. IEEE Trans. On Image Processing, Vol.6. (1997) 1164–1175
10. Lin, C. -Y., Chang, S. -F.: A Robust Image Authentication Method Surviving JPEG Lossy Compression. SPIE Storage and Retrieval of Image/Video Databases, San Jose (1998) 296–307
11. Bartolini, F., Tefas, A., Barni, M. and Pitas, I.: Image authentication techniques for surveillance applications. Proc. of the IEEE, Vol. 89(10). (2001) 1403–1418
12. Costantini, M., Farina, A.: The Fusion of Different Resolution SAR Images. Proc. of the IEEE, Vol.85. (1997) 139–146

Robust Local Watermarking on Salient Image Areas

Yi Feng and Ebroul Izquierdo

Dept. of Electronic Engineering, Queen Mary, University of London
Mile End Road, London, United Kingdom, E1 4NS
{yi.feng, ebroul.izquierdo}@elec.qmul.ac.uk

Abstract. Digital content services and tools have spread all over the world creating an acute need for robust copyright protection and ownership management systems. Robust watermarking technology is playing a crucial roll in these systems developments. This paper reports a robust technique for digital image watermarking. Salient image areas extracted from the pixel domain are used to embed local watermarks in the frequency domain. Relevant image corners are first extracted using well- established scale-space theories for edge and corner detection. Fairly small areas around each corner are used to insert the watermark. The objective is to achieve robustness against local and global geometric transformations as well as conventional image processing attacks while keeping the computational cost low. The DFT is applied on the discrete polar coordinates over asymmetric grids defined on uniform angles and non-uniform radii. The objective is to keep the rotation invariance property of the DFT magnitude while avoiding numerical and interpolation errors on the radii axis. A blind watermark detection process based on statistical correlation is used. Several experiments to validate the robustness of the proposed approach were conducted and are reported in the paper.

1 Introduction

Digital watermarking aims to hide information in digital documents mainly for the purpose of copyright protection. Since effective copyright laws allow content creators to proof ownership in an online distribution system, digital tools are needed to deal with copyright infringement and ownership tracing. Robust digital watermarking is defined by the notion that embedded signatures remains inseparably bound to the object it identifies even when the digital object is severely attacked. This means that a digital watermark must be resilient to various image processing operations and malicious attacks targeting removal of the embedded legal owner identification.

Many image watermarking schemes have been proposed during the last few years. Most of these achieve the robustness against digital-analogue-digital conversion, JPEG compression, noise distortion and other common image processing transformations [1], [2], [3], [4]. However, most of these watermarking schemas are not robust to geometric transformation of the pixel domain. Even a simple rotation, translation or scaling (RST) can easily lead to a negative response of the watermark detector because these transforms affect the synchronization between the watermarked signal and the watermark itself [5]. Theoretically, robustness against RST can be achieved using the Discrete Fourier-Mellin transform [6]. Unfortunately,

F. Petitcolas and H.J. Kim (Eds.): IWDW 2002, LNCS 2613, pp. 189–201, 2003.
© Springer-Verlag Berlin Heidelberg 2003

what appears evident in the continuous domain results on several difficulties and severe numerical problems when practical implementations are attempted on a discrete signal. This aspect is reviewed in section 2.

In this paper we describe a novel watermarking schema in which salient image features extracted from the pixel domain are used to embed local watermarks in the frequency domain. A robust corner detector is used to find relevant image corners. Here well-established scale-space theories for edge and corner detection in computer vision are used. Once relevant corners have been detected in the pixel domain, a fairly small area around each corner is used to insert the watermark. The watermarking process is carried out in the DFT domain. The DFT is applied separately to each local image region. This strategy not only leads to watermarking robustness against local geometric transformations but also strongly reduce the computation workload. Thus, resilience against global and local attacks is achieved while keeping the computational cost low. The DFT is applied on the discrete polar coordinates over asymmetric grids defined on uniform angles θ and nonuniform radii ρ. Therefore, rotations in the spatial domain remain equivalent to circular shiftings along the θ-axis and the DFT magnitude remains invariant to rotations. Variable discretization intervals along the ρ axis are used in order to reduce numerical and interpolation errors.

The watermark detection is based on statistical correlation [4]. The correlation between the transform coefficients extracted from the watermarked and processed (attacked) image, and the embedded watermark is calculated. The presence of the watermark is confirmed if the correlation value is higher than a predefined threshold. The whole process is blind since the original image is not required during the detection stage. Since the performance of the proposed technique strongly relies on the accuracy of corner detection in the attacked image, the threshold used for corner detection, during the watermark extraction, is chosen to be lower than that taken to detect corners in the original image during the embedding process. This strategy leads to the detection of most of the corners corresponding to those used for watermark embedding in the original image. Since the amount of regions used during the detection process neither affect the detection response nor the watermark-signal synchronization, a high correlation from the detector is expected.

Both watermark embedding and detection are presented in section 3. Several results of the experimental validation are reported in section 4. The paper closes with conclusion and further work in section 5.

2   RST Invariance and the Discrete Fourier-Mellin Transform

Consider a grey-scale image I of dimensions $N_1 \times N_2$, $i.e.$ $I(x, y)$ is the intensity value at position (x, y). The discrete Fourier transform is given by:

$$F(x,y) = \frac{1}{\sqrt{N_1 N_2}} \sum_{u=0}^{N_1} \sum_{v=0}^{N_2} I(u,v) e^{\frac{-i2\pi ux}{N_1} \frac{-i2\pi vy}{N_2}} \tag{1}$$

where $e^{\frac{2\pi i \theta}{N_1}} = \cos\theta + i\sin\theta$.

Let $M(x,y)$ represent the magnitude of the Fourier transform and $\Phi(x,y)$ its phase. A well-known property of the Fourier transform is that M is invariant to circular shifting in the spatial domain [7]. The Fourier-Mellin Transform is defined as the Fourier transform on the log-polar coordinates. For a given intensity value $I(x,y)$, the corresponding pixel on log-polar coordinates is given by $I(\mu,\theta)$, where $\mu \in R$ and $\theta \in [0,2\pi)$. The transformation between Cartesian coordinates and log-polar coordinates is given by:

$$\theta = \tan^{-1}(y/x), \quad \mu = \ln\left(\sqrt{x^2 + y^2}\right). \tag{2}$$

Using the Fourier-Mellin transform, image scaling and rotation are given by $I(\mu + \log\sigma, \theta)$ and $I(\mu, \theta + \alpha)$ respectively, where σ is the scaling parameter and α the rotation angle. It is straightforward to show that the magnitude of Fourier-Mellin transform is invariant to rotation and scaling.

Although this transform offers a simple schema to achieve rotation and scaling invariance in the continuous log-polar domain, its discretization is not straightforward. The main difficulty is caused by numerical approximations and sampling errors originated by the conversion between Cartesian and log-polar coordinate systems. Using the log-polar map on uniform grids, some sorts of interpolation are required. The sampling interval defines the number of pixel values to be interpolated and the total number of sampling positions influences the watermarks capacity. The larger the number of sampling values, the larger the capacity. On the other hand, a high number of interpolated values carrying more watermark information will be neglected during the inverse log-polar map transform. Thus, a relevant part of the watermark will not be available for the detection process. Furthermore, the computational complexity will increase proportionally to the number of interpolated values.

In Fig.1, an example of the potential exponential growth of interpolation points on the horizontal axis of the log-polar coordinate system is shown. For an image of the size 512×512 and coordinate system centered in its middle point, the maximum value of μ is less than 3. In the nonuniform grid obtained by exact mapping the Cartesian grid into the log-polar along the direction fixed by a 45 degrees angle, the maximum sampling interval becomes 0.301 while the minimum is 0.003. Taking 0.3 as sampling interval almost no information remains in the transformed grid. Taking 0.003 as sampling interval, a total of 490 values need to be interpolated for a single

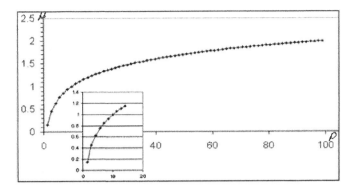

Fig. 1. Relation between $\mu = \ln(\rho)$ and $\rho = \sqrt{x^2 + y^2}$.

value of θ. The huge workload and storage capacity associated with the last case makes it unfeasible for practical applications. Since a number of interpolation points vary for different angles θ, it is extremely difficult to find a trade-off between accuracy, computation and storage. Basically, a direct application of the Fourier-Mellin transform to achieve RST-robustness is unfeasible for practical applications in which the time of response and the storage capacity are limited.

3   Robust Local Watermarks

Another drawback of the reported Fourier-Mellin transform based approaches [5], [6] is their failure to cope with local geometric transformations. An attacker can easily perform local rotation on the watermarked image in order to disable the detection capability of the algorithm. As shown by evaluations conducted using the benchmark software stirmark [8], unsynchronized local transformation can severely reduce the detection capabilities of watermarking based on the Fourier-Mellin transform. To overcome this drawback we proposed to insert watermark into several small salient local areas, which are obtained by robust corner detectors. The watermarking technique is therefore robust against global and local rotation. Robustness against translation, cropping and other geometrical attacks can also be achieved.

3.1 Corner Detection

In principle any robust and accurate corner detector from the literature can be used to extract local salient image regions. In the work presented in this paper two different detectors were used: The Harris corner detector with high accuracy as presented in [9], [10] and the curvature scale-space (CSS) descried in [11]. For the experiments reported in this paper the CSS technique was used. In our implementation edges are first extracted using the Canny detector. Each relevant edge is evolved according to a

Gaussian scale-space paradigm. Thus, each relevant edge is represented by a planar parametric path $\ell : S \subseteq \Re \rightarrow \Re^2$, $\ell(s) = [x(s), y(s)]$, where s represents the arc length. A linear scale-space is obtained by deforming each edge according to the time evolution of:

$$\ell(s, t) = \begin{cases} \ell_0(s) & \text{if} \quad t = 0 \\ (G_{\sqrt{2t}} * \ell_0)(s) & \text{if} \quad t > 0 \end{cases}, \tag{3}$$

where $G_\sigma(w) = (1/2\pi\sigma^2)\exp(-w^2/2\sigma^2)$ is the Gaussian with standard deviation σ and $\ell_0(s) = \ell(s, 0)$. For any t>0,

$$\frac{\partial^n \ell}{\partial s^n} = \frac{\partial^n k}{\partial s^n} * \ell_0. \tag{4}$$

Equation (3) can be expressed in terms of the two components $[x(s), y(s)]$ of $\ell_0(s)$ as:

$$\ell(s, t) = (G_{\sqrt{2t}} * [x(s), y(s)])(s) = [X(s, t), Y(s, t)], \tag{5}$$

with $[X(s, t), \quad Y(s, t)] = [(G_{\sqrt{2t}} * x)(s), \quad (G_{\sqrt{2t}} * y)(s)]$.

The CSS is obtained from the curvature function $\kappa(\ell(s, t))$, which can be defined in terms of the derivatives of the two parametric components $X(s, t)$ and $Y(s, t)$ of $\ell(s, t)$:

$$\kappa(\ell(s, t)) = \frac{\partial^2 Y}{\partial X^2} \bigg/ \left[1 + \left(\frac{\partial Y}{\partial X} \right)^2 \right]^{3/2}. \tag{6}$$

Relevant image corners are defined as points along the edges with high absolute curvature. The scale parameter σ is used to control the amount of corners extracted from the image and the influence of noise.

As shown in Fig. 2a, it can happen that several relevant corners appear in a small image area. In this case salient regions can interest each other as shown in Fig. 2b. Embedding the watermark in all extracted relevant areas will lead to redundant watermarking and strong image distortion. To keep the watermark imperceptible some corners are removed according to the following strategy: The first salient area is build around the corner with the maximum absolute curvature value. Next, the position of the maximum curvature from the remaining corners is considered and a circular area around this point is built. If the two resultant areas intersect, the second salient area in not considered for watermarked embedding. This process is repeated for all the corner points initially selected.

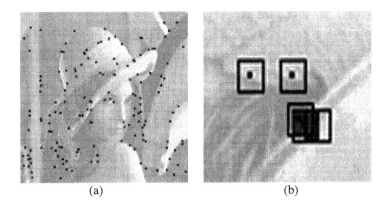

(a)   (b)

Fig. 2. (a) The corners of "Lena" by CSS corner detection. (b) Intersections of local neighbourhoods around corners.

3.2 Polar Map Transform and Inverse Transform

To overcome the implementation difficulties inherent to the discretization of the log-polar map while achieving RST-robustness and low computational cost, polar instead of log-polar coordinates are used. In this case the magnitude of the DFT on polar coordinates, i.e., $\left|\text{DFT}\left[I(\rho,\theta+\alpha)\right]\right|$, is rotation invariant. The DFT is applied separately to small regions defined according to previously extracted image corners. The transformation from Cartesian to polar coordinates is performed using an asymmetric grid defined on uniform angles θ and nonuniform radii ρ. The non-uniform grid along the ρ-axis is defined using variable discretization intervals. The objective is to reduce numerical and interpolation errors caused by approximations over regular grids. The algorithm steps to transform the coordinate systems is outlined in the following:

- For each pixel position (x, y) inside of a salient image area in the Cartesian coordinate system, calculate its direction relative to the horizontal axis and the origin of the Cartesian coordinate system: $\theta_{x,y} = \text{int}(\tan^{-1}(y/x)/\omega)$, where ω is the sampling interval and $\theta_{x,y} \in [0, S]$, where $S = \text{int}(2\pi/\omega)$. Notice that the centre of the coordinate system coincides with the corner used to define the salient image area.

- Calculate the radius of the pixel, $\rho_{x,y} = \sqrt{x^2 + y^2}$, and insert it into an array $\rho[\theta]$.

- Sort the elements of $\rho[\theta]$ according to their magnitude and store corresponding relations between (x, y) and ($\theta_{x,y}$, $\rho[\theta]$) in a look-up table.

- During the inverse polar map transform, for each (θ, ρ) position, retrieve its corresponding pixel (x, y) using the look-up table.

Using this algorithm only simple interpolation without padding is needed during the coordinate conversion process. Furthermore, only few pixels are neglected and the information loss remains low.

3.3 Watermark Embedding

The embedding method is based on the spread spectrum. The frequency of the host image is used as a *communication channel*, and the watermark is viewed as a signal that is transmitted through it and spread over many frequency components so that the energy in any one component is very small and almost undetectable. The frequency coefficients are synchronized with the watermark signals after embedding. However, problems emerge if using the conventional embedding method based on DFT. In this case, it will be necessary to define an ordering relation between the local salient areas. This relation should be extremely robust against distortions and loss few local areas. To overcome this problem the same watermark is used for each image area. The basic algorithm for the embedding process can be outlined as follows:

- Given an image $I(x, y)$, find several corners LC_i $(0 \le i \le n)$ by curvature scale space corner detection. Here n is the number of selected salient areas.
- Use each selected corner LC_i to define of a fairly small block, $IL_i(x_L, y_L)$, $0 \le x_L \le N$, $0 \le y_L \le N$, centred at LC_i .
- For each block, apply polar map transform, which algorithm is defined in section 3.2. $IL_i(\rho,\theta)$ represents the block on polar coordinates, where $\rho \in [0, N/2]$, $\theta \in [0, S]$.
- Apply DFT on each block $IL_i(\rho,\theta)$ and obtain the magnitudes, which are denoted as $M_i(\rho,\theta)$, with $\rho \in [0, N/2]$, $\theta \in [0, S]$.
- Generate a two dimensional watermark $W = \{w_{ij}\}$, where $i \in [1, N/2]$, $j \in [1, S/2]$. Here $w_{ij} = \begin{cases} -1 & \text{if } r_{ij} > 0 \\ 1 & \text{else} \end{cases}$, where $\{r_{ij}\}$ is a random sequence created by a secret key or signature.
- Embed watermark W to $M_i(\rho,\theta)$ according to the formula given below:

$$M'(\rho,\theta) = \begin{cases} M(\rho,\theta) & \text{if } \rho=0 \text{ or } \theta=0 \\ M(\rho,\theta)*(1+\alpha)W(\rho,\theta) & \text{if } \rho \in [1, N/4], \theta \in [1,S] \cdot \\ M(\rho,\theta)+\alpha*M(N/2-\rho,S-\theta)W(N/2-\rho,S-\theta) & \text{else} \end{cases} \quad (7)$$

Equation (7) defines a symmetric watermark and guarantees that the inverse DFT applied on the distorted watermarked image becomes a real number [12].

3.4 Watermark Detection

Assuming that the watermarked image I' will undergo transformations and suffer attacks, the detection proves is performed on a distorted image $\hat{I}$. The watermark detector calculates the correlation coefficient K between the referred watermark $\tilde{W}$ and the sum $\tilde{V}$ of DFT magnitudes $\tilde{V}^{(k)}$, which is extracted from every salient area. The formula to calculate K can be written as Equation (8):

$$K = \frac{\tilde{V} \cdot \tilde{W}}{\sqrt{(\tilde{V} \cdot \tilde{V})(\tilde{W} \cdot \tilde{W})}}, \tag{8}$$

where $\tilde{V} = 1/n \sum_{k=0}^{n} \tilde{V}^{(k)} = 1/n \sum_{k=0}^{n} (\sum_{i=1}^{N/2} \sum_{j=1}^{S/2} \tilde{v}_{ij}^{(k)})$, $\tilde{W} = \sum_{i=1}^{N/2} \sum_{j=1}^{S/2} \tilde{w}_{ij}$,

$\tilde{v}_{ij}^{(k)} = (\overline{v}^{(k)} \cdot v_{ij}^{(k)})$ and $\tilde{w}_{ij} = (\overline{w} \cdot w_{ij})$.

$\overline{v}^{(k)}$ and $\overline{w}$ are the mean values of $\{v_{ij}^{(k)}\}$ and $\{w_{ij}\}$.

The presence of the watermark is confirmed if the correlation is higher than a predefined threshold. As shown by Equation (8), it is expected that the correlation value remain high even if additional signals are added to the calculation. Basically, this is the case when additional not watermarked blocks are considered in the correlation estimation.

$$E^2[K] = \begin{cases} \alpha^2 K & \text{if } \tilde{W} \text{ is synchronised with } \tilde{V} \\ 0 & \text{if } \tilde{W} \text{ is unsynchronised with } \tilde{V} \end{cases}, \tag{9}$$

$$E^2[K] = E^2[(\tilde{V}_s + \tilde{V}_e) \cdot \tilde{W}] = E^2[\tilde{V}_s \cdot \tilde{W}] + E^2[\tilde{V}_e \cdot \tilde{W}] = E^2[\tilde{V}_s \cdot \tilde{W}]. \tag{10}$$

According to Equation (10), the expected value will be the same and correlation coefficient remains high when additional signals $\tilde{V}_e$ are considered along with the watermarked ones $\tilde{V}_s$. Therefore, using more salient areas or corners for the detection will not affect the correlation response.

4 Experimental Results

To validate the performance of the proposed method several computer experiments were conducted using a variety of test images. In this paper some selected results obtained for LENA are reported. Corners were extracted and local areas defined as shown in Fig.3a. Here a high threshold for the sensitiveness of the Canny edge detector and a high scale parameter were used. A total of 151 corners were detected and circles of radius 10 around every corner were defined as salient image areas. After intersecting circles were removed using the strategy described in section 3.1, a total of 46 salient image regions remained. For the watermark detection a lower threshold and scale parameter were applied (50% lower than those used in the embedding stage). The 173 corners extracted from a 45 degrees rotated image are shown in Fig. 3b. Over 98% of correspondences between the corners used in the embedding process and those used for watermark detection were found. This confirms the robustness of the used corner detector.

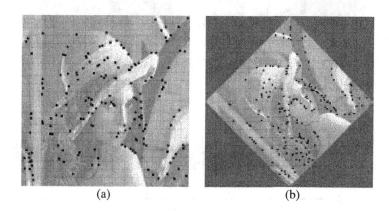

(a)   (b)

Fig. 3. (a) The CSS corner detector applied to LENA with a high sensitivity threshold. (b) CSS corner detection for a rotated image (45 degrees) using a lower sensitivity threshold.

The original and the watermarked images are shown in Fig. 4a and 4b, respectively. In this case parameter controlling the watermark strength was set to 0.2. Fig. 4c shows the normalized correlation between DFT coefficients extracted from the watermarked image and a set of 1000 different random signal containing the watermark.

Since the watermark is embedded into the middle frequency bands it is expected to be robust against JPEG compression. Fig. 5a shows the watermarked LENA after JPEG compression with three different compression ratios. The corresponding correlation responses are given by the four picks of Fig. 5b. The highest pick correspond to the undistorted image.

The watermarking technique is also confirmed to be strongly robust to global rotations with any degree. Fig. 6a and 6b show the rotated watermarked image after rotated by 9 degrees and 45 degrees. The corresponding correlations are shown as the peaks in Fig. 6c.

The proposed method is also expected to be robustness to the geometrical distortions, which applied on part areas of the image. Fig. 7 shows an example for partly rotation. The two part areas 200×200 in the watermarked image, as shown in the high-lined regions in Fig. 7a, were rotated by 0.3 degrees. The rotated degree is

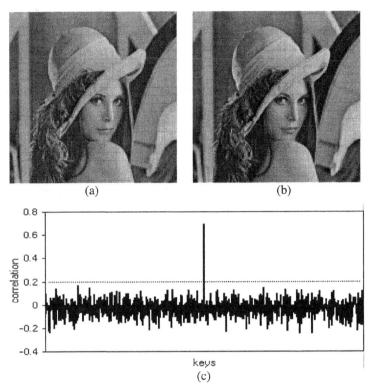

Fig. 4. (a) The original image LENA. (b) The watermarked image. (c) The normalized detection with thousand different watermarks. The dotted line is notated as the threshold.

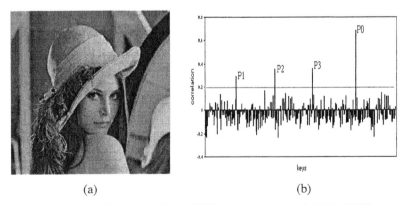

Fig. 5. (a) Compressed Watermarked image LENA (compression ratio 20:1). (b) The detection response correlation for 500 different keys. The main peaks tcorrespond to correct positive detection on the original watermarked image (P0), on JPEG image versions (P1, P2 and P3 for a compression ratio of 20:1 and 17:1 and 15:1 respectively).

less than 1 degree so that the distortion does not reduce the quality of the image. The corresponding correlation is give by Fig. 7b.

The performance of the proposed watermarking methods in the paper against the Strimark benchmarking tests is drawn in Table 1. Fig. 8a shows the watermarked "Lena" attacked by random geometric distortions of Stirmark and the detection result is shown in Fig. 8b.

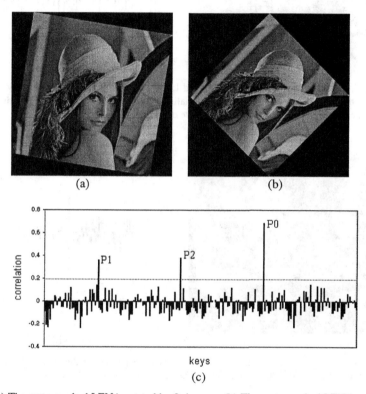

(a)   (b)

(c)

Fig. 6. (a) The watermarked LENA rotated by 9 degrees. (b) The watermarked LENA rotated by 45 degrees. (c) The detection response correlation for 500 different keys. The two peaks correspond to the correct positive detection on rotated watermarked image. (P1 for (a) and P2 for (b)).

5   Conclusions and Further Work

A watermarking schema based on symmetric watermarks embedded in the DFT domain is introduced. The goal is to exploit the rotation invariance property of the magnitude of the DFT coefficients. The DFT is applied on discrete polar coordinates.

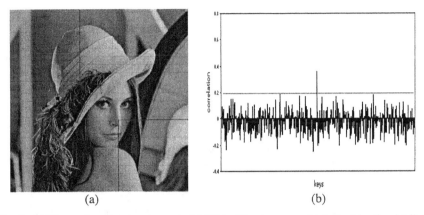

(a)   (b)

Fig. 7. (a) The partly rotated watermarked LENA. (The two areas high-lined by the dot lines are rotated by 0.3 degrees) (b) The normalized detection of Fig. 7a with 500 different keys. The peak corresponds to the correct positive detection.

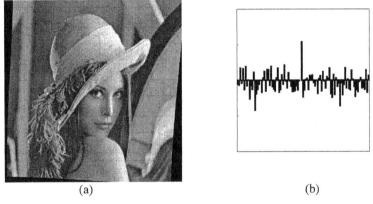

(a)   (b)

Fig. 8. (a) Watermarked LENA attacked by random geometric distortion. (b) The detection result of Fig. 8a with 100 different keys. The peak corresponds to the correct positive detection.

Table 1. Stirmark 3.1 benchmarking of our approach.

Applied Attack	Stirmark Score
Signal enhancement	1.00
Compression	0.90
Cropping	1.00
Rotation	1.00
Random geometrical distortions	1.00

To achieve high accuracy while keeping the computation low, the polar coordinate system is defined in a nonuniform grids: the θ-axis is discretized using regularly distant samples while on the ρ-axis, irregularly sampled points are chosen. A strategy is introduced to avoid loss of information during the conversion from Cartesian to polar coordinate system and vice versa.

The watermark consists of a low amplitude random signal, which is embedded, in the DFT spectrum of fairly small image areas. The centres of these areas are extracted using a corner detection technique based CSS. The watermarking technique is resilient to global rotation, translation and scaling. Moreover, it is also robust against local geometric distortions and conventional image processing attacks.

Possible extensions include the use of a matching technique to shape the strength of the watermark in each salient area. For this, the Just Noticeable distortion over the whole image can be continued and the watermark signal modulated accordingly. Another extension will be to use geometric relations between selected corners to deal with combined attacks, e.g. scaling.

References

1. Cox, I.J., Miller, M.L., Bloom, J.A.: Digital Watermarking. Morgan Kaufmann Publishers, An Imprint of Academic Press, USA. (2002) 41–58
2. Hartung, F., Kutter, M.: Multimedia Watermarking Techniques. Proceedings of the IEEE, Vol. 87, No. 7. (1999) 1079–1107
3. Cox, I.J., Kilian, I., Leighton, F.T., Shamoon, T.: Secure spread spectrum watermarking for multimedia. IEEE Transaction on Image Processing, Vol. 6, No. 12. (1997) 1673-1687
4. Voyatzis, G., Pitas, I.: Image Watermarking for Copyright Protection and Authentication. Handbook of Image & Video Processing. Academic Press Canada. (2000) 733–744
5. Lin, C., Wu, M., Cox, I.J., Bloom, J.A., Miller, M.I., Lui, Y.M.: Rotation, Scale and Translation Resilient Watermarking for Images. IEEE Transaction on Image Processing, Vol. 10. (2001) 767–781
6. Joesph, J.K., Ruanaidh, J.ó., Pun, T.: Rotation, scale and translation invariant spread spectrum digital image watermarking. Signal Processing, Vol. 66, No. 3. (1998) 303–317
7. Bracewell, R.N.: The Fourier Transform and its Applications. McGraw-Hill Book Company New York. (1963) 15–22
8. Petitcolas, F.A.: Watermarking schemes evaluation. IEEE on Signal Processing. Vol. 17, No. 5. (2000) 58–64
9. Harris, C., Stephens, M.: A combined corner and edge detector. Proceedings of the Fourth Alvey Vision Conference. (1988) 147–151
10. Montesionos, P.,Gouet, V., Deriche, R., Pele, D.: Matching color uncalibrated images using differential invariants. Image and Vision Computing on Special Issue BMVC'2000. Elsevier Science, Vol. 18, No. 9. (2000) 659–671
11. Mokhtarian, F., Suomela, R.: Robust image corner detection through curvature scale space, IEEE Transactions on Pattern Analysis and Machine Intelligence, Vol.20, No.12. (1998) 1376–1381
12. V. Solachidis and Pitas, I.: Circularly Symmetric Watermark Embedding in 2-DFT Domain. IEEE Transaction on Image Processing, Vol.10, No.11. (2001) 1741–1753

Image Normalization Using Invariant Centroid for RST Invariant Digital Image Watermarking

Bum-Soo Kim[1], Jae-Gark Choi[2], and Kil-Houm Park[1]

[1] Department of Electronic Engineering, Kyungpook National University,
1370, Sankyug-Dong, Buk-Gu, Daegu, 702-701, Korea,
bskim@palgong.knu.ac.kr, khpark@ee.knu.ac.kr
[2] Department of Computer Engineering, Dongeui University,
Gaya-Dong, Busanjin-Gu, Busan, 614-714, Korea
cjg@dongeui.ac.kr

Abstract. Digital image watermark is an invisible mark embedded in an image that can be used for copyright protection. The current paper proposes a new watermarking scheme by improving image normalization based watermarking (INW). Image normalization is based on the moments of the image, however, in general, RST attacks bring the image boundary cropping and the moments are not preserved original ones. Thereafter the normalized images of before and after are not same form. To solve the cropping problem of INW, Invariant Centroid (IC) is proposed and the only central region(R), which has less cropping possibility by RST, is used for normalization. In addition, the watermark is embedded and detected in the normalized form of the image. Experimental results demonstrated that the proposed watermarking scheme is robust to RST attacks with cropping.

1 Introduction

Digital image watermarking is a state-of-the-art technique for protecting digital media copyright based on embedding an invisible mark directly into a digital image [1-3]. For successful copyright protection, the embedded watermark should be robust to any type of attack. Although conventional watermarking schemes are robust to waveform attacks, such as JPEG compression or filtering to some degree [4-6], they are still vulnerable to geometrical attacks, such as rotation, scaling, and translation (RST). As such, image normalization based watermarking (INW) has been proposed to solve this problem [7]. In this scheme, a standard form, i.e. normalized image, of an image is made from a geometrical transformation [8], then the watermark is embedded and detected in this form, thereby providing robustness to RST attacks. However, if the image is cropped by an RST attack, the normalized image becomes different to the original one, because the centroid and geometric moments used to extract the normalization parameters are changed. As a result, the watermark cannot be detected even if it still remains.

Accordingly, the current paper proposes a new method of digital image watermarking that is against RST attacks including cropping based on the use of

F. Petitcolas and H.J. Kim (Eds.): IWDW 2002, LNCS 2613, pp. 202–211, 2003.
© Springer-Verlag Berlin Heidelberg 2003

an IC. Since the IC of an image does not vary, if it is used to determine the region from which the normalization parameters are extracted, the normalized image will have the same form even if cropping has occurred. Therefore, even though the image has been cropped, the watermark can still be detected.

2   Image Normalization Using IC

In INW, image normalization is performed by parameters extracted from its centroid and central moments, then a watermark is embedded into the normalized image. To normalize an image $I(x, y)$ of $(x, y) \in \Omega$, the centoid and central moments of $I(x, y)$ are calculated first. The centroid $\mathbf{C_0} = (C_{x0}, C_{y0})$ of $I(x, y)$ is calculated as follows:

$$C_{x0} = \int_{\Omega} x f(x, y) dx, \quad C_{y0} = \int_{\Omega} y f(x, y) dy \qquad (1)$$

where $f(x, y) = I(x, y) / \iint_{\Omega} I(x, y) dx dy$, and the (k, r)th order central moment u_{kr} is calculated using the following equation

$$u_{kr} = \iint_{\Omega} (x - C_{x0})^k (y - C_{y0})^r f(x, y) dx dy. \qquad (2)$$

Based on the above equations, if the pixel values are changed or image cropping occurs due to an attack, the centroid and central moments will be different from the original image. As a result, in INW, the normalized forms of the original and attacked image will also be different, which means that the embedded watermark cannot be extracted even if it still remains.

Accordingly, the current paper proposes a robust digital image watermarking scheme using an IC. The proposed scheme for calculating an IC is depicted in Fig. 1. First, the initial centroid $\mathbf{C_0}$ of the image is calculated after performing low pass filtering so as to reduce the effects of waveform attacks, as most waveform attacks, e.g. JPEG compression and noise addition etc., do not affect the low frequency bands. Next, the centroid $\mathbf{C_1}$ is calculated based on a circular region with radius r and center point $\mathbf{C_0}$. The region used to calculate the centroid must be circular so that it will remain unchanged in the case of rotation. $\mathbf{C_1}$ is also used as the center point for another circle with radius r to calculate $\mathbf{C_2}$. A comparison is then made between $\mathbf{C_2}$ and $\mathbf{C_1}$ and the above process is repeated until the centroids converge on the same point, thereby becoming an IC, $\mathbf{C_f} = (C_{xf}, C_{yf})$.

In addition, the central moments are not calculated from entire image, but rather from the central circle region R of $I(x, y)$, because the boundary region of an image can be cropped by RST attacks and this region must remain the same even after the image is attacked. Therefore, in the proposed scheme, the last circle area used to calculate $\mathbf{C_f}$ becomes the central moment calculation region R and Eq. 2 is changed as follows:

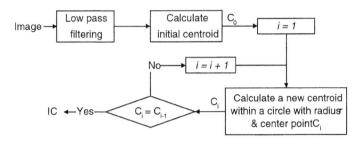

Fig. 1. Scheme for extracting IC

$$u_{kr} = \iint_R (x - C_{xf})^k (y - C_{yf})^r f(x,y) dx dy \tag{3}$$

where $f(x,y) = I(x,y) / \iint_R I(x,y) dx dy$.

Consequently, the resulting normalized images, attacked or not, have the same form as the IC and R remain the same. Also, since the watermark is embedded in the normalized form of the image, the proposed watermarking scheme is robust to attacks.

3 Watermark Embedding and Verification

In the proposed watermarking scheme, the normalized image is made by using IC and a watermark is embedded and detected in frequency domain. To verify copyright of the test image, it is also normalized by the same method in embedding process and copyright is determined based on the presence or absence of the watermark without the original image.

3.1 Watermark Embedding

The proposed watermark embedding scheme is shown in Fig. 2, where the watermark is embedded into the frequency domain of the normalized image. Although there are several ways to transform an image into a frequency domain, the current study uses a 2-dimensional Fourier transform (2-D DFT) with its magnitude spectrum, $M(u,v)$ as the embedding domain, since it is fast and simple. As such, the watermark, $\mathbf{W_k} = \{w_1, w_2, \ldots, w_N\}$ where $w_i \in \{-1, 1\}$, is a pseudo-random binary sequence of length N that is generated by the copyright owners secret key (k). The watermark is then embedded in $\dot{N}$ points of $M(u,v)$ selected based on k and which satisfy the frequency bands $f_L < \sqrt{u_i^2 + v_i^2} < f_H$ using the formula

$$M'(u_i, v_i) = M(u_i, v_i)(1 + \alpha w_i) \tag{4}$$

where α is the embedding strength and $M'(u_i, v_i)$ is the watermarked 2-D DFT magnitude. The watermark is also embedded in $M(-u_i, -v_i)$ because the magnitude of the 2-D DFT is symmetric to the DC.

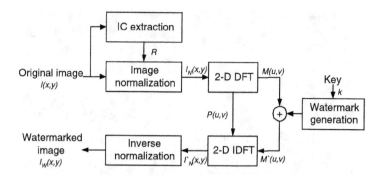

Fig. 2. Proposed watermark embedding scheme

3.2 Watermark Verification

The watermark verification scheme is similar to the watermark embedding scheme. First, the IC and R of the test image are decided, and then the test image is normalized using the parameters extracted from R. Finally, the 2-D DFT magnitude of the test image, $M'(u, v)$ is obtained and the number of N points, $M'(u_1, v_1), \ldots, M'(u_N, v_N)$, is selected using the same key, k, as used in the embedding process, then the similarity with the watermark $\mathbf{W_k}$ is calculated using the formula

$$S = \frac{\sum_{i=1}^{N} w_i M'(u_i, v_i)}{\sqrt{\sum_{i=1}^{N} (M'(u_i, v_i))^2}} \tag{5}$$

and whether or not the watermark is present is determined based on the similarity S compared with a given threshold T.

4 Experimental Results

To evaluate the performance of the proposed watermarking scheme, experiments were conducted using the Lena, Girl, and Pepper (256 × 256) images and the results compared with Barnis method [4] and INW [7]. When determining the IC and R, the radius of the circle r was 64. Also the watermark embedding bands f_L and f_H were 20 and 40, respectively, and the embedding strength α was 0.25. The length N of the watermark was 1000 and the decision threshold T used to determine the presence of the watermark was 3.

Fig. 3 shows the images and watermarked versions used in the experiments. Figs. 3 (a), (c), and (e) are the original images, while (b), (d), and (f) are the watermarked images with PSNRs of 41.5dB, 42.1dB, and 42.5dB, respectively. Fig. 3 demonstrates that the invisibility requirement was satisfied by the proposed scheme.

The most important part of the proposed scheme, i.e. the identification of an IC, was found to be efficient and robust to various attacks, see Fig. 4. Fig.

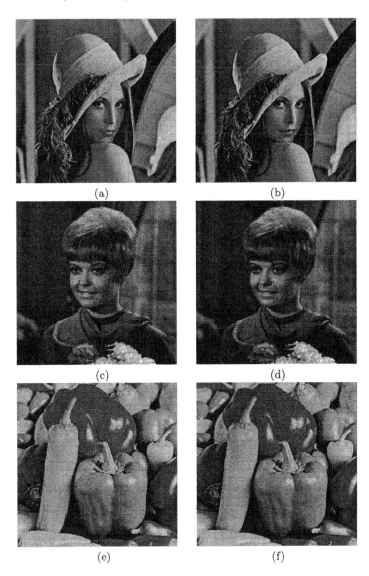

Fig. 3. (a),(c),(e) Original images of Lena, Girl, Pepper; (b),(d),(f) watermarked images of (a),(c) and (e) respectively

4 (a) shows the IC of the original image, while Figs. 4 (b) to (g) represent the robustness of the IC to various attacks, including 3×3 average filtering (Fig. 4 (b)), the addition of 5based on a compression ratio of 70 (Fig. 4 (d)), clockwise rotation of 20 degrees with cropping (Fig. 4 (e)), translation of 30 pixels along the axis (Fig. 4 (f)), and scale changing based on a scaling factor of 0.5 (Fig. 4 (g)), respectively. In Figs. 4 (a)-(g), the IC is marked with a cross and despite various

Fig. 4. ICs marked with cross: (a) original image; (b) 3×3 average filtered; (c) 5(d) JPEG compressed image with compression ratio of 70; (e) 20 degree clockwise rotation of image plus cropping; (f) 30 pixels translated image along x axis; (g) sclaed image based on scaling factor of 0.5

RST and waveform attacks, each IC has a similar position on the hatband. Also, the normalized images of the original and attacked images are represented in Fig. 5. Figs. 5 (a) and (c) are the original image and rotated and cropped image of (a), respectively, however, Figs. 5 (b) and (d), the normalized images of (a) and (c), have the same form since they have the same IC and R.

The 500th watermark, among 1000 watermarks generated using different keys, was embedded in the Lena image, then the similarities between the 1000 watermarks and the watermarked Lena image were computed, as shown in Fig.

6. The results show that the similarity with the 500th watermark was the highest, which also satisfied the threshold. As such, the person with the 500th key can insist on their copyright ownership of the image.

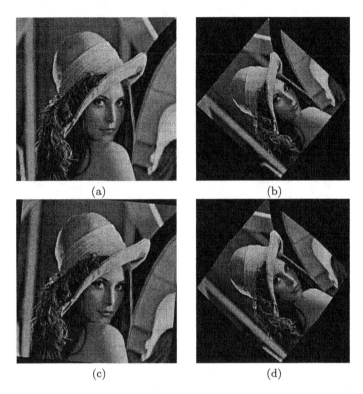

(a)   (b)

(c)   (d)

Fig. 5. Normalized images of original and attacked images: (a) original image; (b) normalized image of (a); (c) rotated and cropped image of (a); (d) normalized image of (c)

The proposed scheme can also detect a watermark after common signal processing, such as JPEG compression, filtering, and noise addition, because the modified 2-D DFT magnitude coefficients are robust frequency bands. Consequently, a watermark can be easily detected after JPEG compression, as represented in Fig. 7.

The watermark should be able to survive an RST attack with cropping. As such, Figs. 8, 9, and 10 show that the proposed watermarking scheme was robust to RST attacks. The similarity after rotation attacks with cropping is depicted in Fig. 8. The conventional methods were unable to provide sufficient similarity to prove the existence of a watermark after a rotation of only 1 degree. However, with the proposed scheme, the similarity value remained basically unchanged even after a rotation attack with cropping and was unaffected by the amount of

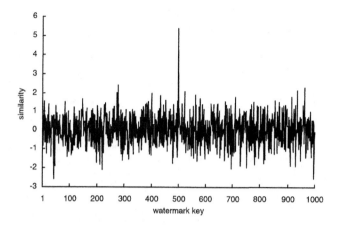

Fig. 6. Similarity of Lena image to watermarks with 1000 different keys

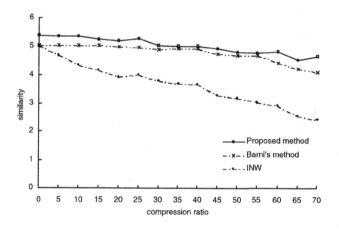

Fig. 7. Similarity after JPEG compression

the rotation angle. The similarities computed using different scaling factors are shown in Fig. 9. The similarities with the proposed method were theoretically uniform, regardless of a scale change, although the similarity was lower when the scale was reduced, as a certain loss of information is unavoidable in a discrete signal. However, when the scaling factor was 0.5, the similarities still satisfied the threshold. In this case, INW also performed well as there was no cropping. Fig. 10 represents the similarities after translation attacks on 40 pixels along the x-axis, in which the proposed scheme proved to be robust to translation. Accordingly, the experimental results confirmed that the proposed watermarking

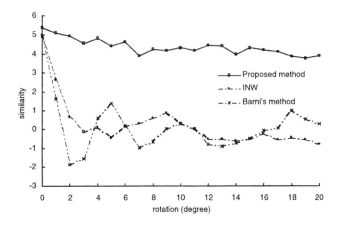

Fig. 8. Similarity after rotation attack with cropping

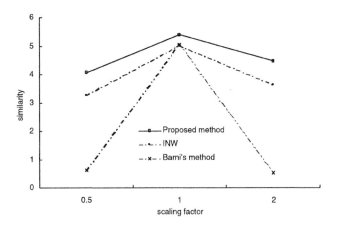

Fig. 9. Similarity after scaling attack

scheme was robust to RST and waveform attacks, because the image normalization parameters were not extracted from the entire image region but rather from a circle-shaped central region, which remained unchanged after waveform and RST attacks.

5   Conclusion

The current paper proposed a new watermarking scheme using region-based image normalization that is robust to RST attacks with cropping. The proposed

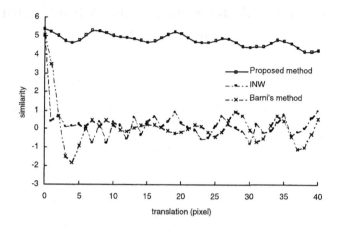

Fig. 10. Similarity after translation attack

scheme determines and uses an IC and R. As such, the normalized result from an attacked image, even after cropping, is the same as that from the original image. Plus, the watermark is embedded in the middle frequency bands of the normalized image. Consequently, the proposed watermarking scheme is robust to both waveform attacks and RST attacks with cropping.

References

1. Swanson, M.D., Kobayashi, M., Tewfik, A,H.: Multimedia data-embedding and watermarking technologies, Proceedings of IEEE, **86** (1998) 1064–1087
2. Bender, W.R., Gruhl, D., Morimoto, N., Lu, A.: Techniques for data hiding, IBM Systems Journal, **35** (1996) 313–336
3. Langelaar, G.C., Setyawan, I., Legendijk, R.L.: Watermarking digital image and video data, IEEE Signal Processing Magazine, **17** (2000) 20–46
4. Barni, M., Bartolini, F., Cappellini, V., Piva, A.: A DCT-domain system for robust image watermarking, Signal processing, **66** (1998) 357–372
5. Cox, I.J., Kilian, J., Leighton, F.T., Shamoon, T.: Secure spread spectrum watermarking for multimedia, IEEE Transactions on Image Processing, **6** (1997) 1673–1678
6. Hsu, C.-T., Wu, J.-L.: Hidden digital watermark in images, IEEE Transactions on Image Processing, **8** (1999) 58–68
7. Alghoniemy, M., Tewfik, A.H.: Geometric distortion correction through image normalization, Proceeding of ICIP, **2** (2000) 1291–1294
8. Pei, S.-H., Lin, C.-N.: Image normalization for pattern recognition, Image and Vision Computing, **13** (1995) 711–724

An Image Watermarking Algorithm Robust to Geometric Distortion

Xiangui Kang [1], Jiwu Huang [1], and Yun Q. Shi [2]

[1] Dept. of Electronics, Zhongshan University, Guangzhou 510275, P. R. China. E-mail:
{isskxg, isshjw }@zsu.edu.cn
[2] Dept. of ECE, New Jersey Institute of Technology, Newark, NJ 07102, USA.
shi@njit.edu

Abstract. In this paper, a robust watermarking algorithm in DWT domain against geometric distortion is proposed. We introduce a distance measure between the distorted and undistorted images/video in order to determine the distortion. We can then inverse the geometric distortion to regain synchronization. An efficient algorithm searching for the synchronization parameters has been developed. Using multi-resolution coarse-fine searching to prune the searching space, the computation of algorithm is reduced drastically. The BCH code and 2-D interleaving are exploited to lower detection error probability. Our watermarking algorithm can successfully resist geometrical distortion, including rotation, scaling, translation, shearing, cropping, jitter attack and linear transformations.

1 Introduction

Watermarking is an effective method for the protection of intellectual property rights (IPR) of multimedia data [1]. There are two kinds of watermarks. The first one is just a pseudo random sequence representing one information bit [1], which is usually used to verify the presence of a known watermark. The second one consists of meaningful information, such as text [2], binary images [3] and grayscale images [4]. In general, as the bit rate of embedded data increases, the robustness of hidden data will decrease under the constraint of invisibility. It is a challenge to guarantee the robustness of the watermark with multiple information bits.

There has been much emphasis on the robustness of watermarks to common signal processing operations such as compression and filtering. Recently, however, it has become clear that even very small geometric distortions may impair the watermark detection [5][6].

Robustness against geometric distortion is a difficult issue in watermarking. There are two different types of solutions to geometrical attacks, non-blind and blind [7]. Though the blind solutions have wider applications and are more challenging, the non-blind solutions find applications such as covert communications and etc. in which the original image/video is available. The non-blind solution proposed by Davoine et al. [8] is to split the original (or the non-geometrically distorted marked) image into a set of triangular patches. This mesh then serves as the reference mesh and be kept in memory for a pre-processing step of mark signal retrieval. As emphasized by the

F. Petitcolas and H.J. Kim (Eds.): IWDW 2002, LNCS 2613, pp. 212–223, 2003.
© Springer-Verlag Berlin Heidelberg 2003

authors, however, this kind mesh based compensation is only efficient in cases involving minor deformations. Johnson et al. [9] proposed to recognize distorted images using salient *image points* (in fact, 5x5 or 11x11 rectangular regions) first, then using the original image to fine-tune image parameters based on *normal flow* (displacement field). But its computational complexity is not reported. In [10], a set of three or more dispersed reference points is established in both the original and marked images. An exhaustive searching for the best matching between these reference points is conducted to determine the approximate horizontal and vertical position distortion of every pixel in the marked image, thus restoring the geometrically distorted stego-image. One example is reported, from which, however, the information about the specific StirMark test functions applied and computational complexity is not available. In this paper, a non-blind solution to resist a quite large range of geometric distortions is proposed that can be rather accurate and fast.

The watermarking in DWT domain has drawn extensive attention because of DWT's merits. Since the DWT coefficients are not invariant under geometric distortion, the existing watermarking in the DWT domain cannot resist geometric transforms.

By introducing a distance (dissimilarity) measure between the attacked image and the unattacked one, the proposed watermarking algorithm in the DWT domain can resist geometric attacks. It incorporates error correcting coding, 2-D interleaving, resynchronization based on the distance measure. The generated watermark, containing 536 information bits, is robust to additive noise and most test functions in StirMark 3.1.

The rest of this paper is structured as follows. In section 2, we describe the watermark embedding using BCH coding and 2-D interleaving[11]. Section 3 describes the extraction algorithm, and the proposed resynchronization using a fast searching algorithm. The experimental results can be found in section 4.The last section is devoted to conclusions.

2 Watermark Embedding Using BCH Codes and 2-D Interleaving

Meaningful watermark, CS, consists of a character string with length L, i. e. CS={CS_i; $0<i<L$}, where CS_i is a character. The data hiding procedure is demonstrated in Fig. 1. According to Cox [1], watermark should be embedded into the DC and low frequency AC coefficients in DCT domain due to their larger perceptual capacity. This embedding strategy has now been well accepted. Huang et al. [12] extend this idea, proposed to embed image watermarks in DC components. In DWT domain, the low frequency subband (LL) is the best approximation to the original image, and most energy of the image is concentrated in LL whereas the high frequency subbands are just the detailed information of the image. Watermark can be regarded as a weak signal (watermark) embedded into the strong background (an original image). If the contrast ratio of the embedded signal is lower than threshold, the perceptual distortion will not be perceived. According to the law of Weber, contrast ratio threshold is proportional to the amplitude of background signal. Since the low frequency coefficients have much larger magnitude than that of high frequency coefficients, they have larger perceptual capacity, and thus allow a stronger watermark to be embedded

without perceptual distortion. We therefore propose to embed watermark into LL subband coefficients.

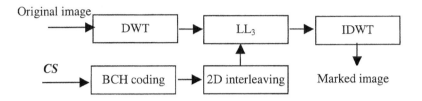

Fig. 1. Information embedding algorithm

To lower detection errors, watermark signal is coded with a BCH $(n,8)$ code. We choose n to be 61. The Hamming distance between two different codewords in the BCH $(61,8)$ code is 27. The code can correct any error as large as 13 bits in a codeword. Each character of the watermark, CS_i, is mapped into a BCH codeword as follows:

$$CS_i \xrightarrow{\ BCH\ coding\ } W_i\{w_{ij}; w_{ij} \in \{0,1\}, 0 \leq j < n, 0 \leq i < L\} \tag{1}$$

where L is the total number of the characters.

To enhance the robustness of watermarking against bursts of errors, 2-D interleaving is applied to the watermark. Bursts of errors do occur when a watermarked image is cropped or jitter attacked to name a few. 2-D interleaving can spread bursts of errors among different codewords [11]. With a simple random error-correction code such as the BCH (61,8), the spread error bits within a codeword may be less than 13 bits so that the bursts of errors can be corrected. The binary string W, consisting of all W_i, is arranged into a 2-D 64x64 array. By exploiting 2-D interleaving technique [11], we obtain an interleaved 2-D array. Scanning this array, say, row by row, we convert the interleaved 2-D array into a 1-D array, X.

First we perform 3-level DWT on the original image. The DWT coefficients in the LL_3 subband are scanned in the same fashion as above to form a 1-D array C. We adopt Equation (2) to embed the binary data X into C to obtain C' [13]. Here $C(i), C'(i)$ denotes the ith element in C, and C', respectively, $0 \leq i < 4096$. In our

$$\begin{cases} C'(i) = C(i) - (C(i) \bmod \alpha) + \dfrac{3}{4}\alpha, & if\ x_i = 1 \quad and \quad (C(i) \bmod \alpha) \geq \dfrac{1}{4}\alpha \\[2mm] C'(i) = \left[C(i) - \dfrac{1}{4}\alpha\right] - \left[(C(i) - \dfrac{1}{4}\alpha) \bmod \alpha\right] + \dfrac{3}{4}\alpha, if\ x_i = 1 \quad and \quad (C(i) \bmod \alpha) < \dfrac{1}{4}\alpha \\[2mm] C'(i) = C(i) - (C(i) \bmod \alpha) + \dfrac{1}{4}\alpha, & if\ x_i = 0 \quad and \quad (C(i) \bmod \alpha) \leq \dfrac{3}{4}\alpha \\[2mm] C'(i) = \left[C(i) + \dfrac{1}{2}\alpha\right] - \left[(C(i) + \dfrac{1}{2}\alpha) \bmod \alpha\right] + \dfrac{1}{4}\alpha, if\ x_i = 0 \quad and \quad (C(i) \bmod \alpha) > \dfrac{3}{4}\alpha \end{cases} \tag{2}$$

experiment, they are all larger than 0. For the watermark to be robust, α should be maximized under the constraint of invisibility. Note that the difference between $C(i)$ and $C'(i)$ is between -0.5α and $+0.5\alpha$. Performing inverse DWT on the modified image, we obtain a watermarked image.

3 Watermark Extraction Based on Resynchronization

It is known that geometric distortion damages geometric synchronization of hidden data that is necessary in watermark extraction. To resynchronize hidden data, we propose to perform an anti-attack operation to remove the geometric distortion on the watermarked image by searching for the minimum distance (best matching) between the attacked, stego-image and a reference image. The reference image can be an uncorrupted marked image or the original image. Fig.2 shows the data detection procedure in the paper.

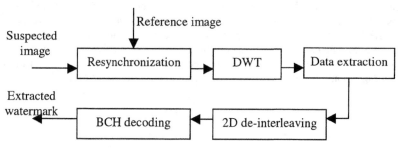

Fig. 2. Information extraction algorithm

3.1 Resynchronization Based on Minimum Distance Searching

The distance d between an image $f(x, y)$ and another image $f'(x, y)$ (both are m×n 2-D array) is defined to be the mean absolute difference of gray values:

$$d = (\sum_{x=1}^{m} \sum_{y=1}^{n} |f(x, y) - f'(x, y)|) / (m \times n) \qquad (3)$$

When we compute the distance between $f(x, y)$ and $f'(x, y)$, we can just use a portion instead of a whole image in practice in order to save computation. The stego-image may be subject to various types of geometrical distortion: RST, shearing and etc. The RST is a combination of rotation, scaling and translation. Consider an image $f(x, y)$ and a rotated, scaled, and translated version of this image, $f'(x, y)$. Then we can write [6]:

$$f'(x, y) = f(\sigma(x\cos\theta + y\sin\theta) - x\_offset, \quad \sigma(-x\sin\theta + y\cos\theta) - y\_offset) \qquad (4)$$

where the RST parameters are θ, σ, and (x_offset, y_offset), respectively. With these parameters determined, the RST distortion can be inverted, or in other words, $f'(x, y)$ can be registered to $f(x, y)$. Ideally at the point of registration, $f'(x, y) = f(x, y)$, the distance reaches the minimum. In practice, at the point of registration, $f'(x, y)$ may be slightly different from the $f(x, y)$ due to image noise, e. g., additive noise, image compression or interpolation, the distance is then a cumulative measure of the various image noise. At any other unregistered point, the distance can be considered as the sum of image noise, and registration noise due to the fact that the pictures are out of registration. It is reasonable to assume that the distance is minimal at the point of registration. As depicted in Fig. 3, which is a surface of the distance between the to-be-checked image (rotation_scale_10.00, refer to Table 1) and the non-distorted image. It is observed from the figure that the minimum distance is reached when the to-be-checked image is rescaled to the size of 442×442, re-rotated counter-clockwise by $\theta = 10°$, and translated with $xo=0$, $yo=0$. So once the minimum distance is found, we can determine the RST parameters. Similarly, shearing and general linear transformation, which both are other geometric test functions in StirMark, can be inverted. Because the geometric distortion is unknown in advance, we apply both operations to the attacked stego-image sequentially and search for the minimum distance to determine which operation among inverse RST and inverse shearing operation should be applied to the attacked image and what parameters of the inverse operation should be chosen in order to regain geometric synchronization.

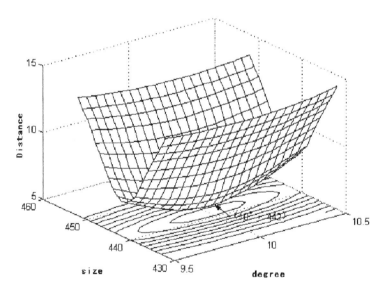

Fig. 3. The distance surface formed by the searching of minimum distance

3.2 Multiresolution Searching for the Resynchronization Parameters

Among the above-mentioned two anti-attack operations, the anti-RST is much more time consuming since it has a 4-dimensional searching space (*size*, θ, *x_offset*, *y_offset*), where *size* is the size of the scaled image (assuming equal scaling along x and y directions) and hence a scaling related parameter, while the anti-shearing operation has a 2-dimensional searching space (shift in X and Y directions). So in what follows, we mainly discuss the searching process of the anti-RST operation. In the whole searching algorithm, we use the bi-linear interpolation.

Anti-RST operation. As shown in Fig.3, the distance function increases monotonically from the point of minimum distance in a region surrounding the point (Fig.3). We decrease the computation drastically using multi-resolution matching and coarse-fine searching. The anti-RST operation is divided into five phases: coarse searching, medium_1 searching, medium_2 searching, fine_1 searching and fine_2 searching. Without loss of generality, we choose the size of the original image to be 512x512. We choose the searching range of *size* to be 512 ~ 256 (the corrupted image is assumed to be cropped less than 75%). The searching range of translations parameters *x_offset*, *y_offset* is determined by the above *size*. For example, if *size* is N, the searching range of *x_offset* or *y_offset* is $-(512-N)/2 ~ + (512-N)/2$. So we choose the maximum searching range of *x_offset* or *y_offset* to be $-128~+128$, and the searching range of rotation angle θ to be $-90°~+90°$. After fine_1 searching, we obtain the final parameters of translation– *x_offset*, *y_offset*. After fine_2 searching, we obtain the final parameters of scaling and rotation – *size*, θ.

Coarse searching at resolution of 64x64. We convert the non-distorted image to the 64x64 resolution first. Then we obtain a 22x22 sub-image, using gray-level interpolation via pixel-filling (also referred to as backward mapping) [14] algorithm from the to-be-checked image, which has been rescaled to the size of *size×size* and re-rotated by an angle θ. It is reasonable to consider that the search with such a large enough sub-image will not miss any matching candidate since the 22×22 sub-image at the 64×64 resolution corresponds to a 176×176 sub-image in the 512×512 image. We then compute its distance to a 22×22 sub-image in the non-distorted image at 64×64 resolution, whose center (reference point) shifts from the center of the non-distorted image by *x_offset* and *y_offset*. There are a lot of fast matching algorithms for the best matching available in literature. For simplicity, however, the full searching is adopted in our algorithm. It contains four nesting cycles (*size*, θ, *x_offset*, *y_offset*), where the cycle of changing *size* is the outermost cycle and the one of changing *y_offset* is the innermost one. In coarse searching, the searching range of *size* is 64~32, *size* is changed by 8 pixels in each step. The rotation angle θ is changed by 5°each step, the searching range of re-rotation angle is -90°~+90°. The maximum searching range of *x_offset* or *y_offset* is $-16~+16$, step size is 1 pixel. In our experiment, the coarse searching on many images converges to the right solution no matter where the searching starts. After coarse searching, the parameters $size_{coarse}$, θ_{coarse}, x_offset_{coarse}, y_offset_{coarse} are determined. This candidate of the best matching is then propagated to medium-1 level of 128×128. A search with smaller ranges and steps is conducted in medium-1 level. This procedure continues finally to fine-2 level.

Medium_1 searching at resolution of 128×128. *size* is changed by 2 pixels wide each step and the searching range of *size* is $(size_{coarse} -8)\times2~(size_{coarse} +8)\times2$ (because we adopt full searching, the following searching is similar). The rotation angle θ is changed by 1°each step, the searching range of re-rotation angle is $(\theta_{coarse}$ -5°)~$(\theta_{coarse}$ +5°). The searching range of x_offset or y_offset is $(x\_offset_{coarse}-2) \times 2 \sim (x\_offset_{coarse}+2) \times 2$, $(y\_offset_{coarse}-2) \times 2 \sim (y\_offset_{coarse}+2) \times 2$ respectively, step-length is 1 pixel wide. After medium_1 searching, $x\_offset_{medium1}$, $y\_offset_{medium1}$, $size_{medium1}$, $\theta_{medium1}$ can be determined. We use the sub-image of size $[0.7(2size_{coarse}-16)]\times[0.7(2size_{coarse}-16)]$ (we adopt 0.7 to decrease the computation but also assure the reliability of the algorithm) to compute the distance in medium_1 searching.

Medium_2 searching at resolution of 256x256. *size* is changed by 1 pixel wide each step and the searching range of *size* is $(size_{medium1}-1) \times 2 \sim (size_{medium1}+1) \times 2$. The rotation angle θ is changed by 0.5°each step, the searching range of re-rotation angle is $(\theta_{medium1}-1°) \sim (\theta_{medium1}+1°)$. The searching range and step-length of x_offset or y_offset are similar to the above. After medium_2 searching, $x\_offset_{medium2}$, $y\_offset_{medium2}$, $size_{medium2}$, $\theta_{medium2}$ can be determined.

Fine_1 searching at resolution of 512x512. *size* is changed by 1 pixel each step and the searching range of *size* is $(size_{medium2} -1) \times 2 \sim (size_{medium2} +1) \times 2$. The rotation angle θ is changed by 0.2°each step, the searching range of re-rotation angle is $\theta_{medium2} -0.4° \sim \theta_{medium2} +0.4°$. The searching range and step-length of x_offset or y_offset are similar to the above. After fine_1 searching, we obtain $size_{fine1}$, θ_{fine1} and translation parameters x_offset, y_offset.

Fine_2 searching at resolution of 512x512. Fine_2 searching contains only 2 nesting cycles *(size, θ)*. *size* is changed by 1 pixel each step and the searching range of *size* is $(size_{fine1} -1) \sim (size_{fine1} +1)$. The rotation angle θ is changed by 0.02°each step, the searching range of re-rotation angle is $\theta_{fine1} -0.10° \sim \theta_{fine1} +0.10°$. Through the fine_2 searching, we can determine scaling and rotation parameters of *size*, and θ. We use the sub-image of size $(0.9size_{fine1}) \times (0.9size_{fine1})$ to compute the distance in fine_2 searching.

Anti-shearing operation. One way to recover the distortion of shearing and/or general linear transformation is to perform the linear transform as Equation (5) on the suspected image.

$$\begin{bmatrix} x \\ y \end{bmatrix} \rightarrow B \begin{bmatrix} x \\ y \end{bmatrix} = \begin{bmatrix} a & b \\ c & d \end{bmatrix} \begin{bmatrix} x \\ y \end{bmatrix}, \tag{5}$$

where $B = \begin{bmatrix} a & b \\ c & d \end{bmatrix}$ denotes the linear transformation matrix. By changing the parameters (a, b, c, d) in a constrained range, search for the minimum distance at multi-resolution. It has a 4-dimensional searching space (a, b, c, d). We propose to perform anti-shearing operation only in a 2-dimensional searching space. Anti-shearing operation includes: 1). By changing the anti-shearing parameters s_x, s_y (the maximum shift in X and Y direction) in a constrained range, we perform the following transform (Equation 6) operations on the suspected image $(M_x \times N_y)$ and search for the minimum distance between the operated image and the reference image. (2) Flip the suspected image and reference image in up/down direction. Similar to the step given above, search for the minimum distance between the flipped and operated image and the flipped reference image. We perform the above searching at multi-resolution. When the distance reaches the minimum, the parameters for resynchronization can be determined.

$$
\begin{bmatrix} x \\ y \end{bmatrix} \rightarrow \begin{bmatrix} \dfrac{511}{N_s + s_x - 1} & 0 \\ 0 & \dfrac{511}{M_s + s_y - 1} \end{bmatrix} \begin{bmatrix} 1 & \dfrac{s_x}{M_s + s_y - 1} \\ \dfrac{s_y}{N_s + s_x - 1} & 1 \end{bmatrix} \begin{bmatrix} x \\ y \end{bmatrix} \tag{6}
$$

3.3 The Computational Aspects and Reliability of the Searching Algorithm

Because the full searching is started in the 64x64 level with a large subimage of 22x22 at the level, the algorithm will not miss possible candidate. Our numerous experiment support this observation. Because the full search in the coarse level is about $(1/8)^4 = 1/4096$ of equivalent search in the finest level, and the search in the remaining levels with smaller search ranges and step sizes, the computation has been reduced drastically. Searching algorithm takes less than 10 seconds on a Pentium PC of 1.4 GHz. In our many tests, the proposed algorithm can recognize the joint RST (with cropping) or shearing distorted images and successfully invert the geometrical distortion (refer to Fig. 5). If the geometrically distorted image is corrupted by JPEG compression with quality factor above 10 and/or additive noise, the resynchronization parameters can also be recovered correctly. It is noted that this searching approach can be used with various system such as the watermarking in DCT domain.

3.4 Blind Data Extraction

First, perform 3-level DWT on the resynchronized suspect marked image. The coefficients of the LL_3 subband are scanned and turned into a 1-D array, which is denoted by C^*. Then we can extract the hidden binary data X^* according to the following formula:

$$
\begin{cases} x^*_i = 1 & if \quad (c^*_i \bmod \alpha) \geq \dfrac{\alpha}{2} \\ x^*_i = 0 & otherwise \end{cases} \tag{7}
$$

Next we perform 2-D De-interleaving, which is the inverse process of 2-D interleaving [11], to X^* to obtain the binary sequence W^*. By partitioning W^* into subsequences with size of $n=61$, we obtain the extracted signals $W^*_i = \{w^*_{ij}, 0 \leq j < n, 0 \leq i < L\}$. Finally, by searching for a codeword that is closest to w^*_i in BCH codebook in the sense of Hamming distance, we can decide the possibly embedded byte CS^*_i.

4   Experimental Results

We have tested the proposed algorithm on various images. The results on 512x512x8 Lena and Baboon images are reported here. In our work, we choose the Daubechies 9/7 biorthorgonal wavelet filter in DWT on image, and we choose α to be 56 for Lena, 64 for Baboon. A string of 67 characters (536 bits) are embedded into the images. The PSNRs of the marked image are 40.2 dB and 39.0 dB for Lena and Baboon respectively (Fig. 4). The watermarks are perceptually invisible. The embedding algorithm takes less than 2s while the whole watermark detection takes about 10s on a Pentium 1.4GHz. This is sufficiently fast for commercial applications. Table 1 shows some tested results with our proposed algorithm on Lena and Baboon using StirMark 3.1. In Table 1, the reported bit error rate (BER) is calculated after the ECC. That is, if a codeword is decoded correctly then all bits within the codeword are considered not in error. The watermark can be error-freely recovered from the marked images when they are attacked by shearing, general linear transform, aspect ratio changes, scaling, Gaussian filtering, jitter attack etc. We can see that the proposed watermarking algorithm can effectively resist the attacks such as JPEG compression, cropping, rotation (auto-crop, auto-scale), sharpening. According to [5], most of simple spread-spectrum based marking schemes cannot resist jitter attack. It is noted that our algorithm can recover embedded characters error-freely for a JPEG compression quality factor of 15%. While the marked image is attacked by a combination of rotation, scaling, cropping, the watermark can still be recovered error-freely if the rotation angle is less than 15°, and the maximum BER is only 0.024 for rotation angle larger than 15° for Baboon. Fig. 5 shows the image undergoes JPEG_50 in addition to a combination of rotation (2°), scaling, cropping and translation (RST), the geometric distortion can still be recovered, the hidden data can be decoded successfully. Note that in [15], the embedded information is just 60 bits in an image of 512x512 or 1024x1024, while the present scheme embeds 536 information bits in an image of 512x512.

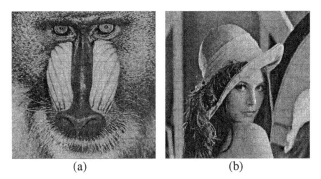

(a)   (b)

Fig. 4. (a) Watermarked Baboon image (39.0 dB, α=64) and (b) Lena (40.2dB, α=56)

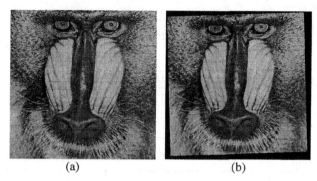

(a)	(b)

Fig. 5. Resynchronization. (a) A distorted version of Fig.4a. JPEG_50 + rotation + cropping + translation + scaling. (b) The recovered image. The hidden data (67 characters) can be recovered with no error

5 Conclusions

In this paper, we propose an algorithm for hiding invisible and robust meaningful watermark in the DWT domain. The main contributions are as follows: (1) Introduction of the distance measure between images, based on which geometric distortion can be inverted, so resynchronization of the hidden watermark can be achieved. By doing so, watermarking algorithms in the DWT domain can resist RST, shearing, general linear transformation etc. (2) A fast automatic resynchronization scheme has been developed. It incorporates multi-resolution matching and coarse-fine searching, achieving low computation complexity. The scheme can be applied to watermarking in DCT domain to resist to geometric attacks as well. (3) Compared with the existing non-blind marking schemes [8], [9], the major advantage of the proposed scheme is that it can cope with large amount of geometric distortion with satisfactory accuracy and it can be implemented very fast. In addition, our proposed scheme can achieve high detection accuracy. For instance, our anti-RST recovers a rotation of 0.02°. (4) Apply BCH codes to reduce the detection error rate. (5) Apply 2-D interleaving technique to the watermark in DWT domain to reduce the bursts of errors caused by some attacks such as cropping, jitter and shearing.

The major progress made in this paper is that the watermarking is robust against geometric distortion and common signal processing, such as JPEG compression, Gaussian filtering etc, due to the proposed fast resynchronization scheme. However, robustness of the present watermark against median filtering, FMLR and randomization-and-bending remains to be improved. According to our experiment, robustness against median filtering and FMLR can be improved by increasing the strength of the watermark (via adaptively embedding the watermark [16]) and soft decoding. The future works for the improvement will be needed.

Table 1. Test Results with StirMark 3.1

StirMark functions	Lena (BER)	Baboon (BER)
17(5)_rows_5(17)_cols_removed (jitter)	0	0
ratio_x_1.00_y_1.20, ratio_x_1.20_y_1.00	0	0
ratio_x_0.80_y_1.00, ratio_x_1.00_y_0.80	0	0
scale_0.50, scale_2.00	0	0
cropping_10, cropping_25	0	0
sharpening_3_3	0	0.017
2x2_median_filter	0.021	0.362
3x3_median_filter	0.065	0.472
FMLR	0.412	0
Gaussian filtering_3_3	0	0
JPEG_15,20,25,30,40,50,60,70,80,90	0	0
linear_1.007_.010_.010_1.012,	0	0
linear_1.013_.008_.011_1.008	0	0
linear_1.01_.013_.009_1.012	0	0
shearing_x_1.0_y_0.0, shearing_x_0.0_y_1.0	0	0
shearing_x_0.0_y_5.0, shearing_x_5.0_y_0.0	0	0
shearing_x_1.0_y_1.0, shearing_x_5.0_y_5.0	0	0
rotation_15°,10°,5°,±2°,±1°,±0.5°,±0.25°,90°	0	0
rotation_scale_15°,10°,5°,±2°,±1°,±0.5°,±0.25°	0	0
rotation_ 30° , rotation_scale_30°	0.047	0.017
rotation_ 45°, rotation_scale_45°	0.132	0.024
stirmark_random_bend	0.459	0.479

Acknowledgments. Authors appreciate, respectively, the support received from NSF of China (69975011, 60172067, 60133020), NSF of Guangdong (980442), Key Project of Science and Technology of National Education Ministry, China, Key Project of Science and Technology of Guangzhou, China, New Jersey Commission of Science and Technology via NJCMR, New Jersey Commission of High Education via NJ-ITOWER, and NSF via IUCRC.

References

1.   Cox, J., Killian, J., Leighton, F. T., Shamoon, T.: Secure spread spectrum watermarking for multimedia. IEEE Transactions on Image Processing, 6(12) (1997) 1673–1687
2.   O'Rauanaidh, J. J. K., and Pun, T.: Rotation, scale and translation invariant spread spectrum digital image watermarking. Signal Processing, 66(3) (1998) 303–317
3.   Tsai, M., Yuang, K. and Chen, Y.: Joint wavelet and spatial transformation for digital watermarking. IEEE Transactions on Consumer Electronics, 46(1) (2000) 241–245

4. Huang, J. and Shi, Y. Q.: Embedding gray level images. Proc. of IEEE Int. Sym. on Circuits and Systems, Vol. V, (2001) 239–242
5. Petitcolas, F. A. P., Anderson, R. J. and Kuhn, M. G.: Attacks on copyright marking systems, Proc.2nd Information Hiding Workshop, Portland (1998)
6. Lin, C. -Y., Wu, M., Bloom, J. A., Cox, I. J., Miller, M. L. and Lui, Y. -M.: Rotation, scale, and translation resilient watermarking for images. IEEE Transactions on Image Processing. 10(5) (2001) 767–782
7. Dugelay, J.-L. and Petitcolas, F. A. P.: Possible counter-attackers against random geometric distortions. Proc. SPIE Security and Watermarking of Multimedia Contents II, Vol. 3971, California, USA (2000)
8. Davoine, F., Bas, P., Hébert, P.-A. and Chassery, J.-M.: Watermarking et résistance aux déformations géométriques". In J.-L. Dugelay, ed., Cinquièmes journées d'études et d'échanges sur la compression et la représentation des signaux audiovisuals (CORESA'99), Sophia-Antipolis, France (1999), Centre de recherche et développement de France Télécom (Cnet), EURÉCOM, Conseil général des Alpes-Maritimes and Télécom Valley
9. Johnson, N. F., Duric, Z. and Jajodia, S: Recovery of watermarks from distorted images. In A. Pfitzmann, ed., preliminary proceedings of the third international information hiding workshop, Dresden, Germany, (1999) 361–375
10. Braudaway, G. W. and Minter, F.: Automatic recovery of invisible image watermarks from geometrically distorted images. Proc. SPIE Security and Watermarking of Multimedia Contents II, Vol.3971, CA, USA (2000)
11. Elmasry, G. F., Shi, Y. Q.: 2-D interleaving for enhancing the robustness of watermark signals embedded in still image. Proc. of IEEE Int. Conf. on Multimedia and Expo. , (2000)
12. Huang, J., Shi, Y. Q. and Shi, Y.: Embedding image watermarks in DC components. IEEE Transaction on Circuits and Systems for Video Technology, 10(6) (2000) 974–979
13. Tsai, M., Yuang, K. and Chen, Y.: Joint wavelet and spatial transformation for digital watermarking. IEEE Transactions on Consumer Electronics, 46(1) (2000) 241–245
14. Castleman, K. R.: Digital image processing. prentice-hall (1997)
15. Pereira, S. and Pun, T.: Robust template matching for affine resistant image watermark. IEEE Transactions on Image Processing, 9(6) (2000) 1125–1129
16. Huang, J. and Shi, Y. Q.: An adaptive image watermarking scheme based on visual masking, Electronics Letters, 34(8) (1998) 748–750

Spatial Frequency Band Division in Human Visual System Based Watermarking

Yong Ju Jung, Minsoo Hahn, and Yong Man Ro

Multimedia Information and Communication Group, Information and Communications
University (ICU), P.O.Box 77. Yusong, Taejon, 305-600, Korea
{yjjung, mshahn, yro}@icu.ac.kr

Abstract. A good watermark is known to be perceptually invisible, undetectable without key and robust to spatial/temporal data modification. In this paper, we utilize the characteristics of the human visual system (HVS) for watermarking. In HVS, the response of visual cortex decomposes the image spectra into perceptual channels that are octave bands in spatial frequency. Based on the octave-bands division, same numbers of bits of the watermark are inserted into each channel. Experimental results show that the proposed method based on HVS method gives strong robustness to the attacks compared with conventional DCT, wavelet and DFT watermarking methods.

1 Introduction

For a good watermarking technology, watermark data suppose to be hidden undetectably by human eyes while they are remained in spite of the damages of the data, such as trials to remove the watermark. To do so, it is important to choose appropriate portions of an image for watermarking insertion, which have significant energy of the image. In general, there are two kinds of embedding and detection technologies of watermark. Those are spatial domain and frequency domain watermarking techniques. In the watermarking technologies in the frequency domain, image data are transformed using various transformations such as Discrete Cosine Transform (DCT) [1,2], wavelet transform [3], Fourier-Mellin transform and Discrete Fourier Transform (DFT) [4,5]. Subsequently a watermark is embedded into visually insensible area. The watermarking methods without original image in the frequency domain are widely used but they are known to be not robust to all attacks.

In this paper, we propose a watermark embedding method in DFT domain. The original image is not required for watermark detection procedure. In the proposed method, watermark is embedded into significant areas according to the amount of information which the areas could contain. The areas are divided by HVS band in DFT domain. In the proposed method, robustness of watermark is superior to that in the conventional methods in terms of external attacks such as compression, filtering, cropping and shifting.

The paper is organized as follows. In section 2, we explain HVS-based frequency layout for the watermark embedding, propose a new watermark embedding and

F. Petitcolas and H.J. Kim (Eds.): IWDW 2002, LNCS 2613, pp. 224–234, 2003.
© Springer-Verlag Berlin Heidelberg 2003

detection method. In section 3, we show experimental results and compare proposed method with existing methods. Finally, we draw conclusion in section 4.

2 Theory

In this paper, we propose a DFT based watermarking technique using the human visual system. In the following section, the HVS-based frequency layout is designed so that a watermark is to be embedded.

2.1 HVS-Based Frequency Layout for the Watermark Embedding

Psychophysical experiments have shown that the response of visual cortex is turned to the band-limited portion of the frequency domain. It gives evidence that the brain decomposes the spectra into perceptual channels that are bands in spatial frequency [6]. As far as spatial vision is concerned, best-adopted sub-band representation of HVS is a division of spatial frequency domain with octave-band division in radial axis and equal-width division in orientation axis (or angular axis). Figure 1 shows an example of band division in the radial direction. In the radial direction, the center frequencies of channels are spaced with octave scale such as $\omega_s = \omega_1 \cdot 2^{-(s-1)}$, $s \in \{1,2,3,4,5\}$ where s is a radial index and ω_1 is the highest center frequency. Two-dimensional HVS-based frequency layout can be represented as shown in Figure 2.

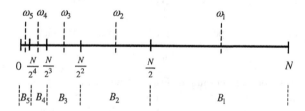

Fig. 1. Channel division in radial direction, where B_s is each band and $\omega_s = \omega_1 \cdot 2^{-(s-1)}$, $s \in \{1,2,3,4,5\}$ where s is a radial index and ω_1 is the highest center frequency.

As shown in Figure 2, HVS-based channels consist of dense channels in low frequency domain and relatively broad channels in high frequency. Namely, the human visual feature is sensitive to the change of low frequency components, and it is insensitive to the change of high frequency components. Based on these features of channel, watermark is embedded in this paper.

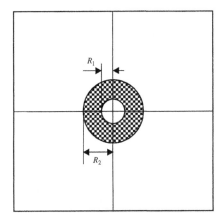 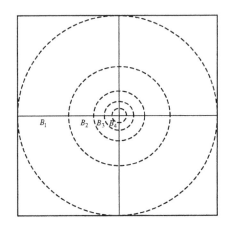

Fig. 2. Conventional DFT domain embedding layout (*left*), HVS-based frequency band layout, where B_s is the sth band (*right*).

2.2 A Watermark Embedding Method in the HVS Layout

In this paper, watermark is embedded in DFT domain which is divided according to the HVS layout, as shown in Figure 2. Let $I(x,y)$ be original image with size of N x M. The Fourier transform of $I(x,y)$ can be written as

$$F(u,v) = \frac{1}{MN} \sum_{x=0}^{M-1} \sum_{y=0}^{N-1} I(x,y) \exp[-j2\pi(ux/M + vy/N)] \cdot \qquad (1)$$

$F(u,v)$ in Eq. (1) has the property of conjugate symmetry such as

$$F(u,v) = F^*(-u,-v), \qquad (2)$$

where $F^*(u,v)$ is complex conjugate $F(u,v)$. Due to this property, the watermark is embedded symmetrically in the DFT domain. The watermark is a 2-D circularly symmetric sequence consisting of values 1 or –1. This sequence is a pseudo-noise (PN) sequence which is used to modulate transmitted data into noise-like wide band signals in spread spectrum communication systems so they blend into the background [7]. PN-sequences are periodic noise-like binary sequences generated by feedback shift register of fixed length [7]. They also are generated with equal probability of 1 and –1 and provide an easy way to generate a unique code for an author's identification [8].

Let $M(u,v)$ be the magnitude of the Fourier transform of $I(x,y)$ and B_s be each band where s is a radial index, *i.e.,* $s \in \{1,2,3,4,5\}$. Let also $W(u,v)$ be a watermark and $M'(u,v)$ be the modified magnitude by embedding the watermark. The proposed embedding algorithm is shown in Figure 3. In the band selection module in Figure 3, the positions where watermark is embedded are determined. Each band has octave width in the radial direction. The watermark sequence is divided equally so that same length (L) of watermark is embedded into the selected bands. So, the length of watermark embedded into i^{th} band and j^{th} band is equal and satisfies the following condition

$$L_{B_i} = L_{B_j},$$ (3)

where L_{B_i} is the length of the watermark sequence inserted in the ith band. And the total length of the inserted watermark is

$$L_{total} = SL_{B_i} = SL_{B_j},$$ (4)

where S is the number of selected bands in the band selection module. In order to preserve complex conjugate symmetry as mentioned in Eq. (2), the watermark must be

$$W(u,v) = W(M-u, N-v).$$ (5)

The watermark is embedded into the random positions of the selected bands by generating a PN sequence. Therefore, the coefficients of the watermarked magnitude M' can be written as

$$M'(u,v) = M(u,v) + aW(u,v),$$ (6)

where a is a weighting factor which determines the strength of the watermark. The weighting factor is adjusted at each band so that one can compromise between the degradation of image fidelity and the robustness of watermark effectively.

The watermarked image $I'(x, y)$ is obtained from the inverse Fourier transform with $M'(u,v)$:

$$I'(x, y) = IDFT(M', P),$$ (7)

where P is the phase of $I(x,y)$.

In conventional DFT method, the watermark is embedded in a ring covering the middle frequencies as shown in Figure 2 [5]:

$$W(r,\theta) = \left\{ \begin{array}{l} 0, \ if \ r < R_1 \ and \ r > R_2 \\ \pm 1, \ if \ R_1 < r < R_2 \end{array} \right\},$$ (8)

where $r = \sqrt{u^2 + v^2}, \theta = \arctan(v/u)$.

On the other hand, in proposed method, the watermark is inserted into the octave bands such that same number of bits of the watermark is assigned in each band. In doing so, more bits of the watermark are embedded into small area of bands. Namely stronger watermark signals are embedded into significant portions, which locate in low-middle frequency region in the frequency domain. This watermark insertion scheme gives the robustness to attacks because the watermark of significant portion can resist against strong attack of image.

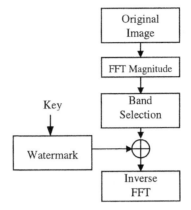

Fig. 3. Watermark embedding algorithm.

2.3   A Watermark Detection Method

The detection process is the inverse order of the watermark insertion process and is based on correlation method. In the proposed method, the original image is not required in the watermark detection procedure. The detection procedure is shown in Figure 4.

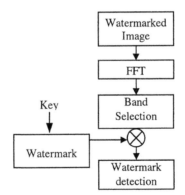

Fig. 4. Watermark detection algorithm.

The correlation c between the watermarked coefficients M' in the frequency bands and the possible watermark W can be used to detect the presence of the watermark. The correlation c can be written as

$$c = \frac{1}{L_{total}} \sum_{u=1}^{N} \sum_{v=1}^{N} W(u,v) M'(u,v), \qquad (9)$$

where L_{total} is the total length of inserted watermark.

3 Experiments

Experiments have been carried out to verify the robustness of the proposed method in this paper. In experiments, A LENA image with size of 512x512 has been used. So parameter of N was 512.

In our experiments we have inserted the watermark in two bands (B_2 and B_3 in Figure 2). Note that a watermark can be inserted in any other bands by adjusting the weighting factors. We generated watermarking inserting scheme as shown in Figure 3. Same number of bits of watermark was inserted in both inner and outer bands in the frequency domain in Figure 2. The weighting factor a was set to 0.3. This parameter was set so that the image quality was not affected by the watermark.

To test the performance of watermarking, we measured correlation between inserted watermark and possible watermarks. Figure 5 shows the response of the watermark detection for 100 randomly generated watermarks. As it is seen, only one watermark has high correlation value so that the watermark is authenticated. As shown in that figure, correlation value is high at the 20th watermark.

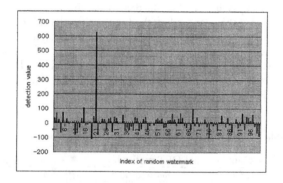

Fig. 5. Detection response (No attack).

We have also measured PSNR to check data loss due to embedding the watermark. Table 1 shows the detection peak value (correlation values) and PSNR with respect to the weighting factor (a). Note that the same number of watermark was inserted in inner band and outer band in the experiment. As shown in the table, for a of 0.3, the detection value and PSNR can be satisfied. The large value of a causes the degradation of the watermarked image.

Table 1. Correlation peak and PSNR vs. the weighting factor (No attack), where L = 18888.

weighting factor (a)	Peak	PSNR
0.1	227.80	50.04
0.2	429.79	46.16
0.3	628.95	43.24
0.4	827.25	40.95
0.5	1026.47	39.11

Table 2. Watermark performance vs. watermark length.

Watermark length	Lena(512x512)		
	PSNR	First peak	Second peak
1000	51.10	52.99	37.29
2000	50.94	59.70	-42.74
5000	49.80	148.70	62.92
10000	48.37	217.79	80.90
18888	46.16	429.79	107.29

Table 2 shows the detection value and PSNR with respect to the number of bits of inserted watermark.

As it is seen, the small number of bits of watermark gives the better resolution. But the detection value is reduced. Note that the watermark length is related with watermark strength. i.e., to improve the image quality (PSNR) watermark strength should be reduced thereby the robustness for the attack is also reduced. Based on the result in Table 2, the proposed algorithm shows more robust to attack than the conventional DFT algorithm [5], i.e., the detection value is larger.

We have compared the proposed method with other algorithm [5]. As the result of our simulation, Table 3 shows peak values of the conventional DFT and the proposed methods with the same quality of a watermarked image. As seen in Table 3, the proposed method shows higher peak values than conventional DFT method. This is because more bits of watermark are embedded into visually significant areas according to the HVS bands in DFT domain.

Table 3. Comparison between the proposed method and other method.

PSNR	Conventional DFT method		Proposed method	
	First peak	Second peak	First peak	Second peak
42dB	460	130	630	120

To verify the robustness of proposed method for various attacks, we performed noise addition, JPEG compression, cropping, median filtering, blurring, and sharpening. Table 4 shows top three peak of correlation value for various attacks.

As seen in Table 4, first peak values are high enough to detect the watermark, even though many attacks. The results in Table 4 show that the proposed method can detect the watermark from degraded images. Table 5 shows the detection value and PSNR with respect to various band selections.

In Figure 7 to Figure 11, degraded images and watermark detection responses are shown. The watermarked image are distorted such as JPEG compression (Figure 7) with a quality factor 5%, blurring (Figure 8), smoothing (Figure 9) with 3 x 3 median filter, sharpening (Figure 10), Gaussian noise addition (Figure 11). As seen in the right side of each figures, watermark is detected in all case though the watermarked images are degraded.

Table 4. Correlation peaks vs. various attacks, where scale factor a=0.3, L=18888.

Various attacks	Lena(512x512)		
	First Peak	Second peak	Third Peak
No attack	628.95	-106.95	105.11
Add noise	570.70	-96.42	-85.21
JPEG(5% quality)	559.63	103.80	-93.66
Center cropping (a=0.4)	232.04	-122.94	96.62
Median filtering (1 x 1)	513.95	-98.32	97.59
blurring	295.21	79.87	-77.52
Sharpening	795.55	-158.96	136.42

Table 5. Watermark performance vs. various band selections. (a=0.3)

Selected bands	Lena (512x512)		
	PSNR	First peak	Second peak
B_1, B_2	45.49	499	-41
B_2, B_3	43.24	628	-106
B_3, B_4	40.62	4449	1376
$B_1, B_2, and\ B_3$	42.92	626	-165
$B_2, B_3, and\ B_4$	40.50	390	142
$B_1, B_2, B_3, and\ B_4$	40.35	2181	791

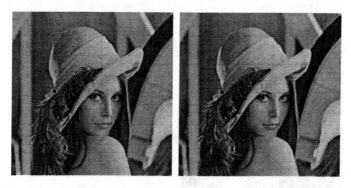

Fig. 6. Original image (Lena 512x512)(Left), Watermarked image (Right).

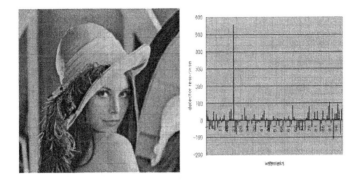

Fig. 7. JPEG compressed version of the watermarked image with 5% quality (*Left*), and the corresponding detection response (*Right*).

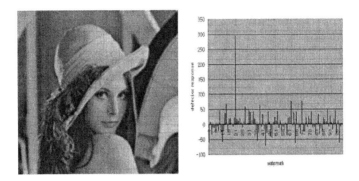

Fig. 8. Blurred watermarked image (*Left*), and the corresponding detection response (*Right*).

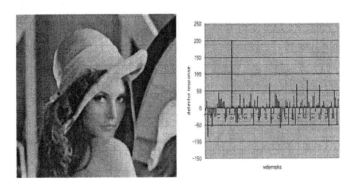

Fig. 9. Smoothed watermarked image with 3 x 3 median filter (*Left*), and the corresponding detection response (*Right*).

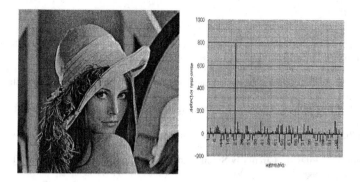

Fig. 10. Sharpened watermarked image (*Left*), and the corresponding detector response (*Right*).

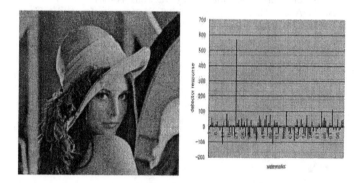

Fig. 11. Watermarked image after adding noise (*Left*), and the detector response (*Right*).

4   Conclusion

In this paper, a DFT based watermarking technique using the human visual system is proposed. Using this division of frequency channel that has been used for MPEG-7 texture descriptor recently, we propose a novel watermarking technique in which watermark is embedded at perceptually significant portions. The performance of the proposed algorithm was compared with other watermarking methods with the same test images. Experimental results show that the proposed HVS-based watermarking method is robust to various attacks, such as JPEG compression, filtering, cropping, multiple watermarking and so on. Although the watermarked images of both the conventional and our proposed method have the same quality in human vision, our method is more robust since watermark is embedded into significant areas according to the amount of information.

References

1. Cox, I. J., Kilian, J., Leighton, F. T., Shamoon, T.: Secure spread spectrum watermarking for multimedia. IEEE Trans. Image processing, Vol. 6. (1997) 1673–1687
2. Piva, A., Barni, M., Bartolini, F., Cappellini, V.: DCT-based watermark recovering without resorting to the uncorrupted original image. Proceedings of ICIP'97, Vol. I. Santa Barbara CA USA (1997) 520–523
3. Inoue, H., Miyazaki, A., Katsura, T.: An image watermarking method based on the wavelet transform. Proc. ICIP'99, Vol. 1. (1999) 296–300
4. Ruanaidh, J. O., Pun, T.: Rotation, scale and translation invariant digital image watermarking. Proceedings of ICIP'97 Vol. I. Atlanta USA (1997) 536–539
5. Solachidis, V., Pitas, I.: Circularly Symmetric Watermark Embedding in 2-D DFT Domain. IEEE Trans. Image Processing, Vol. 10. No. 11. (2001) 1741–1753
6. Daugman, J. G.: High Confidence Visual Recognition of Persons by a Test of Statistical Independence. IEEE Trans. Pattern Analysis and Machine Intelligence, Vol. 15. no.11. (1993)
7. Haykin, S.: Digital Communications, John Wiley and Sons. (1988)
8. Boney, L., Tewfik, A. H., Hamdy, K. N.: Digital Watermarks for Audio Signals. IEEE Proceedings of MULTIMEDIA'96, (1996) 473–480

Two-Step Detection Algorithm in a HVS-Based Blind Watermarking of Still Images

Yong C. Kim[1] and Byeong C. Choi[2]

[1] Dept. of ECE, Univ. of Seoul, Jeonnong, 90, Dongdaemun-gu, Seoul, Korea
yckim@uos.ac.kr
[2] ETRI, 161 Gajeon-dong, Yuseong-gu, Daejeon, Korea
corea@etri.re.kr

Abstract. In this paper, we propose a DCT-based blind watermarking system, with detection performed in a two-step algorithm. In embedding, each bit is inserted in a PN spreading pattern in 12 positions of DCT coefficients of an 8x8 block. The watermark gain, α, is optimized in robustness and invisibility. In detection process, a preliminary decision is obtained by correlation matching and then verified by choosing the more similar spreading pattern with the restored one. Most of bit errors are corrected in verificiation process. The poposed method has been tested for several test images, with attacks including lowpass/median filtering and JPEG compression, but excluding geometrical RST attacks. After verificiation, BER reduces to 0.5% with no attack. Even under heavy JPEG compression, BER stays lower than 9%. Compared with other methods, the proposed method is better in watermark detection and far exceeds others in watermark size.

1 Introduction

Recently, digital watermarking techniques emerge as effective means for protecting intellectual property. By embedding imperceptible digital signature, the owner can secure the property right, They are roughly divided into spatial-domain methods and transform-domain methods. Watermark data are embedded in a wide range of domain, in spatial, in the DCT, in the Fourier, in the fractal domain. Popularly used statistical models for DCT coefficients for images are Gaussian, Laplacian and generalized Gaussian[5,6].

Watermarking methods in early years have often relied on spread-spectrum technology. In the embedding process, watermark data are redundantly spread in a pseudo-random pattern and embedded into the image. In detection, the value of the correlation is computed which measures the similarity between the spreading pattern and the watermarked image. The randomness of images is easily overcome with a high precessing gain in spread spectrum.

Some of the desired characteristics of digital signature are [1,2]:

– Perceptually and statistically invisible.

F. Petitcolas and H.J. Kim (Eds.): IWDW 2002, LNCS 2613, pp. 235–248, 2003.
© Springer-Verlag Berlin Heidelberg 2003

- Robust to attacks including lossy compression.
- Original image not necessary for detection.
- Rich enough to contain meaningful information.

Watermarking can also be divided into non-blind methods and blind methods. Non-blind methods use the original image for the extraction of watermark while blind methods do not require the original image in the detection process. In blind detection, the detection of watermark usually requires the information about parameters in the embedding process. Blind algorithms need to extract such parameters from altered images only and thus are more difficult to implement than non-blind alforithms.

Problem Definition

In this paper, we address two important issues in watermarking, capacity and watermark gain. The value of the watermark gain, α, is an improtant factor. With a large value of α, the robustness of the watermark increases at the expense of invisibility and *vice versa*. Yet, there is no clearly stated algorithm of determining the value of α.

Capacity of watermark is also related with a fair evaluation of a watermarking algorithm[10,11]. Given an image, how many bits can be embedded without degrading the quality of the image? There is a tade-off between the watermark size and robustness. Servetto applied channel capacity theorem for additive Gaussian watermarks and derived an expression for capacity[10]. The capacity of the proposed scheme as computed by eq.(1) is 7912 bits. The actual size of the watermark in our tests are 4096 bits, which is about half of the full capacity.

$$C_W = \frac{nN}{2} log_2(1 + \frac{1}{\sigma^2})$$ (1)

1.1 Performance Measures

We evaluate the performance of the proposed method by two measures, MPSNR (masked PSNR) and BER (bit error rate)[1,4]. MPSNR is the ratio of the peak energy to the distortion from watermarking and is an effective metric for invisibility. BER is the detection error rate for each bit of watermark and includes both false negatives and false positives. BER is an effective measure for robustness.

Performance comparison is presented in two ways. First, we compare the performance between the proposed method and conventional methods such as CM (correlation matching) and binary voting. Second, we compare the overall performance with the results of IA-DCT(image adaptive DCT) non-blind of Zeng [11,12].

1.2   Contribution of This Paper

- The issue of watermark capacity is addressed and about half of the full-capacity watermark is embedded in an image.
- The value of watermark gain, α, is determined on HVS(human visulal system) approach, considering both MPSNR and BER.
- A blind watermarking detection algorithm is developed, which has better performance, compared with other conventional methods[1,2,3].

When compared with previous studies, our method far exceeds others in watermark size. Nevertheless, the detection performance of watermark is better or almost equal. BER of watermark is around 0.5% for standard test images with no attacks.

2   Proposed System

The process of embedding and extraction of the watermark is shown in Fig. 1 and Fig. 2. The original image is DCT transformed block by block. Each bit of the 4096-bit watermark is embedded by a gain of α in the mid-frequency region of the DCT coefficients in one block. The value of α is determined based on HVS such that α is proportional to the standard deviation of the DCT coefficients of the corresponding image block. The amount of modification is dependent on the local image content.

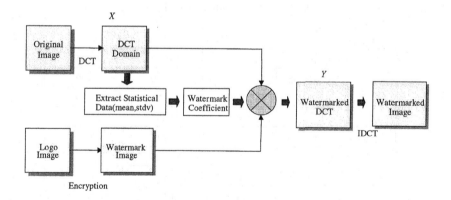

Fig. 1. Embedding of watermark

2.1   Optimal Choice of Watermark Gain

We show the values of MPSNR and BER as α varies in Table 1. Watermark gain α is determined such that it satisfies the threshold both in MPSNR and in

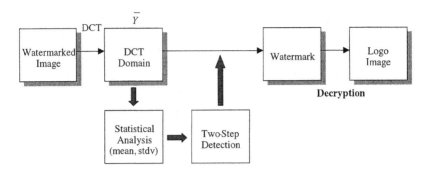

Fig. 2. Extraction of watermark

BER as proposed by Lembrecht [9] and Macq [8]. First, the range of α is examined which maintains MPSNR above 38dB. Then the range of α is examined, which maintains BER below 20% [4]. Of the intersection of these two ranges, the maximum value of α is chosen to solve the problem of faked ownership by inserting another digital signature into a watermarked image. Since the embedding is with maximum allowable strength, one cannot insert another signature without remarkable quality degradation.

Table 1. MPSNR and BER with varying α

Image	α	PSNR(dB)	BER(CM)	E(disdortion)
Airplane	0.25σ	45	0.2633	1.05
	0.333σ	43	0.2249	1.22
	0.5σ	39	0.1251	1.59
	$1\,\sigma$	32	0.0531	2.96
Babara	0.25σ	44	0.2747	1.13
	0.333σ	42	0.1909	1.39
	0.5σ	37	0.0745	1.94
	1σ	30	0.0178	3.8

2.2 Embedding of Watermark Bits

Each bit of the watermark is embedded in 12 positions of the DCT coefficients of a block b of the image as in eq.(2). The 12 frequency positions are numbered as in Fig. 3.

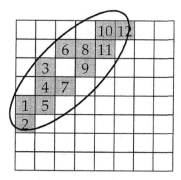

Fig. 3. Watermark embedded in 12 positions

$$Y_i = sgn(X_i)(|X_i| + \alpha P_i^k)$$
$$(i = 1, 2, \cdots, 12 \qquad k = 0, 1) \tag{2}$$

$$\alpha = \beta\sigma \tag{3}$$

$$P^0 = \{1, 0, 1, 0, 1, 1, 0, 0, 0, 1, 1, 0\}$$
$$P^1 = \{0, 1, 0, 1, 0, 0, 1, 1, 1, 0, 0, 1\}$$

X_i and Y_i represent the i-th DCT coefficient of an 8 by 8 block, before watermarking and after watermarking, respectively. The watermark gain α is proportional to σ, which is the standard deviation of 15 DCT coefficiens (the modified ones and neighbors in that block). This way, the absolute value of the DCT coefficient increases in proportion to the local activity. P^0 and P^1 are the spreading pattern for bit 0 and bit 1, respectively.

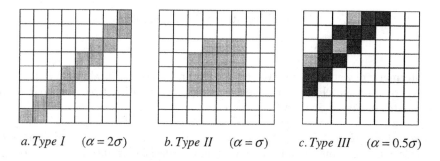

a. Type I $(\alpha = 2\sigma)$ b. Type II $(\alpha = \sigma)$ c. Type III $(\alpha = 0.5\sigma)$

Fig. 4. Three frequency regions tested

Patterns P^0 and P^1 are so selected as to be symmetric and orthogonal to each other. For the design of the spreading pattern, we examined which frequency region is the most effective. After tests for 3 kinds of frequency regions in Fig. 4, type III returned to be to the most effective. The values of α needed for the same BER performance are 2σ for region 1, σ for region 2 and 0.5σ for region 3.

2.3   Detection of Watermark

Since the original image is not available in the extraction of the watermark, we need to make a decision based on the modified (and possibly attacked) DCT coefficients. We assume that i-th DCT coefficient in each block is Gaussian and the 12 coefficients in a single block are jointly Gaussian as in Fig. 5.

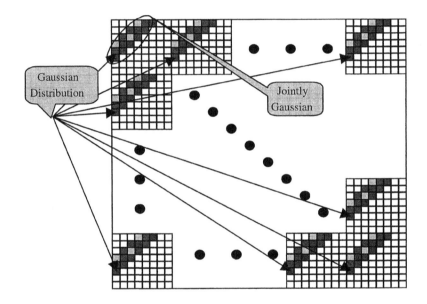

Fig. 5. Distribution of DCT coefficients

Watermark detection is in two-steps. The first step is a preliminary decision by correlation matching and the second step is verification by voting, based on estimates of the original DCT coefficients.

The values of correlation between each of P^0, P^1 and the watermarked coefficients is computed and then a preliminary decision is obtained by choosing the larger of the two as in eq. (4).

$$S_0 = \Sigma |Y_i| P_i^0, \quad S_1 = \Sigma |Y_i| P_i^1 \tag{4}$$

$$if \begin{cases} S_0 > S_1 \rightarrow \text{decide bit} = 0 \\ S_0 < S_1 \rightarrow \text{decide bit} = 1 \end{cases} \tag{5}$$

In our experiments, the BER by preliminary decision alone stays around 5~10%. Most of the wrong decisions can be corrected in the verification process as follows.

1. Estimates($\hat{X}_i$) of the original DCT coefficients are obtained by removing the watermark gain, based on the preliminary decision. The variance of the original coefficients, σ^2, can be easily estimated from that of watermarked coefficients, as in eq.(6), which is detailed in the Appendix. Then the estimate of X_i, is obtained from the watermarked coefficient as in eq.(7).

$$\hat{\sigma}_X^2 = 0.656(\sigma_Y)^2 \tag{6}$$

$$\hat{X}_i = \begin{cases} sgn(Y_i)\{|Y_i| - \hat{\alpha}P_i^0\} & \text{if preliminary decision} = 0 \\ sgn(Y_i)\{|Y_i| - \hat{\alpha}P_i^1\} & \text{if preliminary decision} = 1 \end{cases} \tag{7}$$

2. Watermarked coefficients(Y_i) are scaled by the ratio of estimated coefficient to their mean value as in eq. (8).

$$Y_i^S = w_i Y_i \qquad \text{where} \qquad w_i = |\hat{X}_i|/mean(|\hat{X}_i|) \tag{8}$$

3. Each of the scaled coefficients (Y_i^S) are thresholded with their mean, resulting in a 12-bit pattern. A voting is performed, based on the Hamming distance between that 12-bit pattern and each of P^0, P^1. The final decision is obtained by choosing the one with smaller distance, that is, the embedded watermark bit is concluded to be 1 if the 12-bit pattern is more similar to P^1 than to P^0.

An example is shown in Fig. 6 to illustrate the details. The original bit, 1, is erroneously decoded be 0 in the preliminary decision since $S_0 > S_1$. Scaled coefficients have a mean value of 11. Thresholding the scaled coefficients with the mean, we get a 12-bit pattern, {0 1 0 0 1 0 1 0 1 0 0 1}. Since that pattern is closer to P^1 than to P^0, we conclude that the original watermark bit is 1.

2.4   Why BER Improves in Two-Step Process?

The final decision for each bit comes from the verification. One may doubt: A correct preliminary decision may be erroneously reversed just as a wrong preliminary decision can be corrected. Table 2   show the transition between the preliminary decision and the verification. C(correct)/W(wrong) represents a correct preliminary decision and a wrong verificaiton, in that order. The numbers in the inner columns represent the number of occurrences and the number in the right column is the distance between S_0 and S_1. Most of wrong preliminary decisions are corrected while most of correct preliminary decisions just pass the verification as follows:

– It is rare that a correct preliminary decision will be erroneously reversed when the distance is larger than 5. Most of the erroneous inversions occur when the distance is small.

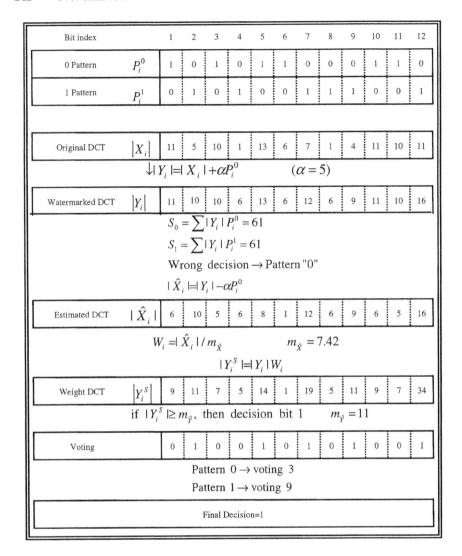

Fig. 6. Intermediate steps in Two-Step method

- The number of erroneous inversions of correct preliminary is 59, only 20% corrected out of 279 wrong preliminary decisions.

What would happen if we make preliminary decision entirely randomly and rely on the verification process only? In experiments, the performance is much lower than with the preliminary decision. The BER goes down to 19% even with no attack.

Table 2. Transition from Preliminary to Verificiation (Barbara, $\alpha = 0.5\sigma$)

Pre/				Distance	
Verifiy	Original	Pre	Verify	< 5	≥ 5
C/C	1	1	1	273	1529
	0	0	0	292	1638
C/W	1	1	0	21	1
	0	0	1	36	1
W/C	1	0	1	178	36
	0	1	0	38	27
W/W	1	0	0	16	1
	0	1	1	8	1

2.5 Capacity of Watermark Data

Converting eq. (1) in terms of the proposed method, N is the number of image blocks, 4096, and n is the number of DCT coefficients, 12. σ^2 is the ratio of watermark energy to the background image (*noise* from a viewpoint of watermark detection) and is equivalent to $1/\beta^2 = 4.0$. The capacity is comquted to be 7912 bits. The actual size of the watermark in our tests is 4096 bits, which is about half of the full capacity.

3 Experimental Results

We experimented the proposed algorithm for 4 images as shown in Fig. 7. They are 8-bit gray level images with 512x512 pixels. Watermark data are 4096 random bits. The subfigures in Fig. 8 are (a) original image, (b) watermarked image, (c) amplified difference and (d) reconstructed image after detecting watermark.

3.1 Comparison with Other Blind Watermarking

The BER performance of the proposed method is shown in Table 3 through Table 6. Tested attacks include sharpening, blurring, median filtering, addition of Gaussian noise and heavy JPEG compression (20% by Photoshop). However, no geometrical attacks such as rotation, shifting or transformation have been tested. In all of 4 images, we use the same $\alpha(= 0.5\sigma)$. For comparison, we use two conventional blind methods, CM(correlation matching) and binary voting. CM is an identical process to the preliminary decision process alone in the proposed method. On the other hand, in binary voting, each of the watermarked coefficients is compared to their mean value and we examine to which of the two, P^0 and P^1, the resulting 12-bit pattern is closer. Thus, binary voting

a. Barbara   b. Airplane

c. Baboon   d. Lena

Fig. 7. Original images

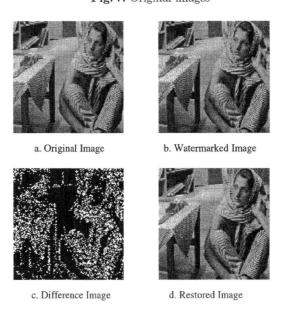

a. Original Image   b. Watermarked Image

c. Difference Image   d. Restored Image

Fig. 8. Watermarking of Barbara

is similar to the verification process, but without any preliminary decision or restoration.

Table 3. BER with watermark attacks (Barbara)

Attacks	CM	Voting	Proposed
None	0.0745	0.0718	0.0091
Sharpen	0.0813	0.0802	0.0066
Blur	0.1289	0.1241	0.0288
Median	0.1833	0.1762	0.0823
Noise(G)	0.1188	0.1214	0.0293
JPEG(20%)	0.1044	0.1001	0.0259

Table 4. BER with watermark attacks(Airplane)

Attacks	CM	Voting	Proposed
None	0.1251	0.1231	0.0511
Sharpen	0.1201	0.1189	0.0239
Blur	0.1861	0.1853	0.0586
Median	0.3769	0.3657	0.1031
Noise(G)	0.2839	0.2847	0.0301
JPEG(20%)	0.3193	0.3557	0.0851

BER produced by the proposed method is 5~10 times lower than the conventional methods. With no attack on watermarked images, BER by two-step method is in the range of 0.002~0.05, while BER by CM or voting is in the range of 0.05~0.125. With an attack of heavy JPEG compression, two-step method has BER of 0.02~0.09, while CM or voting has BER of 0.1~0.3.

3.2   Comparison with Other Non-blind Methods

We compare our method with the performance of IA-DCT watermarking of Zeng. In IA-DCT, the PSNR was 30dB with watermark size of 512 bits. The proposed method has a PSNR of 38 dB with a 4096-bit watermark size. Yet, the BER has a performance gain of 5~10%. A summary is in Table 7, where a normalized correlation is used as the performance metric in order to have a fair

Table 5. BER with watermark attacks(Baboon)

Attacks	CM	Voting	Proposed
None	0.0501	0.0525	0.0002
Sharpen	0.0569	0.0584	0.0007
Blur	0.1023	0.1013	0.0029
Median	0.3127	0.3232	0.0173
Noise(G)	0.1257	0.1269	0.0015
JPEG(20%)	0.1455	0.1751	0.0886

Table 6. BER with watermark attack(Lena)

Attacks	CM	Voting	Proposed
None	0.0732	0.0745	0.0039
Sharpen	0.0867	0.0874	0.0073
Blur	0.1528	0.1514	0.0127
Median	0.3748	0.3625	0.0626
Noise(G)	0.2769	0.2813	0.0056
JPEG(20%)	0.3406	0.2965	0.0912

comparison with published results. The proposed *blind* method appears to have better performance both in robustness and in capacity and equal performance in invisibility, than published *non-blind* methods.

Table 7. Comparison with other non-blind methods

Methods	Info(bits)	PSNR[dB]	JEPG(20%)	Blur(0.2)	Sharp(0.5)
IA-DCT	512	30	0.4953	0.9534	0.8255
IA-DWT	512	34	0.3387	0.9066	0.8744
Proposed	4096	38	0.9088	0.9414	0.9761

4   Conclusion

In this paper, we presented a DCT-based blind watermarking system, with a two-step detection algorithm. Each bit of 4096 watermark data is embedded as pseudo-random patterns in 12 of DCT coefficients of an 8 by 8 block. The watermark gain, α, is optimized in terms of robustness and invisibility. In the extraction process, a preminary decision is obtained by correlation matching and then verified by voting for the more similar spreading pattern with the restored one. Most bit errors are corrected in the verification process. The proposed method has been tested on several test images with attacks. BER is around 0.5% in case of no attack on watermarking. BER in worst case stays lower than 9% with heavy JPEG compression. Compared with others, the proposed method is better in watermark detection performance and far exceeds others in watermark size.

References

1. R. Wolfgang and C. Podilchuk, "Perceptual watermarks for digital images and video ", Proceedings of IEEE, Vol.87, No.7, July 1999
2. W. Zeng and B. Liu, "A statistical watermark detection technique without using original images for resolving rightful ownerships of digital images", IEEE Transaction on image processing, Vol.8, No.11, November 1999
3. J. Raunaidh, and G. Csurka, "A bayesian approach to spread spectrum watermark detection and secure copyright protection for digital image libraries", IEEE Computer Vision and Pattern Recognition, 1999
4. F. Petitcolas and R. Anderson, "Evaluation of copyright marking systems", Proceedings of IEEE Multimedia Systems'99, vol. 1, pp. 574–579, 7–11 June 1999, Florence, Italy
5. F. Muller, "Distribution shape of two dimensional DCT coefficients of natural images", Electronics Letters, Vol. 29, Oct. 1993, pp. 1935–1936
6. E. Lan, and J. Goodman, "A mathematical analysis of the DCT coefficient distributions for images", IEEE Transactions on Image Processing, Vol.9, No.10, October 2000
7. G. Langelaar, I. Setywan and R. Lagendijk, "Watermarking digital image and video data", IEEE Signal Processing Magazine, 20–46 September 2000
8. S. Comes, O. Bruyndonckx, and B. Macq, "Image quality criterion based on the cancellation of the masked noise", ICASSP-95, Vol.4, pp. 2635–2638
9. C. Branden Lambrecht and O. Verscheure, "Perceptual quality measure using a spatio-temporal model of the human visual system", in Proceedings of the SPIE, Vol. 2668, pp. 450–461, January 28 February 2 1996
10. S. Servetto, C. Podilchuk and K. Ramchandran, "Capacity issues in digital image watermarking", ICIP 98, Vol.1, pp. 445–449
11. M. Barni, F. Bartolini, A. De Rasa, and A. Piva, "Capacity of full frame DCT image watermarks", IEEE Transactions on image processing, Vol. 9, No. 8, August 2000
12. W. Zhihui, and X Liang, "An evaluation method for watermarking techniques", 2000 IEEE International Conference on Multimedia and Expo, Vol.1, pp. 373–376

Appendix

$$Y_i = \begin{cases} X_i + \alpha P_i \ (X_i \geq 0) \\ X_i - \alpha P_i \ (X_i < 0) \end{cases}$$

$$E(Y) = \int_{-\infty}^{0} (x - \alpha P) \, f_X(x) \, dx + \int_{0}^{\infty} (x + \alpha P) \, f_X(x) \, dx$$
$$= 0 \quad \text{(assuming} \quad f_X(x) = G(0, \sigma_X))$$

$$E(Y^2) = \int_{-\infty}^{0} (x_2 - 2x\alpha P + \alpha^2 P^2) f_X(x) dx + \int_{0}^{\infty} (x_2 + 2x\alpha P + \alpha^2 P^2) f_X(x) dx$$
$$= E(x^2) + \alpha^2 E(P^2) + 4\alpha E(P) \int_{0}^{\infty} x f_X(x) dx$$
$$\simeq 1.524 \sigma_X^2$$

$$\sigma_Y^2 = E(Y^2) - E(Y)^2 \simeq 1.524 \sigma_X^2$$
Therefore, $\hat{\sigma}_X^2 = 0.656 \sigma_Y^2$

Content Adaptive Watermark Embedding in the Multiwavelet Transform Using a Stochastic Image Model

Ki-Ryong Kwon[1], Seong-Geun Kwon[2], Je-Ho Nam[3], and
Ahmed H. Tewfik[4]

[1]Division of Electronic and Computer Engineering, Pusan University of Foreign
Studies, 55-1 Uam-dong, Nam-gu, Pusan 608-738, Republic of Korea,
krkwon@taejo.pufs.ac.kr
[2]School of Electrical Engineering and Computer Science, Kyungpook National
University, 1370 Sangyuk-dong, Buk-gu, Daegu 702-701, Republic of Korea
[3]Broadcasting Media Research Department, ETRI, 161 Gajeong-dong, Yuseong -gu,
Daejeon 305-350, Republic of Korea
[4]Dept. of Electrical and Computer Engineering, University of Minnesota, 4-174
EE/CSci Building 200 Union Street S.E. Minneapolis, MN55455,
tewfik@ece.umn.edu

Abstract. Content adaptive watermark embedding algorithm using a stochastic image model in the multiwavelet transform is proposed in this paper. Usually, watermark is embedded with the same embedding strength regardless of local properties of the cover image, so the visible artifacts are taken placed at flat regions. A watermark is embedded into the perceptually significant coefficients (PSCs) of each subband using multiwavelet transform. The PSCs in high frequency subband are selected by SSQ, that is, by setting the thresholds as the one half of the largest coefficient in each subband. The perceptual model is applied with a stochastic approach based on noise visibility function (NVF) that has local image properties for watermark embedding. This model uses stationary Generalized Gaussian model characteristic because watermark has noise properties. The watermark estimation use shape parameter and variance of subband region, it is derive content adaptive criteria according to edge and texture, and flat region.

Keywords: Multiwavelet, successive subband quantization, perceptually significant coefficients, noise visibility function, stochastic image model

1 Introduction

The proliferation of digital contents and media has made it easy to copy, store, and distribute various kinds of digital contents. At the same time, this ease of manipulation has also prompted unauthorized duplication and distribution of valuable contents. Digital watermarking might be used to protect the copyright of multimedia data from illegal copying and watermarks are imperceptible signals that are embedded into the media to be protected. As such, digital watermarks can help to identify the

F. Petitcolas and H.J. Kim (Eds.): IWDW 2002, LNCS 2613, pp. 249–263, 2003.
© Springer-Verlag Berlin Heidelberg 2003

source or ownership of the media, the legitimacy of its usage, and the type of the contents or multimedia data in various applications.

The most important requirements in the data embedding systems are the robustness and transparency, but unfortunately these are in the relation of trade-off [1]. First of all, the watermark must be robust against attacks that are applied to the watermarked media for the purposes of editing, storage, and even circumventing watermark detection. Generally, these attacks are categorized into the lossy compression, filter, noise-addition, and geometrical modification. Secondly, the watermark must be embedded in a transparent way to avoid degrading the perceptual quality of the host media. In another words, Users should not detect existence of the watermark in the watermarked media statistically and visually.

According to the HVS (human visual system), human eyes are less sensitive to changes in the neighborhood of the edges than the smooth regions of the image [2]. This phenomenon is called the spatial masking effect and can be exploited in the watermark embedding, that is, by increasing the embedding strength in the edges and high textured areas of the image, and reducing it in smooth regions.

Swanson et al. [3] proposed watermarking method in the DCT domain using property of human perceptual system. This algorithm is used in the context of image compression using the perceptual based quantizers. Podilchuk et al. [4] developed a content adaptive scheme, where the embedding strength is adjusted for each DCT and wavelet coefficients. Kutter [5] have developed content adaptive watermarking schemes on the basis of luminance sensitivity function using the HVS. Ruanaidh et al. [6] have applied transfer modulation features of HVS in the transform domain to solve the problem of the compromise between the robustness and transparency. This method embeds the watermark into the Fourier coefficients in a middle frequency band with the same embedding strength assuming that the image spectra have isotropic characteristic. This assumption is caused by lead to some visible artifacts of images in the flat regions since it is an isotropic property of image spectra. Delaigle et al. [7] proposed perceptual modulation function to overcome the problem of visibility of the watermark around the edges. This method is developed based on a content adaptive criterion that may easily be applied to any watermarking techniques in coordinate, Fourier, DCT or wavelet domains as perceptual modulation function. Voloshynovskiy et al. [8] proposed adequate stochastic modeling for content adaptive digital image watermarking. By knowing stochastic models of the watermark and the host image, one can formulate the problem of watermark estimation/detection according to the classical MAP (maximum a posteriori probability) and stochastic models and also estimate the capacity issue of the image watermark scheme.

The conventional watermarking techniques using global information of the cover image embed the watermark into the host image with the same embedding strength regardless of its local property. Therefore, this embedding technique leads in practice to visible artifacts in the flat regions. In order to reduce these artifacts, the embedding strength has to be decreased. This reduces the robustness of the watermark against several attacks, since the image region that generates the most visible artifacts determine the final maximum strength of the watermark to be embedded.

A content adaptive watermarking has been proposed using a stochastic image model based on multiwavelet transform. This algorithm utilizes the local properties of image to determine the optimal embedding area using successive subband quantization and perceptual model for the more strongly embedding. Multiwavelet can be seen as vector-valued wavelets that offer simultaneous orthogonality, symmetry, compactly support, and vanishing moments, which are impossible with single wavelet systems. One of the great challenges to the successful watermark embedding in the orthogonal multiwavelet is to construct the space spanned by the multiscaling function with a higher approximation order usually leads to better energy compaction than single wavelets. Also it can reduce the checkboard artifacts in the reconstructed image. Multiwavelet used in this paper is DGHM multiwavelet with approximation order of 2. To embed watermark, the original image is decomposed into 4 levels using a discrete multiwavelet transform, then a watermark is embedded into the PSCs of each subband. The PSCs in high frequency subband are selected by SSQ, that is, by setting the thresholds as the one half of the largest coefficient in each subband. After the PSCs in each subband are selected by SSQ, perceptual model based on a stochastic approach is utilized to embed watermark. This is based on the computation of a noise visibility function that has local image properties proposed by [8]. Using perceptual model, the proposed watermarking algorithm embeds watermark by the SSQ at the texture and edge region for the stronger watermark. This method uses stationary Generalized Gaussian model characteristic because watermark has similar characteristic. The watermark estimation uses shape parameter and variance of subband region, it is derive content adaptive criteria according to edge and texture, and flat region. The experimental results of the proposed watermark embedding method confirmed the excellent invisibility and robustness.

2   Adaptive Watermark Embedding in the Multiwavelet Transform

2.1 Multiwavelet Transform

Multiwavelet is a new addition to realize as vector-valued filter banks leading to wavelet theory. Multiwavelet has many advantages such as compactly support, orthogonality, symmetry, and vanishing moments [9]. That is, it can simultaneously provide perfect reconstruction (orthogonality), good performance at the boundaries (linear-phase symmetry), and high order of approximation (vanishing moments). But a single wavelet cannot possess all these properties at the same time. Other feature of multiwavelet is an efficient, robust, and compact representation than single wavelets.

One of the great challenges to successful watermark embedding in orthogonal multiwavelet is to construct the space spanned by the multiscaling function with a higher approximation order usually leads to better energy compaction than single wavelets. And it contributes the reduction of checkboard artifacts in the reconstructed image. For a tree-structured vector filter bank in multiwavelet transforms, the lowpass and highpass properties for the two vector filters are not as clear as those for the two filters in single wavelet transforms. Therefore, the prefilters and postfilters are a necessary step for discrete multiwavelet filter banks [10]. The prefilters are constructed for multiwavelet based on matrix filter banks that preserve certain properties of the central filter bank. The prefilters must be compatible with the central matrix filter banks in order to fully exploit the underlying properties of the multiwavelet filter banks. Prefilters of DGHM multiwavelet used in this paper is the 2nd-order quasi-interpolation [11].

The block diagram of orthogonal multiwavelet filter in this paper is shown Fig. 1. Multiwavelet has multiresolution analysis (MRA) which is the same concept as the scalar wavelets. $H_0(Z)$, $H_1(Z)$ are analysis filter banks, $G_0(Z)$, $G_1(Z)$ are synthesis filter banks. $P(Z)$ and $P^{-1}(z)$ are prefilter and postfilter banks. A basis for V_0 is generated by translates of vector form of N scaling functions $\phi_1(t-k), \phi_2(t-k), \cdots, \phi_N(t-k)$. The scaling vector $\mathbf{\Phi}(t) = [\phi_1(t), \cdots, \phi_N(t)]^T$, will denote a compactly supported orthogonal scaling vector of length N with a matrix dilation equation

$$\mathbf{\Phi}(t) = \sqrt{2} \sum_{k \in Z} \mathbf{H}[k]\mathbf{\Phi}(2t-k). \tag{1}$$

Where, the multiwavelet coefficients $\mathbf{H}[k]$ are N by N real matrices.

An orthonormal basis $W_0 = V_{-1} \oplus V_0$ is generated by N wavelets vector $\mathbf{\Psi}(t) = [\varphi_1(t), \cdots, \varphi_N(t)]^T$, satisfying the matrix wavelet equation

$$\mathbf{\Psi}(t) = \sqrt{2} \sum_{k \in Z} \mathbf{G}[k]\mathbf{\Psi}(2t-k). \tag{2}$$

The $\mathbf{G}[k]$ is also N by N real matrix. The scaling vectors with H and G from matrix finite impulse response (FIR) filters have orthogonality, stability, smoothness, and good approximation property.

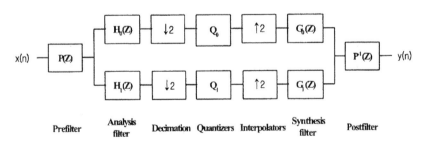

Fig. 1. Multiwavelet scheme with orthogonal filter bank.

In the Fourier domain, the matrix frequency responses for H and G is denoted by $\hat{H}(\omega)$, $\hat{G}(\omega)$, respectively.

$$\hat{H}(\omega) = \frac{1}{\sqrt{2}} \sum_{k \in Z} H_k e^{-jk\omega} \text{ and } \hat{G}(\omega) = \frac{1}{\sqrt{2}} \sum_{k \in Z} G_k e^{-jk\omega} \tag{3}$$

The power complimentary condition can be expressed as

$$\hat{H}(\omega)\hat{H}^*(\omega) + \hat{H}(\omega+\pi)\hat{H}^*(\omega+\pi) = I_N$$

$$\hat{G}(\omega)\hat{G}^*(\omega) + \hat{G}(\omega+\pi)\hat{G}^*(\omega+\pi) = I_N$$

and

$$\hat{H}(\omega)\hat{G}^*(\omega) + \hat{H}(\omega+\pi)\hat{G}^*(\omega+\pi) = 0_N$$

where * denotes complex conjugate transpose, whereas I_N and 0_N are N by N identity and null matrices, respectively.

Multiwavelet system is a matrix valued multirate filter bank. The DGHM multiwavelet system is constructed by two scaling function $\phi_1(t), \phi_2(t)$ and two wavelets $\varphi_1(t), \varphi_2(t)$ having the four coefficients symmetric paraunitary filter bank:

$$\Phi(t) = \begin{bmatrix} \phi_1(t) \\ \phi_2(t) \end{bmatrix} = C[0]\Phi(2t) + C[1]\Phi(2t-1) + C[2]\Phi(2t-2) + C[3]\Phi(2t-3) \quad (4)$$

$$\Psi(t) = \begin{bmatrix} \varphi_1(t) \\ \varphi_2(t) \end{bmatrix} = D[0]\Phi(2t) + D[1]\Phi(2t-1) + D[2]\Phi(2t-2) + D[3]\Phi(2t-3), \quad (5)$$

There are properties of the DGHM scaling function, as follow.
- They have compactly support (the intervals [0, 1] and [0, 2])
- Both scaling functions are symmetric and the wavelets form a symmetric/anti-symmetric pair
- The system has second order of approximation

In the time domain, filtering to be follow by downsampling is described by an infinite lowpass matrix with double shift;

$$L = \begin{bmatrix} \ddots & & & & & & \\ & C[3] & C[2] & C[1] & C[0] & 0 & 0 \\ & 0 & 0 & C[3] & C[2] & C[1] & C[0] \\ & & & & & & \ddots \end{bmatrix}$$

Each of the filter taps $C(k)$ is a 2×2 matrix.

The continuous time function $f(t)$ in the multiresolution vector space V_0 can be expanded as a linear combination

$$f(t) = \sum_n v_{1,n}^{(0)} \phi_1(t-n) + v_{2,n}^{(0)} \phi_2(t-n) \quad (6)$$

The superscript (0) denotes an expansion 'at scale level 0'. Therefore, their coarse approximation (component in V_{-1}) is computed with the lowpass part of multiwavelet filter bank. Prefilter for DGHM multiwavelet uses a 2nd-order quasi-interpolation prefilter.

$$
\begin{bmatrix}
\vdots \\
\begin{bmatrix} v_{1,n}^{(-1)} \\ v_{2,n}^{(-1)} \end{bmatrix} \\
\begin{bmatrix} v_{1,n+1}^{(-1)} \\ v_{2,n+1}^{(-1)} \end{bmatrix} \\
\vdots
\end{bmatrix}
= L
\begin{bmatrix}
\vdots \\
\begin{bmatrix} v_{1,n}^{(0)} \\ v_{2,n}^{(0)} \end{bmatrix} \\
\begin{bmatrix} v_{1,n+1}^{(0)} \\ v_{2,n+1}^{(0)} \end{bmatrix} \\
\vdots
\end{bmatrix}.
\tag{7}
$$

2.2 Successive Subband Qantization

The PSCs in the high frequency subbands are selected by SSQ, that is, by the subband adaptive threshold [12,13]. It is selected by setting the thresholds as the one half of the largest coefficient in each subband. Then, for each selected coefficient in the high frequency subbands, the maximum amount of the watermark is embedded to the extent of satisfying the transparency according to the perceptual model of that coefficient.

To select the PSCs, a subband adaptive threshold is used as follows

$$
TH_i = 2^{\lfloor \log_2 T_i \rfloor} - 1
\tag{8}
$$

where T_i represents the largest coefficients in each subband and $\lfloor X \rfloor$ represents the largest integer which is no greater than X. The watermark is embedded only to the PSCs greater than the subband adaptive threshold. As such, a constantly weighted watermark, which has the largest value without the introduction of a visual artifact, is embedded into the PSCs in the subband. Whereas, for the PSCs in the high frequency subbands, the watermark is embedded based on NVF so as to provide transparency and robustness.

The SSQ is performed to select the PSCs in the high frequency subbands. The procedure of SSQ is as follow:

1. Set the initial threshold T_s of each subband to one half of the maximum amplitude value of the coefficients inside the same subband. Set all coefficients as unselected.
2. Select the subband with the maximum value of T_s, the within the selected subband examine all unselected coefficients with the current threshold T_s and select those coefficients which are greater than T_s as the PSCs.
3. Change the new threshold of the selected subband to one half.
4. Repeat Step 2 and 3 until all required PSCs are selected.

3 Stochastic Multiresolution Model

This paper presents perceptual model with a stochastic multiresolution that can be applied to watermark embedding in the multiwavelet domain. This embedding method is based on the computation of a noise visibility function (NVF) that has local properties of image based on [9]. Adaptive watermarking algorithm using Stationary GG perceptual model embeds watermark into the texture and edge region for more strongly embedded watermark by the successive subband quantization. This method uses the modified stationary GG model because watermark has similar characteristic with this model. The watermark embedding use the shape parameter and variance of each subband of multiwavelet domain, which is derived according to edge and texture, flat region. The block diagram of the proposed watermarking model is shown of Fig. 2.

Based on global information of the image, the watermark modeled as the random noise is embedded with the same strength into the whole host image regardless of the local properties of the image. This embedding may produce visible artifacts at the regions that are characterized by small variability of reconstructed image. In order to decrease these artifacts, the given embedding strength has to be decreased. However, this reduces remarkably the robustness of the watermark against various kinds of attacks, since the image regions which generate the most visible artifacts determine the final maximum strength of the watermarked signal to be embedded. Perceptual model is applied with an effective solution that embeds the watermark into the host image according to the local properties of the image. This approach has the advantage that it is applicable for very different types of images.

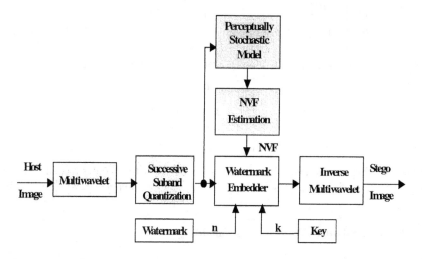

Fig. 2. The block diagram of proposed watermark embedding model in the multiwavelet domain.

3.1 NVF with Stationary Generalized Gaussian Model

In the case of stationary Generalized Gaussian model, NVF can be written as

$$NVF(i, j) = \frac{w(i, j)}{w(i, j) + \sigma_x^2(i, j)} \tag{9}$$

where $w(i, j)$ is variable weighting function, $\sigma_x^2(i, j)$ denotes the local variance of the image in a window centered at $(i, j), 1 \leq i, j \leq M$. The watermark is an *i.i.d.* (independent identically distributed) Gaussian process with unit variance, i.e. $N(0, 1)$.

$$w(i, j) = \gamma \left[\eta(\gamma)^\gamma \frac{1}{\|a(i, j)\|^{2-\gamma}} \right] \tag{10}$$

where $a(i, j) = \dfrac{x(i, j) - \overline{x(i, j)}}{\sigma_x}$, $\eta(\gamma) = \sqrt{\dfrac{\Gamma(\frac{3}{\gamma})}{\Gamma(\frac{1}{\gamma})}}$ and $\Gamma(t) = \int_0^\infty e^{-u} u^{t-1} du$ is the

Gamma function.

The parameter γ is shape parameter. This distribution is the same as Gaussian one for shape parameter, 2 and Laplacian one, 1. The shape parameter for real image is in Fig. 3. The stationary GG model is as following.

$$p_x(x) = \left[\frac{\gamma \eta(\gamma)}{2\Gamma(\frac{1}{\gamma})} \right]^{\frac{N}{2}} \cdot \frac{1}{|\det R_x|^{\frac{1}{2}}} \cdot \exp\{ -\eta(\gamma)(|C x|^{\frac{\gamma}{2}})^T R_x^{-\frac{\gamma}{2}} |C x|^{\frac{\gamma}{2}} \}. \tag{11}$$

where R_x is autocovariance function for stationary GG model. C is a high-pass filter.

$$R_x = \begin{bmatrix} \sigma_x^2 & 0 & \cdots & 0 \\ 0 & \sigma_x^2 & 0 & \vdots \\ \vdots & & 0 & \ddots & 0 \\ 0 & & 0 & 0 & \sigma_x^2 \end{bmatrix} \tag{12}$$

Adaptive shape parameters are utilized according to each subband and the approximation of shape parameters for Lena and Barbara images are as shown in Fig. 3.

3.2 Content Adaptive Watermark Embedding

The final equation with adaptive watermark embedding of middle and high level subbands is following formulate:

$$X' = X + (1 - \beta)(1 - NVF) \cdot w \cdot S_{ET} + \beta \cdot NVF \cdot w \cdot S_F \tag{13}$$

where X', X and w denote the watermarked image, original image, and watermark. S_{ET} denotes the watermark strength of texture and edge regions. S_F denotes the watermark strength of flat region. β is smoothing factor. The above rule embeds the watermark in highly textured areas and areas containing edges stronger than in the flat regions. In a strong edge region, where NVF approaches 1, the strength of the embedded watermark approaches zero. As a consequence of this embedding rule, the watermark information is nearly lost in these areas. Therefore, to avoid this problem,

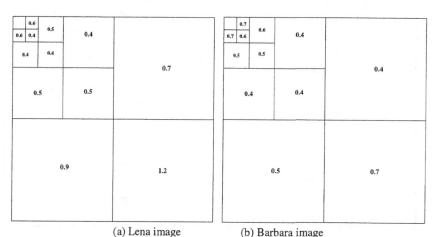

(a) Lena image   (b) Barbara image

Fig. 3. The approximation of shape parameters.

we proposed to modify the above rule, and to increase the watermark strength in these areas to a level below the visibility threshold. The proposed adaptive watermark embedding can be required into these methods to achieve the trade-off between the goals of increasing the robustness by increasing the watermark strength and at the same time, decreasing the visual artifacts introduced by the watermarking process.

4   Experimental Results

To illustrate the main features of the proposed adaptive watermark embedding method in the multiwavelet domain, the simulation was performed on several images of 512×512 size. The multiwavelet decomposed the original image into 4 levels. The used watermark is *i.i.d.* Gaussian random sequence with unit variance, $N(0,1)$ and its length is 1000. The security key is 200th. The highest frequency subband is thrown up watermark embedding step. The first step of experiments, PSCs are selected by SSQ. It is selected by setting the thresholds as the one half of the largest coefficient in each subband. The second step, stationary GG perceptual model with adaptive watermarking algorithm embed at the texture and edge region by SSQ. The third step, NVF has to do estimation according to the stationary GG model.

The PSNR of the watermarked images produced by modeling watermark as stationary GG model with various embedding strength in the multiwavelet domain are compared with non-stationary model in Table 1. As can be noticed from this figure, the performance of the watermarked image with non-stationary GG model is a little better than that of stationary Gaussian model.

Table 1. The PSNR of multiwavelet according to watermark strength variation.

| Watermark Strength | PSNR[dB] : Lena(512×512) | | | |
| | Stationary | | Non-Stationary | |
	Multiwavelet	Biorthogonal	Multiwavelet	Biorthogonal
10	**53.08**	**51.91**	**53.16**	**51.05**
20	**47.06**	**46.28**	**47.14**	**45.36**
30	**43.54**	**42.85**	**43.62**	**41.90**
40	**41.04**	**40.39**	**41.12**	**39.43**
50	**39.10**	**38.46**	**39.18**	**37.51**
60	**37.52**	**36.89**	**37.60**	**35.93**
70	**36.18**	**35.56**	**36.26**	**34.60**
80	**35.02**	**34.40**	**35.10**	**33.45**
90	**34.00**	**33.38**	**34.08**	**32.43**
100	**33.08**	**32.47**	**33.16**	**31.52**

Table 2. The PSNR[dB] values for the several watermarked images.

Image	Multiwavelet (SSQ+ Perceptual Model)	Multiwavelet (SSQ+Modified Perceptual Model)	Multiwavelet (HVS)	Biorthogonal (HVS)
Lena	41.90	42.60	41.20	38.89
Boat	42.62	43.99	40.08	38.32
Barbara	38.18	38.41	36.48	37.49
Baboon	38.18	38.06	35.23	36.91
Bank	38.68	38.83	35.42	36.37
Bridge	40.12	40.23	37.10	36.45
Cablecar	44.20	44.19	42.41	43.05
Goldhill	42.06	43.98	39.51	40.66
Sail	42.62	44.07	41.39	38.59
Pepper	39.47	39.43	34.95	37.72
Woman	40.12	40.12	38.79	36.31
Altoro	40.12	44.05	35.26	32.06

Table 3. JPEG compression with a quality factor varying 10% to 90%.

Multiwavelet Lena(512×512)										
Quality		10	20	30	40	50	60	70	80	90
PSNR	Non-Stationary	30.93	33.35	34.60	35.24	35.92	36.48	37.05	37.62	38.37
	Stationary	30.83	33.21	34.38	35.08	35.62	36.14	36.75	37.56	38.86
C.R	Non-Stationary	22.33	28.20	29.95	30.37	30.52	30.62	30.83	30.85	30.91
	Stationary	23.87	28.80	30.28	30.70	30.78	30.90	31.06	31.08	31.14

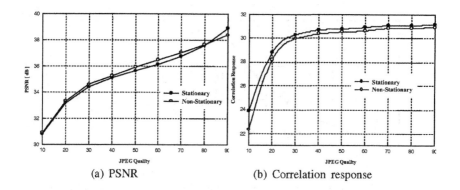

(a) PSNR   (b) Correlation response

Fig. 4. The robustness test of JPEG attack.

The PSNR value of the several watermarked images with respect to the original image is shown the Table 2. The image comparisons using experiment are SSQ and perceptual model in the multiwavelet domain, SSQ and modified perceptual model in the multiwavelet domain, only multiwavelet and HVS, and biorthogonal wavelet and HVS.

To establish the robustness of the watermarked image against lossy compression, JPEG coding with a quality factor varying 10% to 90% was performed and the resultant PSNR and correlation responses are shown in Fig. 4. Table 3 is JPEG compression with a quality factor varying 10% to 90%. As the PSNR comparison of JPEG, non-stationary model is excellent PSNR with a quality factor between 20% and 80% than stationary model, and correlation response of stationary model is better than non-stationary. The result knows the resilience of the watermarking scheme against the JPEG compression.

To evaluate the robustness of the watermarked image under cropping attack, we randomly cropped a region with size of a 10% to 90% from the watermarked image and then compressed it by JPEG with a quality factor varying 80%. The result knows the resilience of the watermarking scheme against the combination of cropping and JPEG compression as shown in Fig. 5. Table 4 is Cropping attack with cropping ratio varying 10% to 90% after JPEG compression Q=80%. For the cropping attack, the stationary and non-stationary models are similar to PSNR and correlation response for the cropping ratio.

Table 4. Cropping attack with cropping ratio varying 10% to 90% after JPEG compression Q=80%.

		10	20	30	40	50	60	70	80	90
		\multicolumn{9}{c}{Multiwavelet Lena(512×512)}								
	Quality	10	20	30	40	50	60	70	80	90
PSNR	Non-Stationary	38.289	38.938	39.767	40.82	42.292	44.29	46.959	50.13	55.883
	Stationary	38.532	39.172	40.002	41.048	42.51	44.501	47.166	50.366	56.056
C.R	Non-Stationary	27.854	25.742	23.666	20.532	17.419	13.846	10.161	7.441	4.0745
	Stationary	28.057	25.903	23.821	20.672	17.558	13.915	10.203	7.5042	4.0899

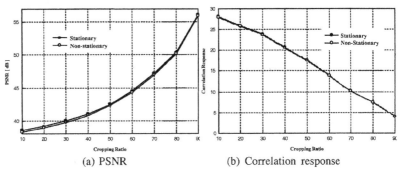

(a) PSNR   (b) Correlation response

Fig. 5. The robustness test against cropping attack after JPEG compression Q=80%.

The correlation responses of the image with no attack, Gaussian attack, median filtering, and sharpening attacks for stationary and non-stationary models are shown in Fig. 6 and Fig. 7. Table 5 is PSNR and correlation response according to various attacks. As shown by the results, stationary model is a little excellent correlation response than non-stationary model. But PSNR of non-stationary model is a little better than stationary model.

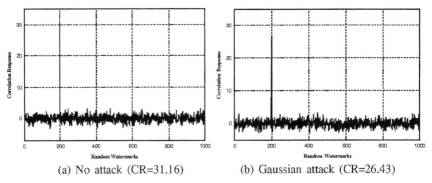

(a) No attack (CR=31.16)   (b) Gaussian attack (CR=26.43)

Fig. 6. (a), (b) Correlation responses for the various attacks in the stationary model.

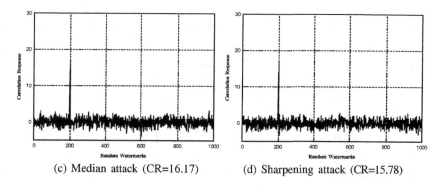

(c) Median attack (CR=16.17)   (d) Sharpening attack (CR=15.78)

Fig. 6. (c), (d) Correlation responses for the various attacks in the stationary model.

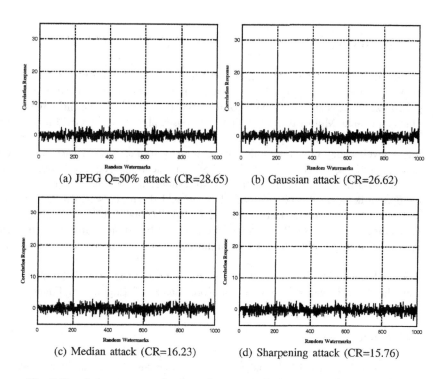

(a) JPEG Q=50% attack (CR=28.65)   (b) Gaussian attack (CR=26.62)

(c) Median attack (CR=16.23)   (d) Sharpening attack (CR=15.76)

Fig. 7. Correlation responses for the various attacks in the non-stationary model.

Table 5. PSNR and correlation response according to various attacks.

LENA 512 x 512				
	Stationary		Non-Stationary	
	PSNR[dB]	CR	PSNR[dB]	CR
3x3 Gaussian.	34.05	27.24	34.15	26.42
3x3 Sharpening	22.45	17.05	22.46	15.81
3x3 Median	31.06	17.44	31.10	16.18
FMLR	32.59	17.39	32.64	16.12
Cropping 50%	48.52	17.46	48.52	17.47
JPEG Q=50	35.79	30.53	35.79	30.52

5   Conclusions

In this paper, adaptive watermark embedding based on the multiwavelet domain has been presented. This approach is based on a stochastic model that uses stationary generalized Gaussian model with local image properties to determine the optimal embedding area. Multiwavelet used in the proposed algorithm is DGHM multiwavelet with approximation order 2. To embed watermark, the original image is decomposed into 4 levels using a discrete multiwavelet transform, then a watermark is embedded into the PSCs of each subband. The PSCs in the high frequency subband were selected by SSQ, that is, by setting the thresholds as the one half of the largest coefficient in each subband. Watermark is embedded into the selected PSCs with the perceptual model and stochastic model. The experimental results about the proposed embedding method with SSQ and perceptual model based on multiwavelet transform techniques were found to be excellent in the aspect of transparency and robustness.

Acknowledgements. This work was supported by grant No. (R01-2002-000-00589-0) from the Basic Research Program of the Korea Science & Engineering Foundation.

References

1.   I.Cox, J.Kilian, T.Leighton, and T.Shamoon.: Secure Spread Spectrum Watermarking for Multimedia. NEC Research Institute Tech Rep. 95–10, (1995)
2.   J.Huang and Y.Shi.: Adaptive Image Watermarking Scheme Based on Visual Masking. Electronic Letters, Vol. 34, No. 8 (1998) 748–750
3.   M. Swanson, B. Zhu, and A. Twefik.: Transparent Robust Image Watermarking. IEEE International Conference on Image Processing ICIP96, Vol. 3 (1996) 211–214
4.   C.Podilchuk and W.Zeng.: Image Adaptive Watermarking Using Visual Models. IEEE Journal on Selected Areas in Communication, Vol. 16, No. 4 (1998) 525–539

5. M. Kutter: Watermarking Resisting to Translation, Rotation and Scaling. Proc. of SPIE, Boston, USA, (1998)

6. J. Ruanaidh and T. Pun.: Rotation, Scale and Translation Invariant Spread Spectrum Digital Image Watermarking. Journal of Signal Processing, Vol. 66, No.3 (1998) 303–317

7. J.F.Delaigle, C.De Vleeschouwer, and B.Macq.: Watermarking Algorithm Based on a Human Visual Model. Signal Processing, Vol.66 (1998) 319–335

8. Sviatoslav Voloshynovskiy, A. Herrigel, N. Baumgaertner, and T. Pun.: A Stochastic Approach to Content Adaptive Digital Image Watermarking. Proc. of Third Information Hiding Workshop (1999)

9. V. Strela, P. N. Heller, G. Strang, P. Topiwala, and C. Heil.: The Application of Multi-wavelet Filterbank to Image Processing. IEEE Trans. On Image Processing, Vol. 8, No. 4 (1999) 548–563

10. X. G Xia, J. S. Geronimo, D. P. Hardin, and B. W. Suter.: Design of Prefilters for Discrete Multiwavelet Transforms. IEEE Trans. on Image Processing, Vol. 44, No. 1 (1996) 25–35

11. Douglas P. Hardin and David W. Roach.: Multiwavelet Prefilters I: Orthogonal Prefilters Preserving Approximation order p $\leq$2. IEEE Trans. On Circuits and Systems II, Vol. 45 (1998) 1106–1112

12. In-Sung Ha, Seong-Geun Kwon, Seung-Jin Lee, Ki-Ryong Kwon, and Kuhn-Il Lee.: A New Wavelet-Based Digital Watermarking Using the Human Visual System and Subband Adaptive Threshold. IS&T's 2001 PICS conference Proceedings, Montreal Canada (2001)

13. K.R. Kwon and A.H. Tewfik.: Adaptive watermarking using successive Subband quantization and perceptual model based on multiwavelet transform. Proc. of SPIE, Vol. 4675–37 (2002)

Author Index

Ahn, Byung-Ha   170
Atallah, Mikhail   130

Byun, Sung-Cheal   170

Chan, Y.K.   22
Charbon, Edoardo   147
Choi, Byeong C.   235
Choi, Jae-Gark   202
Chua, Hock Chuan   64, 91
Cox, Ingemar J.   13

Doërr, Gwenaël J.   13
Donoho, David L.   113

Feng, Yi   189
Flesia, Ana Georgina   113

Guan, Yong Liang   64, 91

Hahn, Minsoo   224
Hong, Jin Woo   31
Hu, Junquan   179
Hu, Yongjian   22
Huang, Daren   179
Huang, Jiwu   179, 212

Ichalkaranje, Nikhil   81
Izquierdo, Ebroul   189

Jain, Lakhmi   40, 81
Jung, Yong Ju   224

Kang, Hyun Soo   31
Kang, Xiangui   212

Kim, Bum-Soo   202
Kim, Kwang Yong   31
Kim, Yong C.   235
Kwon, Ki-Ryong   249
Kwon, Seong-Geun   249
Kwong, Sam   22

Lee, Sang-Kwang   170
Lin, Xinggang   105

Miller, Matt L.   13
Moulin, Pierre   1

Nam, Je-Ho   249

Pan, Jeng-Shyang   40, 81
Park, Kil-Houm   202
Prabhakar, Sunil   130
Pranata, Sugiri   91

Ro, Yong Man   224

Sattar, Farook   51
Shao, Yafei   105
Shi, Yun Q.   179, 212
Sion, Radu   130

Tewfik, Ahmed H.   170, 249
Torunoglu, Ilhami   147

Wahadaniah, Viktor   64
Wang, Feng-Hsing   40, 81
Wu, Guowei   105

Yu, Dan   51

Lecture Notes in Computer Science

For information about Vols. 1–2543

please contact your bookseller or Springer-Verlag

Vol. 2325: B. Falsafi, T.N. Vijaykumar (Eds.), Power-Aware Computer Systems. Proceedings, 2002. X, 213 pages. 2003.

Vol. 2544: S. Bhalla (Ed.), Databases in Networked Information Systems. Proceedings 2002. X, 285 pages. 2002.

Vol. 2545: P. Forbrig, Q, Limbourg, B. Urban, J. Vanderdonckt (Eds.), Interactive Systems. Proceedings 2002. XII, 574 pages. 2002.

Vol. 2546: J. Sterbenz, O. Takada, C. Tschudin, B. Plattner (Eds.), Active Networks. Proceedings, 2002. XIV, 267 pages. 2002.

Vol. 2547: R. Fleischer, B. Moret, E. Meineche Schmidt (Eds.), Experimental Algorithmics. XVII, 279 pages. 2002.

Vol. 2548: J. Hernández, Ana Moreira (Eds.), Object-Oriented Technology. Proceedings, 2002. VIII, 223 pages. 2002.

Vol. 2549: J. Cortadella, A. Yakovlev, G. Rozenberg (Eds.), Concurrency and Hardware Design. XI, 345 pages. 2002.

Vol. 2550: A. Jean-Marie (Ed.), Advances in Computing Science – ASIAN 2002. Proceedings, 2002. X, 233 pages. 2002.

Vol. 2551: A. Menezes, P. Sarkar (Eds.), Progress in Cryptology – INDOCRYPT 2002. Proceedings, 2002. XI, 437 pages. 2002.

Vol. 2552: S. Sahni, V.K. Prasanna, U. Shukla (Eds.), High Performance Computing – HiPC 2002. Proceedings, 2002. XXI, 735 pages. 2002.

Vol. 2553: B. Andersson, M. Bergholtz, P. Johannesson (Eds.), Natural Language Processing and Information Systems. Proceedings, 2002. X, 241 pages. 2002.

Vol. 2554: M. Beetz, Plan-Based Control of Robotic Agents. XI, 191 pages. 2002. (Subseries LNAI).

Vol. 2555: E.-P. Lim, S. Foo, C. Khoo, H. Chen, E. Fox, S. Urs, T. Costantino (Eds.), Digital Libraries: People, Knowledge, and Technology. Proceedings, 2002. XVII, 535 pages. 2002.

Vol. 2556: M. Agrawal, A. Seth (Eds.), FST TCS 2002: Foundations of Software Technology and Theoretical Computer Science. Proceedings, 2002. XI, 361 pages. 2002.

Vol. 2557: B. McKay, J. Slaney (Eds.), AI 2002: Advances in Artificial Intelligence. Proceedings, 2002. XV, 730 pages. 2002. (Subseries LNAI).

Vol. 2558: P. Perner, Data Mining on Multimedia Data. X, 131 pages. 2002.

Vol. 2559: M. Oivo, S. Komi-Sirviö (Eds.), Product Focused Software Process Improvement. Proceedings, 2002. XV, 646 pages. 2002.

Vol. 2560: S. Goronzy, Robust Adaptation to Non-Native Accents in Automatic Speech Recognition. Proceedings, 2002. XI, 144 pages. 2002. (Subseries LNAI).

Vol. 2561: H.C.M. de Swart (Ed.), Relational Methods in Computer Science. Proceedings, 2001. X, 315 pages. 2002.

Vol. 2562: V. Dahl, P. Wadler (Eds.), Practical Aspects of Declarative Languages. Proceedings, 2003. X, 315 pages. 2002.

Vol. 2565: J.M.L.M. Palma, J. Dongarra, V. Hernández, A. Augusto Sousa (Eds.), High Performance Computing for Computational Science – VECPAR 2002. Proceedings, 2002. XVII, 732 pages. 2003.

Vol. 2566: T.Æ. Mogensen, D.A. Schmidt, I.H. Sudborough (Eds.), The Essence of Computation. XIV, 473 pages. 2002.

Vol. 2567: Y.G. Desmedt (Ed.), Public Key Cryptography – PKC 2003. Proceedings, 2003. XI, 365 pages. 2002.

Vol. 2568: M. Hagiya, A. Ohuchi (Eds.), DNA Computing. Proceedings, 2002. XI, 338 pages. 2003.

Vol. 2569: D. Gollmann, G. Karjoth, M. Waidner (Eds.), Computer Security – ESORICS 2002. Proceedings, 2002. XIII, 648 pages. 2002. (Subseries LNAI).

Vol. 2570: M. Jünger, G. Reinelt, G. Rinaldi (Eds.), Combinatorial Optimization – Eureka, You Shrink!. Proceedings, 2001. X, 209 pages. 2003.

Vol. 2571: S.K. Das, S. Bhattacharya (Eds.), Distributed Computing. Proceedings, 2002. XIV, 354 pages. 2002.

Vol. 2572: D. Calvanese, M. Lenzerini, R. Motwani (Eds.), Database Theory – ICDT 2003. Proceedings, 2003. XI, 455 pages. 2002.

Vol. 2574: M.-S. Chen, P.K. Chrysanthis, M. Sloman, A. Zaslavsky (Eds.), Mobile Data Management. Proceedings, 2003. XII, 414 pages. 2003.

Vol. 2575: L.D. Zuck, P.C. Attie, A. Cortesi, S. Mukhopadhyay (Eds.), Verification, Model Checking, and Abstract Interpretation. Proceedings, 2003. XI, 325 pages. 2003.

Vol. 2576: S. Cimato, C. Galdi, G. Persiano (Eds.), Security in Communication Networks. Proceedings, 2002. IX, 365 pages. 2003.

Vol. 2578: F.A.P. Petitcolas (Ed.), Information Hiding. Proceedings, 2002. IX, 427 pages. 2003.

Vol. 2580: H. Erdogmus, T. Weng (Eds.), COTS-Based Software Systems. Proceedings, 2003. XVIII, 261 pages. 2003.

Vol. 2581: J.S. Sichman, F. Bousquet, P. Davidsson (Eds.), Multi-Agent-Based Simulation II. Proceedings, 2002. X, 195 pages. 2003. (Subseries LNAI).

Vol. 2582: L. Bertossi, G.O.H. Katona, K.-D. Schewe, B. Thalheim (Eds.), Semantics in Databases. Proceedings, 2001. IX, 229 pages. 2003.

Vol. 2583: S. Matwin, C. Sammut (Eds.), Inductive Logic Programming. Proceedings, 2002. X, 351 pages. 2003. (Subseries LNAI).

Vol. 2584: A. Schiper, A.A. Shvartsman, H. Weatherspoon, B.Y. Zhao (Eds.), Future Directions in Distributed Computing. X, 219 pages. 2003.

Vol. 2585: F. Giunchiglia, J. Odell, G. Weiß (Eds.), Agent-Oriented Software Engineering III. Proceedings, 2002. X, 229 pages. 2003.

Vol. 2586: M. Klusch, S. Bergamaschi, P. Edwards, P. Petta (Eds.), Intelligent Information Agents. VI, 275 pages. 2003. (Subseries LNAI).

Vol. 2587: P.J. Lee, C.H. Lim (Eds.), Information Security and Cryptology – ICISC 2002. Proceedings, 2002. XI, 536 pages. 2003.

Vol. 2588: A. Gelbukh (Ed.), Computational Linguistics and Intelligent Text Processing. Proceedings, 2003. XV, 648 pages. 2003.

Vol. 2589: E. Börger, A. Gargantini, E. Riccobene (Eds.), Abstract State Machines 2003. Proceedings, 2003. XI, 427 pages. 2003.

Vol. 2590: S. Bressan, A.B. Chaudhri, M.L. Lee, J.X. Yu, Z. Lacroix (Eds.), Efficiency and Effectiveness of XML Tools and Techniques and Data Integration over the Web. Proceedings, 2002. X, 259 pages. 2003.

Vol. 2591: M. Aksit, M. Mezini, R. Unland (Eds.), Objects, Components, Architectures, Services, and Applications for a Networked World. Proceedings, 2002. XI, 431 pages. 2003.

Vol. 2592: R. Kowalczyk, J.P. Müller, H. Tianfield, R. Unland (Eds.), Agent Technologies, Infrastructures, Tools, and Applications for E-Services. Proceedings, 2002. XVII, 371 pages. 2003. (Subseries LNAI).

Vol. 2593: A.B. Chaudhri, M. Jeckle, E. Rahm, R. Unland (Eds.), Web, Web-Services, and Database Systems. Proceedings, 2002. XI, 311 pages. 2003.

Vol. 2594: A. Asperti, B. Buchberger, J.H. Davenport (Eds.), Mathematical Knowledge Management. Proceedings, 2003. X, 225 pages. 2003.

Vol. 2595: K. Nyberg, H. Heys (Eds.), Selected Areas in Cryptography. Proceedings, 2002. XI, 405 pages. 2003.

Vol. 2597: G. Păun, G. Rozenberg, A. Salomaa, C. Zandron (Eds.), Membrane Computing. Proceedings, 2002. VIII, 423 pages. 2003.

Vol. 2598: R. Klein, H.-W. Six, L. Wegner (Eds.), Computer Science in Perspective. X, 357 pages. 2003.

Vol. 2599: E. Sherratt (Ed.), Telecommunications and beyond: The Broader Applicability of SDL and MSC. Proceedings, 2002. X, 253 pages. 2003.

Vol. 2600: S. Mendelson, A.J. Smola, Advanced Lectures on Machine Learning. Proceedings, 2002. IX, 259 pages. 2003. (Subseries LNAI).

Vol. 2601: M. Ajmone Marsan, G. Corazza, M. Listanti, A. Roveri (Eds.) Quality of Service in Multiservice IP Networks. Proceedings, 2003. XV, 759 pages. 2003.

Vol. 2602: C. Priami (Ed.), Computational Methods in Systems Biology. Proceedings, 2003. IX, 214 pages. 2003.

Vol. 2604: N. Guelfi, E. Astesiano, G. Reggio (Eds.), Scientific Engineering for Distributed Java Applications. Proceedings, 2002. X, 205 pages. 2003.

Vol. 2606: A.M. Tyrrell, P.C. Haddow, J. Torresen (Eds.), Evolvable Systems: From Biology to Hardware. Proceedings, 2003. XIV, 468 pages. 2003.

Vol. 2607: H. Alt, M. Habib (Eds.), STACS 2003. Proceedings, 2003. XVII, 700 pages. 2003.

Vol. 2609: M. Okada, B. Pierce, A. Scedrov, H. Tokuda, A. Yonezawa (Eds.), Software Security – Theories and Systems. Proceedings, 2002. XI, 471 pages. 2003.

Vol. 2610: C. Ryan, T. Soule, M. Keijzer, E. Tsang, R. Poli, E. Costa (Eds.), Genetic Programming. Proceedings, 2003. XII, 486 pages. 2003.

Vol. 2611: S. Cagnoni, J.J. Romero Cardalda, D.W. Corne, J. Gottlieb, A. Guillot, E. Hart, C.G. Johnson, E. Marchiori, J.-A. Meyer, M. Middendorf, G.R. Raidl (Eds.), Applications of Evolutionary Computing. Proceedings, 2003. XXI, 708 pages. 2003.

Vol. 2612: M. Joye (Ed.), Topics in Cryptology – CT-RSA 2003. Proceedings, 2003. XI, 417 pages. 2003.

Vol. 2613: F.A.P. Petitcolas, H.J. Kim (Eds.), Digital Watermarking. Proceedings, 2002. XI, 265 pages. 2003.

Vol. 2614: R. Laddaga, P. Robertson, H. Shrobe (Eds.), Self-Adaptive Software: Applications. Proceedings, 2001. VIII, 291 pages. 2003.

Vol. 2615: N. Carbonell, C. Stephanidis (Eds.), Universal Access. Proceedings, 2002. XIV, 534 pages. 2003.

Vol. 2616: T. Asano, R. Klette, C. Ronse (Eds.), Geometry, Morphology, and Computational Imaging. Proceedings, 2002. X, 437 pages. 2003.

Vol. 2617: H.A. Reijers (Eds.), Design and Control of Workflow Processes. Proceedings, 2002. XV, 624 pages. 2003.

Vol. 2618: P. Degano (Ed.), Programming Languages and Systems. Proceedings, 2003. XV, 415 pages. 2003.

Vol. 2619: H. Garavel, J. Hatcliff (Eds.), Tools and Algorithms for the Construction and Analysis of Systems. Proceedings, 2003. XVI, 604 pages. 2003.

Vol. 2620: A.D. Gordon (Ed.), Foundations of Software Science and Computation Structures. Proceedings, 2003. XII, 441 pages. 2003.

Vol. 2621: M. Pezzè (Ed.), Fundamental Approaches to Software Engineering. Proceedings, 2003. XIV, 403 pages. 2003.

Vol. 2622: G. Hedin (Ed.), Compiler Construction. Proceedings, 2003. XII, 335 pages. 2003.

Vol. 2623: O. Maler, A. Pnueli (Eds.), Hybrid Systems: Computation and Control. Proceedings, 2003. XII, 558 pages. 2003.

Vol. 2625: U. Meyer, P. Sanders, J. Sibeyn (Eds.), Algorithms for Memory Hierarchies. Proceedings, 2003. XVIII, 428 pages. 2003.

Vol. 2626: J.L. Crowley, J.H. Piater, M. Vincze, L. Paletta (Eds.), Computer Vision Systems. Proceedings, 2003. XIII, 546 pages. 2003.

Vol. 2627: B. O'Sullivan (Ed.), Recent Advances in Constraints. Proceedings, 2002. X, 201 pages. 2003. (Subseries LNAI).

Vol. 2631: R. Falcone, S. Barber, L. Korba, M. Singh (Eds.), Trust, Reputation, and Security: Theories and Practice. Proceedings, 2002. X, 235 pages. 2003. (Subseries LNAI).

Vol. 2633: F. Sebastiani (Ed.), Advances in Information Retrieval. Proceedings, 2003. XIII, 546 pages. 2003.